ANTHOLOGY
— for —
MUSIC IN THE MEDIEVAL WEST

Margot Fassler

University of Notre Dame

and

Yale University

W. W. NORTON & COMPANY
NEW YORK • LONDON

W. W. Norton & Company has been independent since its founding in 1923, when William Warder Norton and Mary D. Herter Norton first published lectures delivered at the People's Institute, the adult education division of New York City's Cooper Union. The firm soon expanded its program beyond the Institute, publishing books by celebrated academics from America and abroad. By mid-century, the two major pillars of Norton's publishing program—trade books and college texts—were firmly established. In the 1950s, the Norton family transferred control of the company to its employees, and today—with a staff of four hundred and a comparable number of trade, college, and professional titles published each year—W. W. Norton & Company stands as the largest and oldest publishing house owned wholly by its employees.

Editor: Maribeth Payne
Associate Editor: Justin Hoffman
Editorial Assistant: Michael Fauver
Developmental Editor: Harry Haskell
Manuscript Editor: Jodi Beder
Managing Editor, College: Marian Johnson
Project Editor: Jack Borrebach
Electronic Media Editor: Steve Hoge
Assistant Media Editor: Stefani Wallace
Marketing Manager, Music: Christopher J. Freitag
Production Managers: Ashley Horna and Ben Reynolds
Photo Editor: Stephanie Romeo
Permissions Manager: Megan Jackson
Text Design: Jillian Burr
Composition: Jouve International—Brattleboro, VT
Manufacturing: Quad/Graphics—Fairfield, PA

ISBN 978-0-393-92022-2

W. W. Norton & Company, Inc., 500 Fifth Avenue, New York, NY 10110, 0017
wwnorton.com

W. W. Norton & Company Ltd., Castle House, 75/76 Wells Street, London W1T 3QT

For Joe, Rachel, Frank, Susan, Ella, Jenny, Stephanie, Jonathan, and Katie;
Philip, François, and Simon

CONTENTS

CONCORDANCE

— for —

MUSIC IN THE MEDIEVAL WEST

PREFACE

This anthology is a companion to my book *Music in the Medieval West*, the first volume in the series Western Music in Context: A Norton History. The anthology includes scores and analytical commentaries for a broad range of sacred and secular compositions, and can be used on its own or in conjunction with *Music in the Medieval West*. It will be useful for performers and for classes in performance practice, on both the graduate and the undergraduate levels, as well as for those who like to listen to medieval music with a "score" (even if the music they hear is somewhat different from what is on the page, as it inevitably will be).

Music in the Medieval West and the anthology are designed to promote intertextual investigation and listening, an approach that was fundamental to the making and apprehension of music in the Middle Ages. Medieval musicians worked with small cells, formulae, phrases, and melodies, using and reusing them in ways that resemble the work of great graphic designers. The analyses in the anthology identify these fundamental building blocks for singing, composing, and improvisation. Several tunes have been chosen to illustrate how these basic elements were reworked across the centuries; for example, the hymn *Ave maris stella*, the Kyrie *Cunctipotens genitor*, the Responsory *Stirps Jesse*, the antiphon *Ave regina caelorum*, and the rondeau *Prendés i garde* are encountered in multiple guises. Lady Fortune makes repeated appearances, always in a different context. We meet the Virgin Mary on many levels. And one genre, the sequence, composed from the ninth century through the end of period studied here (and well beyond), has been chosen as a touchstone for ongoing developments in medieval melodic and polyphonic repertories.

Because no performance practice alive and well today is as varied as that associated with medieval repertory, the anthology attempts to encourage well-informed experimentation. It includes a mixture of commonly anthologized works and works rarely or never anthologized before, giving users opportunities both for making comparisons and for striking out anew. Like the multifaceted musical repertories it records, the anthology introduces users not only to a wide variety of music and ways of setting and proclaiming texts, but also to some of the methods used for transcribing and editing this repertory.

There is not now, and never has been, one way of working with and out of the medieval sources. From matters of orthography to the questions of whether or not to superimpose rhythmic values or how and when to add accidentals, every scholar and performer will have decisions to make. This is as true for a simple hymn tune as for a complex late-fourteenth-century polyphonic piece from the Chantilly Codex. For example, in our scores we have been careful to follow the editions chosen, whether they are modern chant books or transcriptions made directly from the sources. But when we print the texts alone, with English translations, we sometimes make concessions in the interest of clarity and consistency, especially in regard to capitalization and orthography.

The commentaries in the anthology often discuss the decisions editors have made, so that students will be aware of the choices they too will face in dealing with medieval sources. For each piece in the anthology, we cite both the original manuscript(s) and modern editions used in preparing the scores. URLs provided on the author's website encourage further engagement with digitized reproductions of primary sources. A Medieval Music Primer, which is appended to both the anthology and *Music in the Medieval West*, offers a guide for working not only with some of the most important modern chant books, but also with notational practices encountered in medieval manuscripts.

A wide range of recording options gives students and instructors flexibility in listening to anthology selections. StudySpace, Norton's online resource for students, provides links to stream all anthology selections either from Naxos (accessible via an institutional or individual subscription) or from iTunes and Amazon (via links to purchase and download recordings). The Playlist on StudySpace also includes 10 new performances recorded specifically for this text by Michael Anderson and the Schola Antiqua Chicago. Many of these recordings are discussed in the anthology, and an even greater number are listed on the author's website.

My hope is that this volume will encourage users to sing and play from the original sources and to make their own transcriptions. With so many original manuscripts now online, vast repertories of gorgeous melodic and polyphonic works are available to anyone with the requisite skills for study and performance. These manuscripts are in the public domain, making them an especially valuable resource for musicians in an age increasingly shackled by restrictive copyright laws. When it comes to music of the medieval West, it is like the old song says: the best things in life are free.

I wish to thank numerous individuals who read through the anthology (or parts of it) and offered excellent advice, including Michael Anderson, Rebecca A. Baltzer, Calvin M. Bower, Susan Boynton, Anna-Maria Busse Berger, Peter Jeffery, Peter Lefferts, Michael Long, Rebecca Malloy, Susan Rankin, Kate Kennedy Steiner, and Jerome Weber. Scholars who provided editions and helped with or provided translations were generous in their assistance; thanks to Rebecca A. Baltzer, Isabelle Fabre, Nicolas Kamas, Hailey LaVoy, Michael Long, and Susan Rankin. Michael Anderson made recordings of several examples that were not otherwise available. Anna de Bakker and Jeffery Cooper provided splendid assistance with the author's website.

I am grateful to the staff of the library of the Medieval Institute at Notre Dame, Marina Smyth and Julia Schneider; to Robert Simon, Music Librarian; and to David Gura, curator of Medieval and European Manuscripts, both of the Hesburgh Library, University of Notre Dame. I am thankful as well for the assistance of the staff of the Mendel Music Library at Princeton University, especially to Music Librarian Darwin Scott, and to Suzanne Lovejoy and the staff of the John Herrick Jackson Music Library of Yale University. For the leave time I needed to complete this book, I am most grateful to Yale University, the Institute of Sacred Music, and the University of Notre Dame.

At W. W. Norton I am particularly grateful for the careful copyediting and proof-reading of Jodi Beder and Harry Haskell, both of whom improved the anthology immeasurably. Harry Haskell and Justin Hoffman have done brilliant work coordinating the scores and recordings, grappling with the complex problems of permissions, and helping to assemble and set the scores.

Margot Fassler

ANTHOLOGY

— for —

MUSIC IN THE MEDIEVAL WEST

ANONYMOUS

Ave maris stella

Strophic hymn
Text, 9th century?; melody, by the 10th century

1

Aue maris stella	Hail, star of the sea,
dei mater alma,	tender mother of God
atque semper Uirgo,	and ever virgin,
felix celi porta.	happy door of heaven.

2

Sumens illud "aue"	Putting on that "ave"
Gabrielis ore	from the mouth of Gabriel,
funda nos in pace	changing the name "Eve,"
mutans nomen Eue.	establish us in peace.

3

Solue uincla reis,	Dissolve the chains for the prisoners,
profer lumen cecis,	bring light to the blind,
mala nostra pelle,	rout our evils,
bona cuncta posce.	request many good things.

Paris, BN 15181, f. 467, a breviary from the Cathedral of Notre Dame, Paris, c. 1300

4

Monstra te esse matrem	Announce yourself to be mother
sumat per te precem	that He may take up your petition
qui pro nobis natus	Who, born for us,
tulit esse tuus.	you carried as your own.

5

Virgo singularis	Singular virgin,
inter omnes mitis	sweet among all,
nos culpis solutos	absolve us from sins,
mites fac et castos.	make us sweet and chaste.

6

Vitam presta puram	Show the pure life,
iter para tutum	prepare the safe journey,
ut uidentes Jesum	that, seeing Jesus,
semper colletemur.	we may be always glad together.

7

Sit laus deo patri	Let there be praise to God the Father,
summo Christo decus	and glory to the most high Christ,
spiritui sancto	with the Holy Spirit,
tribus honor unus.	one honor to all three.
Amen.	Amen.

Ave maris stella is a medieval hymn, or sacred song, probably composed in the ninth century; such a work would have been sung in hours of prayer in monasteries and cathedrals. It has two components, its text and its melodies, for the text was set to more than one tune. To date it, we can point to the first known manuscript witness. It is possible to track this early attestation thanks to the wonders of technology: great numbers of digitized medieval manuscripts are now online, including those from the Abbey of St. Gall in modern-day Switzerland. (See the author's website, Chapter 1, for links to this digital resource.) From this database, we can choose St. Gall, manuscript 95, a ninth-century copy of a work by Ambrose of Milan (see Anthology 2).

On the back of the first page, or folio, of the manuscript, a scribe has copied the opening lines of the hymn text, without music notation. At this stage in its history, the music belonged to an oral tradition, so it is not possible to say what melody the copyist would have sung. The melody (reproduced in *Music in the Medieval West*, Ex. 1.1) begins to appear in tenth-century sources, one of the earliest of which (Paris, BN lat. 1240) was found in the south of modern-day France. (See Primer I.2 for a discussion of manuscript designations.) Hence at least part of the text was in existence around 1,100 years ago, and within a century or so, it had been associated with a particular melody.

The score used for this anthology is transcribed from a thirteenth-century manuscript, and the spellings of the text and even the letters that are used follow medieval conventions; the *v* in "Ave," for example, becomes a *u*. As a result, the thirteenth-century text looks quite different from the version of the hymn found in the *Liber Usualis*, which uses the spellings found in classical Latin texts (see Chapter 1 of *Music in the Medieval West*).

The verses of *Ave maris stella* fall into groupings of four lines called strophes, and each of these strophes is sung to the same melody. Each of the three feet (metrical units) in each line has a strong accent followed by a weak one (in quantitative verse, this would be the pattern long-short, called a trochee). *Ave maris stella* is a rhythmical verse. It does not follow ancient metrical rules, but simply consists of an alternating series of stressed and unstressed syllables. (For example, the first syllable of "mala nostra pelle" in strophe 3 is short, not long, as in an ancient trochee; "dei" in the second line of strophe 1 is also short-long; here both of these short syllables receive an accent.) What matters in this poetry is syllable counting and regular patterns of accent: it is qualitative rather than quantitative. The melody given here was extremely popular from the twelfth century forward and in every region of Europe. It makes an engaging partner for the text, stretching and playing with it, moving out of its rhythmic sphere, and then coming home to join with the text on the final powerful line of each strophe.

Metrical (and rhythmic) verse is out of fashion among contemporary American poets; people often think of such verse as singsong, although in song lyrics, accentual, rhymed verse has never gone out of style. When accentual poetry is sung to a skillful melody that transforms ongoing rhythms of the verse, the effect is of pleasurable interplay between two dimensions of a single art. The first melodic line of *Ave maris stella* seems to emphasize the second syllable of each foot, in direct opposition to the implicit accentual patterns of the text. In line 2, however, the accent of the text and the emphasis of the melody are synchronized. In line 3 they are once again at odds, with the unaccented "-go" of "Uirgo" set to a downward leap and a long melisma (a melody sung to a single syllable). In line 4 the textual and musical dimensions come powerfully together again.

When we study medieval chant, we should remember that in this literature pitch is a relative concept, a matter of whole- and half-step relationships in modal formulas, rather than of "absolute" pitch or measurable frequencies, as is the case with contemporary music. So, instead of saying D, meaning a particular sound or pitch class, we should say "protus quality," relating to *maneriae* (or pairs of scales) and mode (see Anthology 3 and Primer III.2). For the sake of convenience, however, we will use the term *pitch* throughout our discussions.

The first pitch of *Ave maris stella* is D, followed by a leap up a fifth to an ornamented A. The second text line features a downward leap back to D, now ornamented in a way that reflects the decoration on the preceding A. Line 3 seems at first to echo the shape of line 2, but instead of closing on D, as expected, it moves down to the C below, creating an unstable cadence with no sense of finality. Line 4 circles around and ultimately settles powerfully on D as the home pitch of the hymn melody, also called the final.

The fifth was a pure or "perfect" interval to medieval ears (see Chapter 2 of *Music in the Medieval West*). *Ave maris stella* can be situated at any pitch, but it comes to life when it is sung with perfect fifths that ring clearly, with no "beats" between the notes such as occur when the pure interval is raised or lowered according to later systems of temperament. Modern interpreters have to make decisions about the rhythm of the music, as rhythm is not expressed in square notation. (See Primer II.1 for a guide to reading chant notation.) On the album *Gregorian Chants for Marian Festivals*, notes grouped in melismas are treated as part of a single gesture and are therefore sung quickly, although certain syllables are emphasized ("*stel*-la," for example). A jazz version of the melody, found on *Sacred Hungarian Folk Songs and Gregorian Chants*, features countermelodies in the instruments. In the early-fifteenth-century Codex Faenza, the melody is in a lower voice, while the upper part spins an ornamental filigree. The choir that sings the chant before the rendition on *Codex Faenza: Instrumental Music of the Early 15th Century* follows an "equalist" interpretation, giving almost every note the same value, a practice associated with the Benedictine monks of the Abbey of Solesmes in northern France (see Primer II.1).

AMBROSE OF MILAN (C. 339–397)

Eterne rerum conditor
Hymn in Ambrosian meter
Text, 4th century; music, 9th through 15th centuries

2.1 NEVERS, FRANCE, 12TH CENTURY

2.2 MILAN, ITALY, 14TH CENTURY

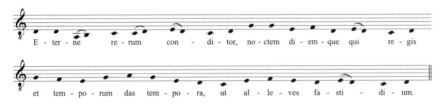

2.3 CISTERCIAN MANUSCRIPT, LATE 12TH CENTURY

2.4 RHEINAU, GERMANY, 1459

2.1: Paris, BN n.a. lat. 1235, ff. 154r–154v

2.2: Milan, Biblioteca Trivulziana 347, pp. 156–59

2.3: Heiligenkreuz, Stiftsbibliothek 20, f. 224

2.4: Zurich, Zentralbibliothek, Rheinau 21, ff. 91v–92r

1

Eterne rerum conditor,*
noctem diemque qui regis
et temporum das tempora,
ut alleues fastidium.

Eternal creator of the
world, you govern night and day, and give
changes of time and season to relieve our
boredom.

2

Praeco diei iam sonet
noctis profunde pervigil
nocturna lux uiantibus,
a nocte noctem segregans.

Let the bird that has been like a light to
travelers during the night, and marked off
for them the night-watches, herald the day,
calling on the sun to shine.

3

Hoc excitatus lucifer
soluit polum caligine,
hoc omnis horrorum** chorus
viam nocendi deserit.

When the cock crows, the sun wakes up
and frees the skies from darkness; when he
crows, all night-prowlers leave the path of
sin.

4

Hoc nauta vires colligit
pontique mitescunt freta,
hoc ipse petra ecclesie
canente culpam diluit.

At cock-crow the sailor again finds
courage, then angry seas become calm; and
the very Rock of the Church [St. Peter] has
washed away his sin.

5

Surgamus ergo strenue,
gallus iacentes excitat,
et somnolentes increpat,
gallus negantes arguit.

Let us rise then promptly. The cock
arouses the sleepers, loudly upbraids the
sleepy, and puts to shame the slug-a-bed.

6

Gallo canente spes redit,
egris salus refunditur,
mucro latronis conditur,
lapsis fides revertitur.

When he crows, hope comes back, a
feeling of health returns to the sick, the
robber sheathes his sword, and trust makes
its way back to sinful souls.

*Spellings as in Paris, lat. 1235.

**A mistake in the manuscript: should be *erronum*.

7

Hiesu, labentes respice	Look on us, Jesus, when we waver and
et nos uidendo corrige,	with a glance correct us; for if you look on
si respicis, lapsus cadunt,	us, our sins fall from us and our tears wash
fletuque culpa solvitur.	away our guilt.

8

Tu lux refulge sensibus	Be a shining star to our minds and drive
mentisque somnum discute,	sloth away from our souls. May our first
te nostra vox primum sonet,	sound be to praise you; so may we open
et ora solvamus tibi.*	our mouths for you.

*A final strophe in praise of the Trinity was not part of Ambrose's original and is not included here.

Ambrose, bishop of Milan in the late fourth century, is known as the father of Latin hymnody. *Aeterne rerum conditor* (medieval spelling, *Eterne*) was attributed to him by his student Augustine of Hippo. Like Augustine, Ambrose was fascinated by the subject of time. The Christian liturgy is, in a sense, a study of human action in a world governed by the turnings of the hours. In this text, Ambrose calls on the singer to put himself in tune with a new day. As the light brings hope and dispels fear and gloom, sleepers awake with renewed energy, leaving their past errors behind and putting themselves right with God. It is clear why this hymn was important in the early morning hours of monastic prayer. (See Primer IV.3 for an outline of the hours in the Divine Office.)

In classical meter iambs and trochees are measured in pairs of feet (dipodes). Each line in *Eterne rerum conditor* has two pairs, and so is called iambic diameter. When this same verse is adapted for accentual poetry, it is reckoned as iambic tetrameter (counting four feet to the line). Unlike *Ave maris stella* (see Anthology 1), which is an example of accentual poetry, *Eterne rerum conditor* correctly follows the patterns of long and short pertaining in quantitative classical Latin verse. Iambic dimeter would become a popular choice for hymn texts from late antiquity through the Middle Ages, and hymns written in it were sometimes assigned to Ambrose. As "Ambrosian meter" came to be used throughout Europe, it should not be surprising that many melodies were composed to suit such texts, and that accentual poetry with lines of four accentual iambs was often used for later Latin hymn texts. The four versions of *Eterne rerum conditor* reproduced here show how multiple settings of a text are sometimes indicative of larger musical understandings or relationships between one region and another. The texts have variants within them as well. These are sometimes in error (as in strophe 3 of the text); at other times they reveal local variants with acceptable meanings.

Anthology 2.1 is from twelfth-century Nevers in central France, and the melody found here is that found in most recordings today. Bearing in mind that pitch is a relative concept in this repertory (see Anthology 1), we can say that the piece is "in D"—that is, D is the final pitch. But the final is a long time coming; each of the first three lines cadences on the fifth (A), the fourth (G) above D, or F.

In Anthology 2.2, taken from a fourteenth-century Milanese manuscript (but reflecting the ancient use of Milan), every line of the hymn cadences on the final, making it more static in character than the melody in Anthology 2.1. Anthology 2.3 is found in a late-twelfth-century Cistercian source from the monastery of Heiligenkreuz in Austria. But it is very close to the melody of Anthology 2.2, and we may wonder why this would be so. The Cistercian Order, founded in the early 1100s, tried to recover the hymns of earlier centuries, long before music was being written down. The monks reasoned that the hymns associated with Ambrose and the rite centered in Milan that bears his name had higher authority than more recent hymns. Moreover, the Cistercians followed the plan of life known as the *Rule of St. Benedict,* which endorsed the singing of "Ambrosian" hymns, and so borrowed melodies from the Milanese (Ambrosian) liturgy, as can be seen in their setting of this hymn text.

The first three versions of the hymn melody are in D. Anthology 2.4, from a hymnal from Rheinau dated to 1459, contains yet another chant with an entirely different character. This melody begins and ends on E (see Primer III.2 for discussion of the modes). The melodies in D feature intervals a fifth above and a fourth below D, but the fifth above E is B, a pitch that made medieval musicians nervous, unless used as an ornament. When sounded with the fourth below it, F, the interval is not a perfect fourth, but rather an augmented fourth. When B is sounded with the fifth above it, also F, the fifth is diminished, once again not perfect. These imperfect intervals—called "tritones" because they are made of three whole steps and lie between the perfect intervals of the fourth and fifth—were to be avoided wherever possible. In fact, B occurs only twice in the entire Rheinau melody. The final E comes as something of a surprise at the end, quite unlike the strong motion to the final D in the other three melodies.

Selected Mass Propers

Frankish monophonic liturgical chants
Texts, by the late 8th century; music, late 8th and 9th centuries

The Mass Propers are those chants whose texts are proper, that is, particular to a given feast or season. Great numbers of them had to be composed to accommodate the many feasts of the church year. There are six genres of Proper Mass chants: Introits, Graduals, Alleluias, Tracts, Offertories, and Communions; their order in the service is shown in Primer IV.1, Table P3. These are the first surviving repertories of Western music. Their texts were compiled in the late eighth and ninth centuries, and copies of some chants with notation survive from the second half of the ninth century. Because the earliest of these melodies were fixed before the dividing of Charlemagne's kingdom at the Treaty of Verdun in 843, they spread throughout much of Europe. Although the contours of most of these early melodies were the same everywhere Frankish chant was sung, small variants were always present to give even these ancient pieces regional characters.

A brief overview of select Proper chants of Easter as found in the *Graduale Triplex* (see Primer I.4) shows that the basic characters of the Proper chant genres vary. The natures of these genres have to do with the ways in which they were performed and historically understood. As discussed in Chapter 3 of *Music in the Medieval West*, they represent three ways of proclaiming texts (most of which were taken from the psalms): antiphonal singing, which depended on the choir; responsorial singing, which involved a soloist working with a select choir; and the unique style of the Tracts, which were sung verse by verse to melismatic but highly formulaic melodies. The Introit, the opening piece of the Mass liturgy, is an example of antiphonal psalmody. Introit melodies are fairly simple in character, and their verse and Doxology (a formula of praise to the Trinity) are sung to a psalm tone (see Primer III.3). The Graduals and Alleluias are much more ornate, the text decorated by fairly long melismatic passages; these are examples of responsorial psalmody. The Offertory chant looks responsorial in character, whereas the Communion chant is antiphonal, although its intoned verse dropped out fairly early. Tracts are the only chants in the repertory that are sung without any kind of tone. Because they are sung in place of the Alleluia during the pre-Easter season called Lent, and on other penitential occasions, there is no Tract among the Proper chants for Easter studied here. (For further discussion of Tracts, see Chapter 3 of *Music in the Medieval West*.)

3.1 *RESURREXI:* INTROIT FOR EASTER (ANTIPHONAL)

Graduale Triplex, 196–97

ANTIPHON

Resurrexi, et adhuc tecum sum, alleluia: posuisti super me manum tuam, alleluia: mirabilis facta est scientia tua, alleluia, alleluia.	I have arisen and am still with you, alleluia: you have put your hand on me, alleluia: your knowledge has become wonderful, alleluia, alleluia.

PSALM VERSE

Domine probasti me, et cognovisti me: tu cognovisti sessionem meam, et resurrectionem meam.	Lord, you have tested me and known me; you have known my sitting down and my rising up. Psalm 139 (138):18, 6, 1–2*

*For psalms, the number in parentheses indicates the Vulgate (based on the Greek), where it differs from that of the New Revised Standard Edition and many other English Bibles (based on Hebrew).

DOXOLOGY

Gloria Patri et Filio et Spiritui Sancto. Sicut erat in principio, et nunc et semper, et in saecula saeculorum. Amen.

Glory be to the Father, and to the Son, and to the Holy Spirit, as it was in the beginning, is now, and ever shall be, world without end. Amen.

Resurrexi, an Introit for Easter Sunday, is an antiphonal chant, as all Introits are. It has the following form: (1) antiphon; (2) intoned psalm verse; (3) antiphon (all or in part); (4) intoned Doxology, sometimes followed by another verse; and (5) antiphon. (See Primer I.4 for further discussion of this chant.)

The text of the antiphon *Resurrexi*, taken from Psalm 139 (138), demonstrates how biblical texts could be adapted to fit the meanings of particular feasts, in this case Easter. In its very simplest sense, the text was chosen because verse 18 contains the word "resurrexi" (I arose). The text in liturgical context becomes prophecy, introducing a sense of coming and foreshadowing. But if you seek this chant text in the Vulgate or in English Bibles, neither the text nor the translation will be found. That is because the Introit text is ancient and comes from a Roman version of the psalter that predates Jerome's Vulgate.

The music of the Introit is in two contrasting styles. The antiphon is a fairly short melody in the fourth mode, which means it has a final of E. As described in Primer III.2, the modes (or scales, each of which has its own character) were conceptualized in pairs, and from the twelfth century forward each pair was called a *maneria*, or a fashion of doing things. The two scales in each pair end on the same final; the first of the pair is a higher scale, called "authentic," and the second is a lower scale, called "plagal." *Resurrexi* is plagal, the lower of the pair on E. But each mode is more than a range of notes: it also has particular formulas that are characteristic of it. In the case of modes 3 and 4, avoidance of the final E and of the B a fifth above it is typical, a concept introduced in our study of the hymn setting from Rheinau (see Anthology 2.4). The verse, usually taken from a psalm, and the Doxology are both sung to a tone, which is a slightly more elaborate version of the psalm tones explained in Primer III.3 and Anthology 4.

The melody of the Introit antiphon *Resurrexi* is highly reiterative, placing great emphasis on the pitches D and F, and allowing the choir to surround the final of the mode without lighting on it. The melody often moves to A as well, the reciting tone employed for the psalm verse. It is instructive to count the number of times the final E sounds at the end of a phrase in this antiphon, for they are few indeed: once at the end of the first long phrase (on "alleluia"), then at the very end of the antiphon, also on "alleluia." This creates a musical parallel between the second phrase, beginning on the words "et adhuc" and ending on "alleluia," and the very end of the piece, one that underscores the word "alleluia" as well as creating a powerful sense of closure for the piece as whole.

3.2 *VIDERUNT OMNES:* GRADUAL FOR CHRISTMAS (RESPONSORIAL)

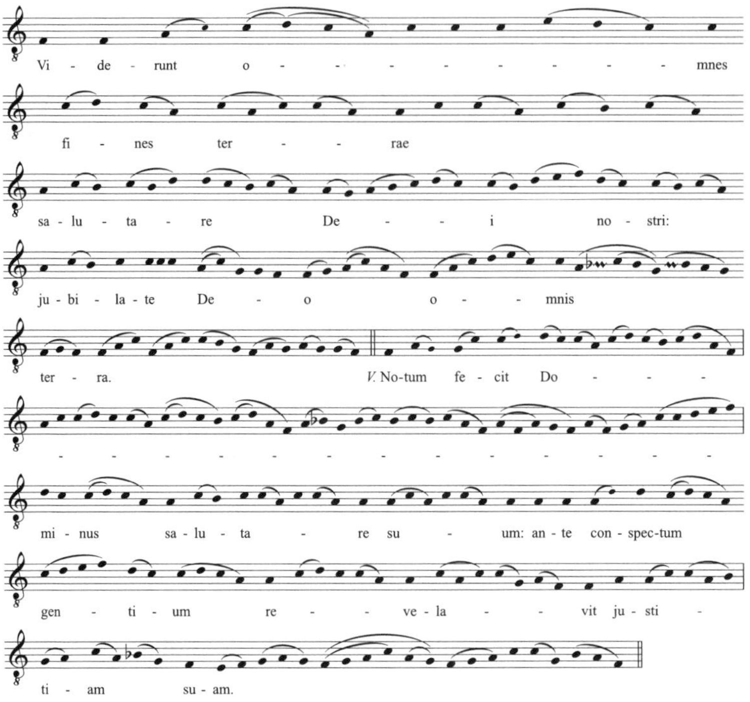

[Musical notation: chant melody with text underlaid]

Vi - de - runt o - mnes

fi - nes ter - rae

sa - lu - ta - re De - i no - stri:

ju - bi - la - te De - o o - mnis

ter - ra. *V.* No-tum fe - cit Do -

mi - nus sa - lu - ta - re su - um: an - te con - spec-tum

gen - ti - um re - ve - la - vit ju - sti -

ti - am su - am.

Liber Usualis, p. 409

RESPOND

Viderunt omnes fines terrae salutare
Dei nostri: jubilate Deo omnis terra.

All the ends of the earth have seen the salvation of
our God: sing joyfully to God, all the earth.
Psalm 98 (97):3 and 4

VERSE

Notum fecit Dominus salutare suum: ante
conspectum gentium revelavit justitiam suam.

The Lord has made His salvation known: He has
revealed His justice in the sight of the gentiles,
alleluia.
Psalm 98 (97):2

Viderunt omnes, for the third Mass of Christmas (this feast is the only day in the
medieval church year with three Masses), is a Gradual—that is, it was sung on
the steps, or *gradus*, leading to the altar. (Figure 9.4 in *Music in the Medieval West*
shows a setting in four-voice organum from a mid-thirteenth-century manuscript; the pitches of the Gradual are in the lowest voice, or tenor.) In the Mass

liturgy, this Gradual would have been sung after the first reading, as can be seen from the outline of the Mass liturgy in Primer IV.1. *Viderunt omnes* is an example of responsorial psalmody; it is made up of two parts, a respond, sung by the most skilled members of the choir, and a verse, sung by a soloist. The form was as follows: (1) respond; (2) verse; and (3) a section of the respond called the *repetendum*. (See also the discussion of the Easter Gradual *Haec dies* in Primer II.2.)

Viderunt omnes is a useful piece to show how the medieval modes worked, for they functioned characteristically within each genre of chant. Recall that in the oldest layers of chant, melodies came first, shaped by styles of singing appropriate to each liturgical action. Later came modes, music theory, and notation, and surely melodic formulas were tamed to suit the new technology. *Viderunt omnes* belongs to a family of Graduals sung to a particular group of modal formulas—in this case, the tritus maneria expressed in mode 5, the authentic, or higher, scale with a final of F. Each of the four pairs of scales (protus, deuterus, tritus, and tetrardus) has distinctive qualities that offered a way of remembering basic melodic types.

One of the most important ways that medieval chant is organized is by the "chains of thirds" principle, not described by medieval theorists, but nonetheless useful today. According to this simple analytical idea, one chain of pitches an interval of a third apart forms a strong grouping for the organization of melodic phrases, and this is counterbalanced by the chain of thirds that neighbors it. Melodies built this way often begin by making sure the ear is well established in the main chain of thirds, and then depart from it. At this point the ear will feel out of joint and anticipate a return to the main chain of thirds, something that will happen at important cadences or ends of phrases. Chant can seem at first to be somewhat meandering until the ear gets used to the ways it is utilizing mode, the "glue" that sustains it. In *Viderunt omnes* (mode 5), the expectation is that the chain of thirds will be anchored by what sounds like a major triad, F–A–C. Indeed, the music begins by establishing the chain of thirds that moves from F to A to C; after ornamenting the C, it leaps up to the E above, another third. The chant melody moves up and down on these thirds, not departing in a prolonged way until near the cadence on "Dei nostri." Here the subsidiary chain of thirds takes over, moving from G to B to D and up to F, the last note of "Dei" and the highest pitch in the entire chant, a dramatic moment before the return to the third (C to A) that closes out this phrase. Mode 5 features triadic figures that pop between the notes F, A, and C (as on the word "omnis" in this melody). This characteristic was also encapsulated in short melodies sung to nonsense syllables that were used to prepare singers for particular modes. Before beginning to sing a chant in a particular mode, a singer might exercise musical memory through a characteristic formula. For example, compare the opening of *Viderunt omnes* to one of the mode 5 formulas (Ex. A1). By singing through this little melody in Example

Alb, we can get a sense of how medieval singers and their teachers may have practiced their chants (and improvised new ones) when memory was still the foundation of a developing notational practice. Formulas such as this were also keys to the development of psalm singing and the differentiae used to close out the singing of each verse (see Anthology 4 and Primer III.3).

Example A1: (a) Opening of _Viderunt omnes_; (b) formula for mode 5

(a)

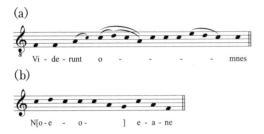

(b)

3.3 _PASCHA NOSTRUM:_ ALLELUIA FOR EASTER (RESPONSORIAL)

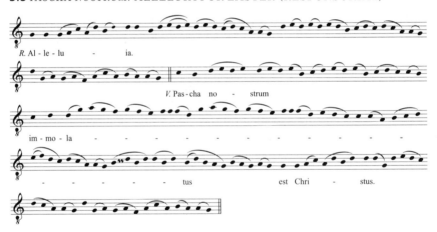

Graduale Triplex, pp. 197–98

RESPOND

Alleluia.   Alleluia.

VERSE

Pascha nostrum immolatus est Christus.   Christ our Pasch has been sacrificed.
                                              1 Corinthians 5:7

Alleluia, a Hebrew word meaning "praise God," was sung in many guises throughout all nonpenitential seasons, and most frequently during paschal time (after the octave of Easter—the eight-day period beginning on the feast day—through to Pentecost). Proclaimed in the Office as an antiphon, this praiseful word was used to punctuate many chant texts in the Office and the Mass, and also occurs most significantly as one of the Proper Mass chants, sung just before the sequence (if one was sung) and then the intonation of the Gospel text. So popular was this genre of chant that a second Mass Alleluia was sung in the place of the Mass Gradual for several weeks after Easter. The Alleluia *Pascha nostrum*, found among the Propers for Easter Sunday, illustrates the formal structure of the Mass Alleluia and demonstrates many of the stylistic features often employed in this genre. This particular chant was sung throughout Europe on Easter Sunday from the late eighth century, and sometimes on the Sunday after Easter as well.

The Mass Alleluias constitute a vast repertory of Frankish melodies, many of which were composed slightly after the establishment of the earliest layers of Mass Proper chants. Musicians were still creating Alleluias in abundance after the splitting of Charlemagne's kingdom into three parts, as can be seen by the great regional variety in the repertories. As Alleluias are responsorial psalmody, they are highly melismatic, but the melismas are often tamed into artful phrases that may repeat, a feature not found to such an extent in any other Proper chant genre. Another distinguishing aspect of the genre is that many Alleluias, even from the very earliest time, were given multiple textual settings.

The long melisma that closes out the respond is sometimes known as the *jubilus*. The chant was performed in several ways, but by the later Middle Ages the form was usually as follows:

Respond: Alleluia (soloist) and repeat of Alleluia plus jubilus (soloist plus choir)

Verse: (soloist, with the choir perhaps joining for the final melisma)

Respond: Alleluia plus jubilus (choir)

In *Pascha nostrum*, the soloistic setting of the word "alleluia" is repeated and followed by the jubilus, vocalized on the vowel "a." The jubilus contains three long melismas. The second is an expansion of the first, while the final cadential melisma is approached by a dramatic descent of a fifth. The verse explores the upper part of the range of this mode 7 piece. At the very end, the cadential formula employed in the jubilus recurs, giving *Pascha nostrum* a rounded form. The Alleluias are discussed in Chapter 4 of *Music in the Medieval West*, along with Ordinary chants, tropes, and sequences.

ANONYMOUS

Ecce apparebit Dominus and Laudate Dominum
Antiphon with intoned psalm verses
9th century

4.1 *ECCE APPAREBIT DOMINUS:* ANTIPHON FOR ADVENT

Ec - ce ap - pa - re - bit Do - mi - nus, et non men - ti - e - tur: si mo-ram fe - ce - rit, ex - spec - ta e - um, qui - a ve - ni - et, et non tar - da - bit, al - le - lu - ia.

4.2 *LAUDATE DOMINUM* (PSALM 147 [146])

intonation flex (for very long lines) mediant termination

Lau - da - te Do - mi-num quo - ni - am bo - nus est psalmus: De - o no-stro sit ju - cun-da de - co - ra - que lau - da - ti - o.

Ae - di - fi - cans Je - ru - sa - lem Do - mi - nus: dis - per - si - o - nes Is - ra - el - is con - gre - ga - bit.

Qui sa - nat con - tri - tos cor - de: et al - li - gat con - tri - ti - o - nes e - o - rum.

Qui nu - me - rat mul - ti - tu - di-nem stel - la - rum: et o - mni-bus e - is no - mi - na vo - cat.

Ma-gnus Do-mi-nus no-ster, et ma-gna vir-tus e - ius: et sa - pi - en - ti - ae e - ius non est nu - me-rus.

4.1: *Liber Usualis*, p. 116
4.2: *Antiphonale monasticum*, p. 196

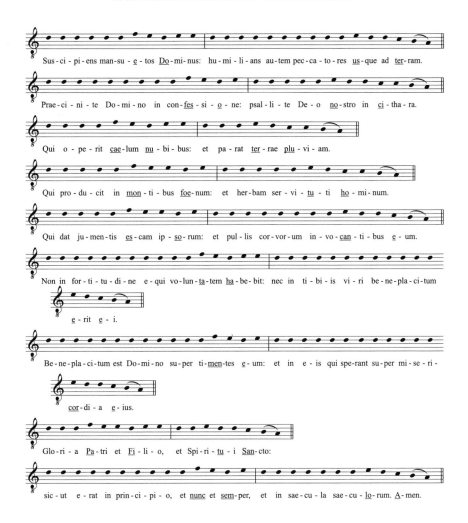

Sus - ci - pi - ens man-su - e - tos Do - mi - nus: hu - mi - li - ans au - tem pec - ca - to - res us - que ad ter - ram.

Prae - ci - ni - te Do - mi - no in con - fes - si - o - ne: psal - li - te De - o no - stro in ci - tha - ra.

Qui o - pe - rit cae - lum nu - bi - bus: et pa - rat ter - rae plu - vi - am.

Qui pro - du - cit in mon - ti - bus foe - num: et her - bam ser - vi - tu - ti ho - mi - num.

Qui dat ju - men - tis es - cam ip - so - rum: et pul - lis cor - vor - um in - vo - can - ti - bus e - um.

Non in for - ti - tu - di - ne e - qui vo - lun - ta - tem ha - be - bit: nec in ti - bi - is vi - ri be - ne - pla - ci - tum

e - rit e - i.

Be - ne - pla - ci - tum est Do - mi - no su - per ti - men - tes e - um: et in e - is qui spe - rant su - per mi - se - ri -

cor - di - a e - ius.

Glo - ri - a Pa - tri et Fi - li - o, et Spi - ri - tu - i San - cto:

sic - ut e - rat in prin - ci - pi - o, et nunc et sem - per, et in sae - cu - la sae - cu - lo - rum. A - men.

ANTIPHON

Ecce apparebit Dominus, et non mentietur: si moram fecerit, expecta eum, quia veniet, et non tardabit, alleluia.

Behold, the Lord will come; He will not prove false. If He makes a delay, wait for Him; for He will come and not be slow, alleluia.

Habbakuk 2:3, Douay/Reims Bible

PSALM VERSES

Laudate Dominum quoniam bonus est psalmus:* Deo nostro sit jucunda decoraque laudatio.

Praise the Lord, because a psalm is good: to our God be joyful and comely praise.

Aedificans Jerusalem Dominus:*
dispersiones Israelis congregabit.
Qui sanat contritos corde:* et alligat
contritiones eorum.
Qui numerat multitudinem stellarum:* et
omnibus eis nomina vocat.
Magnus Dominus noster, et magna virtus
eius:* et sapientiae eius non est numerus.
Suscipiens mansuetos Dominus:*
humilians autem peccatores usque ad
    terram.
Praecinite Domino in confessione:* psallite
Deo nostro in cithara.
Qui operit caelum nubibus:* et parat terrae
    pluviam.
Qui producit in montibus foenum:* et
herbam servituti hominum.

Qui dat jumentis escam ipsorum:* et pullis
corvorum invocantibus eum.
Non in fortitudine equi voluntatem habebit:*
nec in tibiis viri beneplacitum erit ei.

Beneplacitum est Domino super timentes
eum:* et in eis qui sperant super
misericordia eius.

The Lord builds up Jerusalem: He will
gather together the dispersed of Israel.
Who heals the broken of heart, and binds
up their bruises.
Who tells the number of the stars: and calls
them all by their names.
Great is our Lord, and great is His power:
and of His wisdom there is no number.
The Lord lifts up the meek, and brings the
wicked down even to the ground.

Sing to the Lord with praise: sing to our
God upon the harp.
Who covers the heaven with clouds, and
prepares rain for the earth.
Who makes grass to grow on the
mountains, and herbs for the service of
    men.
Who gives to beasts their food: and to the
young ravens that call upon him.
He shall not delight in the strength of the
horse: nor take pleasure in the legs of a
    man.
The Lord takes pleasure in them that fear
Him: and in them that hope in His mercy.
Psalm 147 (146):1–12

DOXOLOGY

Gloria Patri et Filio et Spiritui Sancto. Sicut erat
in principio, et nunc et semper, et in saecula
saeculorum. Amen.

Glory be to the Father, and to the Son, and to the Holy
Spirit, as it was in the beginning, is now, and ever
shall be, world without end. Amen.

Medieval Office psalmody was an art of memory. The psalm tones had to be
committed to memory from an early age, and they in turn would aid in learning the texts of the entire psalter, 150 poems. The tones are formulas, one in
each mode, used to intone the psalms in the Divine Office, or hours of prayer
(see Primer IV.3 for an outline of the Office and Primer III.3 for the psalm
tones). Each tone has a reciting pitch, a beginning formula, a mediant (middle
phrase), and a termination formula (*differentia*), all of which must be fitted
to the Latin texts. The common practice was to sing the antiphon, followed

by the entire psalm with its Doxology, and then to repeat the antiphon. The intonation formula is sung only for the first verse of the psalm; for subsequent verses, the singers enter on the reciting tone (for the *Magnificat* and the *Benedictus*, every verse was intoned). There is a ninth tone as well, the *tonus peregrinus* (wandering tone), which uses a lower reciting pitch for the last half of the psalm verse.

In the accompanying scores, a psalm from the Office is paired with an antiphon from the season of Advent, so the musical connection can be seen. The text of the antiphon *Ecce apparebit Dominus* is a paraphrase of the minor prophet Habbakuk referring to the idea, appropriate to Advent, that God will come and not be late. It is combined with the 11 verses of *Laudate Dominum*, one of the psalms regularly sung at Vespers in accordance with the *Rule of St. Benedict* (SR 17:163; 2/9:27). The entire psalm has been written out to the tone for mode 7, using the termination formula that ends on A. Since, as we have seen, the concept of pitch in this chant repertory is relative, the final can be established wherever it is comfortable for the choir.

The mode 7 psalm tone recites on D and has a mediant (midpoint cadence) comprising the last two accents of the half verse, as can be seen underscored in the text above (and marked by asterisks in the Latin text). The singer, having identified these accents, must move up from the reciting tone a full step for the first of these accented syllables, and drop from the reciting tone one step for the second. The notes in parentheses show what to do to accommodate extra syllables. The termination formula that ends on A also has two accents, telling the singers to move up one note for the first accent, return to the reciting tone, and then move down a pitch for the second accent. The purpose of the termination formula—in this case, a descent to A—is to link the psalm verse smoothly to the pitches of the antiphon that follows. Here too we have underscored the accented syllables both in the score and in the text example. But differentiae do not rely only on pitches and tonality; they also have different ways of treating the texts. While many differentiae rely on accents in this manner, incorporating the patterns found in the final word of the verse, others depend on syllable counting only, and so have *cursive* cadences, like the final cadence for the psalm tone for the Introit *Resurrexi* (see Anthology 3.1). In such cases this pattern serves for all verses of the psalm, regardless of word accent, and is applied to the last four syllables, whatever they might be. The slight variation in rendering caused by the differentiae is one of the great delights of singing to the tones.

The mode 7 antiphon *Ecce apparebit Dominus* has the reciting tone of D as a goal in several of its phrases, and the final of G is strongly emphasized as well. Just as the text of the antiphon is interactive with the text of the psalm, so too the music of the antiphon reinforces the psalm tone. (The same is generally true of all psalms and their antiphons.) Twice near the end of the piece, the voices descend to D an octave below the reciting tone, creating a kind of musical rhyme between the phrases "quia veniet" et "non tardabit." Such ways of emphasizing the octave, fifth, and fourth of the mode are foundational to the melodic style of medieval psalmody.

The way to learn the practice is by singing antiphonally with the tone to the psalm text, matching the underscored accented syllables to the musical inflections. Learning to sing the intoned psalmody is essential, as this is the most important practice in all of medieval music and underlies much of the chant repertory. This musical-textual performance technique was emphasized in standard pedagogy of the Middle Ages to the point where it became second nature. It was so much a part of the culture that a chorister, canon, monk, or nun could sing the entire psalter using all nine psalm tones as adapted in his or her local practice and never have to think about how many accents were necessary for a given cadence.

Stirps Jesse

Great responsory for Matins

Early 11th century

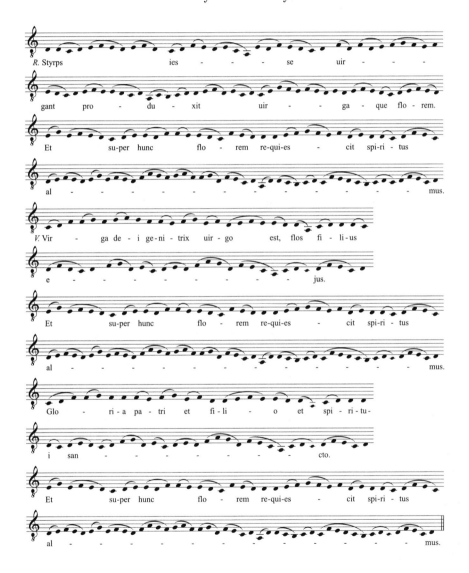

R. Styrps ... ies - - se uir - - -

gant pro - du - xit uir - ga - que flo - rem.

Et su-per hunc flo - rem re-qui-es - cit spi-ri - tus

al - - - - - - - - - mus.

V. Vir - ga de - i ge-ni - trix uir - go est, flos fi - li - us

e - - - - - jus.

Et su-per hunc flo - rem re-qui-es - cit spi-ri - tus

al - - - - - - - - - - - mus.

Glo - ri - a pa - tri et fi - li - o et spi - ri - tu -

i san - - - - - - cto.

Et su-per hunc flo - rem re-qui-es - cit spi-ri - tus

al - - - - - - - - - mus.

Rome, Biblioteca Apostolica Vaticana Vat. lat. 4756, ff. 328v–329r; Margot Fassler, *The Virgin of Chartres: Making History through Liturgy and the Arts* (New Haven: Yale University Press, 2010), 415.

RESPOND

Styrps iesse* uirgam produxit uirgaque florem.	The shoot of Jesse produced a rod, and the rod a flower.
Et super hunc florem requiescit spiritus almus.	And over this flower rests the nurturing spirit.

VERSE

Uirga dei genitrix virgo est, flos filius ejus.	The shoot is the virgin Genetrix of God, and the flower is her Son.
Et super hunc florem requiescit spiritus almus.	And over this flower rests the nurturing spirit.

DOXOLOGY

Gloria patri et filio et spiritui sancto.	Glory to the Father and to the Son and to the Holy Spirit.

REPETENDUM

Et super hunc florem requiescit spiritus almus.	And over this flower rests the nurturing spirit.

Stirps Jesse is spelled variously in medieval sources; see Anthology 27.

Stirps Jesse is a great responsory, as distinguished from the short, formulaic pieces for the Office known as lesser responsories. It was created for the Office of Matins and sung for that most favored of saints, the Virgin Mary. Like all great responsories, it was designed to come after a reading, as can be seen from the plan of the Office in Primer IV.3. Office responsories have three sections: the respond, the verse, and the Doxology, which was usually sung only for the final responsory of a nocturn (and usually only the first half of the text, as here). A nocturn was a grouping of psalms, readings, and responsories, the precise number depending on whether the liturgy was monastic or cathedral, and on the importance of the feast as well. If it was the final responsory of a nocturn, *Stirps Jesse* usually would have been performed as follows:

> Respond (intoned by a soloist, with the choir joining in)
>
> Verse (soloist)
>
> Repetendum (final section of the respond, sung by the choir)
>
> Doxology (half) (choir)
>
> Repetendum (choir)

Stirps Jesse was composed in Chartres, probably in the first half of the eleventh century, and soon became attributed to Bishop Fulbert, who was renowned as a teacher. Many of his students were well trained in music and became leaders of monastic and cathedral choirs throughout Europe. Wherever they went, music that was associated with Chartres Cathedral and their beloved teacher traveled as well. By the early twelfth century, *Stirps Jesse* was established in the chant repertory throughout Europe. Through such famous pieces, historical characters were developed: Bishop Fulbert, for example, became a composer and musician through the power of a melody ascribed to him (whether he wrote it or not). The fame of Chartres Cathedral as a center for musical composition was kept alive for centuries through the singing of this beautiful melody.

A set of tones for the verses of great responsories was sung throughout Europe, and the responds themselves were often highly formulaic. *Stirps Jesse* is free of such restraints. Its text consists of four lines in hexameter, and its freely composed melody is graced with a glorious melisma on the words "flos filius eius" (the flower, her Son).

The first part of the responsory gives voice to two texts from the Old Testament: Isaiah 11:1–2, a description of the shoot of Jesse and the resting of the spirit upon it; and Numbers 17, a description of the flowering rod of Aaron. The text of the verse proclaims that the Virgin is the rod and the flower, her Son (see also *Stirps Jesse florigeram*, Anthology 13). When the repetendum is sung, the spirit mentioned in Isaiah comes to rest over Mary's son. Although neither text is sung to a tone, the music for the Gloria is the same as that used for the verse, a practice common among musicians in the school of Fulbert. So the music for "flos filius eius" is the same as that for "spiritui sancto" (to the Holy Spirit), showing through music that the Spirit rests upon the Son. Musical balance is achieved through the melismatic endings of each major section.

The mode 2 melody provides an example of the tension commonly found in medieval melodies between neighboring chains of interlocking thirds, a principle as true in Frankish chant (see the analysis of *Viderunt omnes* in Anthology 3.2) as in melodies from the tenth and eleventh centuries. In this case, each phrase is some kind of exploration of the third created by D and F, the points of resolution (and the final and reciting tones of the mode, respectively), and A–C–E–G, the chain of thirds that pulls in the opposite direction. Each phrase circles away from D–F, only to return, in one way or another, at its close. The leap on the word "produxit" from D down to A, the lowest pitch in the mode, is the most dramatic. The B–D–F chain of thirds cannot be used because of the tritone between B and F, so B occurs rarely, always as a neighbor note to C.

The enduring popularity of *Stirps Jesse* is reflected in the large number of available recordings. The women of the Vox Silentii, attentive to the medieval rules on music and performance for Bridgettine nuns (see Chapter 12 of

Music in the Medieval West), sing the piece very slowly and allow the listener to focus on the ways the music underscores the text. A group of powerful images appears in the mind, promoting a meditation on the mysteries their juxtapositions represent. The highly reverberant acoustic mimics that of a small stone chapel or other semi-enclosed area. The performance lasts more than five minutes, even without the Doxology and repetendum, which surely would have been rendered in the Middle Ages. The Schola Hungarica recording, by contrast, clocks in at just under three minutes and offers the responsory as part of a series of modally ordered works found in a medieval Hungarian manuscript.

ANONYMOUS

Cunctipotens genitor
Kyrie with prosula
10th century

6.1 KYRIE

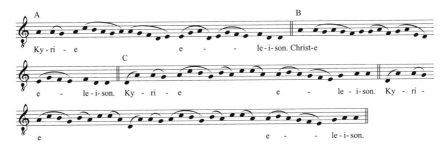

6.2 PROSULA

6.1: *Liber Usualis*, p. 25
6.2: Paris, BN lat. 887, f. 56r; David Bjork, *The Aquitanian Kyrie Repertory of the Tenth and Eleventh Centuries*, ed. Richard Crocker (Aldershot: Ashgate, 2003), 221–23; translation by Calvin M. Bower. We have made diligent efforts to contact the copyright holder to obtain permission to reprint this selection. If you have information that would help us, please write to Permissions Department, W. W. Norton & Company, Inc., 500 Fifth Avenue, New York, NY 10110.

5 Plas - ma - tis hu - ma - ni fac - tor lap - si re - pa - ra - tor

e - lei - son.

6 Ne tu - a dam - ne - tur Ie - su fac - tu - ra be - ni - gne

e - lei - son.

7 Am - bo - rum sac - rum spi - ra - men ne - xus a - mor - que

e - lei - son.

8 Pro - ce - dens fo - mes vi - te fons pu - ri - fi - cans vis

e - lei - son.

9 Pur - ga - tor cul - pe ve - ni - e lar - gi - tor o - pi - mae

of - fen - sas de - le sanc - to nos mu - ne - re re - ple

spi - ri - tus al - me.

A	Cunctipotens genitor deus omnicreator eleison.	All-powerful Father, O God, Creator of all things, have mercy.
A	Fons et origo boni pie luxque perennis eleison.	Font and origin of the good, O holy one, and light everlasting, have mercy.
A	Salvificet pietas tua nos bone rector eleison.	May Your holiness rescue us, O good sovereign, have mercy.
B	Christe dei splendor virtus patrisque sophia eleison.	O Christ, splendor of God, strength and wisdom of the Father, have mercy.
B	Plasmatis humani factor lapsi reparator eleison.	Creator of human substance, restorer of those who fall, have mercy.
B	Ne tua damnetur Iesu factura benigne eleison.	Lest your handiwork be damned, O kind Jesus, have mercy.
C	Amborum sacrum spiramen nexus amorque eleison.	Holy inspiration of them both, their unity and love, have mercy.

C   Procedens fomes vite fons purificans
      vis eleison.

C′   Purgator culpe venie largitor opimae
      offensas dele sancto nos munere reple
      spiritus alme.

Emanating flame, fountain of life, purifying
    power, have mercy.

Great purifier of sin, bestower of pardon, erase our
  offenses, fill us through Your holy gift,
    O nourishing Spirit, have mercy.

The *Kyrie eleison* is a genre of penitential Ordinary chants that are sung near the beginning of the service. Although there were many uses of the text in earlier liturgical development, by the late ninth century the Kyrie of the Mass had a ninefold structure, divided into three sections (**AAABBBCCC′**) that often cohere both musically and textually. The parallel musical plan for *Cunctipotens genitor* is a good example of carefully patterned formal organization, one that would not be found in any genre of Mass proper chants.

Cunctipotens genitor is a southern French chant that first shows up in the tenth century with its prosula (an interpolated poetic text). It belongs to the Mass Ordinary, the pieces whose core texts do not change: Kyrie, Gloria, Credo, Sanctus, Agnus Dei, and *Ite missa est*. Except for the Credo, many pieces in these genres were outfitted with some kind of musical gloss—either tropes or prosulae—which gave them greater specificity. *Cunctipotens genitor* is unlike most others of this genre, date, and region in that its text is metrical (essentially dactylic). Many other chants utilized syllable counting and accent to mark out the lines, rather than the feet of classical meters. Moreover, *Cunctipotens genitor* advances a Trinitarian theme, with the first three lines addressed to the Father, the next three to the Son, and the last three to the Holy Spirit. The music, however, has much in common with other D-mode Kyries and even exhibits some characteristics that can be found in contemporary sequences (see Anthology 7).

Among the most intriguing aspects of medieval melodies created in the late ninth and tenth centuries are the endless ways they reflect the modes, which by this time were a well-established part of musical understanding. The development of the psalm tones, too, helped to reinforce the pitches that constituted the reciting tones in each mode, giving these pitches a secondary level of importance. Most melodies for the Mass Ordinary were first created in abundance while these musical developments were gaining ground; as a result, they are different in character from the earlier Frankish chant repertories, especially from the Mass Propers, many of which were in circulation before the coming of the modes and of musical notation. In addition, the genres of Ordinary chants are not psalmodic, so the understandings connected with antiphonal and responsorial practices do not apply. Comparison of *Cunctipotens genitor* with examples of the earlier Frankish chant traditions reveals many differences in style and general formal conception. The phrases of the Kyrie are clipped and tonally direct by comparison with the reiterative style of the Gradual *Viderunt omnes* (see Anthology 3.2).

Our anthology selection provides two musical understandings of *Cunctipotens genitor*, one without syllables added (from the *Liber Usualis*) and the other with the prosula. It will be seen that the melodies are slightly different. The names given to Kyrie melodies in the *Liber Usualis* and elsewhere are the openings of their medieval Latin prosulae, which in some cases were probably composed along with the melodies themselves. Kyries could also be provided with tropes (additions of both text and music), usually of an introductory type. How the prosula text was performed in the Middle Ages is a matter of speculation. It seems clear that there were several possibilities, including alternating texted lines with vocalized melismas or having one voice proclaim the text while others vocalized.

A high level of repetition in various sections of the melody sustains the piece's large-scale form. Melody **A**, repeated three times to the words "Kyrie eleison" (Lord, have mercy), falls into three phrases: an ornamented A, a descent to E (which, as it is a tone above the anticipated final, offers a sense of incompleteness), and a further descent to D via a cadential leap of a minor third. Melody **B** for the three "Christe eleison" (Christ, have mercy) lines is strongly tied to melody **A** through the use of this cadential phrase. Melody **C**, for the final three "Kyrie eleison" phrases, contains a great deal of repetition and has two versions, one for text lines 7 and 8, and the last for line 9.

The cadential phrase that links melodies **A** and **B** can be found in melody **C** as well, but in the middle of the line, and a fifth higher. The phrase that contains these notes is featured in lines 7 and 8, and repeated twice in the opening of line 9 as well. But the cadential phrase of melody **C** that closes out lines 7, 8, and 9 ends on the pitch A, a fifth away from the expected final of D. This use of the fifth in a final position emphasizes the powerful relationship between D and A. Both of these pitches have a whole tone below and a whole tone and semitone above them. Medieval ears delighted in listening to pitches that relate in this way.

7

ANONYMOUS AND NOTKER THE STAMMERER (C. 840-912)

Rex omnipotens and *Sancti Spiritus*

Sequences

Late 9th century

The sequence is a through-composed genre, an essentially syllabic setting of a text that unfolds in couplets, preceded (and sometimes ended) by a single-line strophe. Although each couplet has different music, the two lines are paired by the use of common music, yielding the form **ABBCCDD**, and so on. The sequence was sung after the Alleluia and before the intoning of the Gospel in the Mass, and sometimes was used for other liturgical occasions as well.

Neat relationships between the jubilus (the long melisma on the final vowel of the word "alleluia") of a particular Alleluia and any given sequence melodies can be difficult to discern. In any case, early sequences always appear to be text syllables set to a jubilus, with the word "alleluia" playing a role in the development of both text and melody. The Alleluia jubilus is characterized by phrase repetitions, and this feature may be the historical reason that the sequence is composed of repeating musical phrases (see Anthology 3.3). In addition to the jubili, a number of very long melodies based on the Alleluia were in circulation both east and west of the Rhine. *Occidentana*, the source of the two sequences considered here, is one of these melodies. The "parent" Alleluia melody was sung on both the feasts of the Ascension and Pentecost.

7.1 *REX OMNIPOTENS*

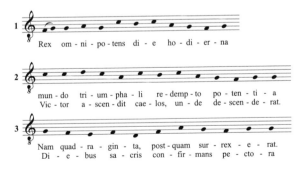

Paris, BN lat. 1118, f. 187; Richard Crocker, *The Early Medieval Sequence* (Berkeley: University of California Press, 1977), 190–91 and 200–201.

4. A - po - sto - lo - rum, pa - cis ca - ra re - lin - quens os - cu - la.
Qui - bus et de - dit po - te - sta - tem la - xan - di cri - mi - na.

5. Et mi - sit e - os in mun - dum bap - ti - za - re cunc - tas a - ni - mas
In pa - tris et fi - li - i et sanc - ti spi - ri - tus cle - men - ti - a:

6. Et con - ve - scens prae - ce - pit e - is ab Hier - o - so - ly - mis
Ne ab - i - rent, sed ex - pec - ta - rent pro - mis - sa mu - ne - ra.

7. "Non post mul - tos e - nim di - es mit - tam vo - bis spi - ri - tum
Et e - ri - tis mi - hi te - stes in Hier - ru - sa - lem. Ju - de - a
pa - ra - cli - tum in ter - ra.
si - ve et Sa - ma - ri - a."

8. Cum hoc dix - is - set, vi - den - ti - bus il - lis e - le - va - tus est et nu - bes cla - ra
Su - sce - pit e - um ab e - o - rum o - cu - lis: in - tu - en - ti - bus il - lis a - e - ra.

9. Ec - ce ste - te - re a - mic - ti du - o vi - ri in ves - te al - ba
Jux - ta di - cen - tes: "Quid ad - mi - ra - mi - ni cae - lo - rum al - ta?

10. Je - sus e - nim hic, qui as - sump - tus est a vo - bis ad pa - tris dex - te - ram.
Ut a - scen - dit, i - ta ve - ni - et quae - rens ta - len - ti com - mis - si lu - cra."

11. O de - us ma - ris, po - li, ar - vi, ho - mi - nem, quem cre - a - sti, quem frau - de
Hos - tis ex - pu - lit pa - ra - di - so et cap - ti - va - tum se - cum trax - it ad
sub - do - la
tar - tar - a.

12. San - gui - ne pro - pri - o quem re - de - mi - sti de - o
Ju - dex cum ve - ne - ris ju - di - ca - re sae - cu - lum
Il - luc et pro - ve - his, un - de pri - ma cor - ru - it pa - ra - di - si gau - di - a.
Da no - bis pe - ti - mus sem - pi - ter - nam re - qui - em in sanc - to - rum pa - tri - a.

13. In qua ti - bi can - te - mus om - nes "al - le - lu - ia."

1	Rex omnipotens die hodierna	On this day the all-powerful king,
2a	mundo triumphali redempto potentia	having redeemed the world by His triumphant might,
2b	Victor ascendit caelos, unde descenderat.	ascends a victor to heaven, whence He had come.
3a	Nam quadraginta, postquam surrexerat,	Throughout forty holy days after His resurrection
3b	Diebus sacris confirmans pectora	He strengthened the hearts
4a	Apostolorum, pacis cara relinquens oscula,	of the Apostles, to whom, leaving the sweet kiss of peace,
4b	Quibus et dedit potestatem laxandi crimina,	He gave the power to forgive sins
5a	Et misit eos in mundum baptizare cunctas animas	and sent them into the world to baptize all souls
5b	In patris et filii et sancti spiritus clementia:	in the mercy of the Father, the Son, and the Holy Spirit.
6a	Et convescens praecepit eis, ab Hierosolymis	And, eating with them, He told them not to leave Jerusalem,
6b	Ne abirent, sed expectarent promissa munera.	but to await the promised gifts.
7a	"Non post multos enim dies mittam vobis spiritum paraclitum in terra.	"For not many days from now I will send to you on earth the Spirit, the Paraclete [Comforter],
7b	Et eritis mihi testes in Hierrusalem, Judea sive et Samaria."	and you will be My witnesses in Jerusalem, Judea, and Samaria."
8a	Cum hoc dixisset, videntibus illis elevatus est et nubes clara	And when He had said this, He ascended while they watched,
8b	Suscepit eum ab eorum oculis: intuentibus illis aera.	and a bright cloud took Him up from their eyes, with them gazing into the air.
9a	Ecce, stetere amicti duo viri in veste alba	Behold, two men, dressed in white robes, stood by
9b	Juxta dicentes: "Quid admiramini caelorum alta?	and said, "Why are you gazing up into high heaven?
10a	Jesus enim hic, qui assumptus est a vobis ad patris dexteram,	This Jesus, who is taken from you to the right hand of the Father,
10b	Ut ascendit, ita veniet quaerens talenti commissi lucra."	as He ascended so shall He come, seeking interest on the entrusted coin."
11a	O deus maris, poli, arvi, hominem, quem creasti, quem fraude subdola	O God of ocean, air, and field, the human whom You created,
11b	Hostis expulit paradiso et captivatum secum traxit ad tartara,	and whom by guile the foe drove out of paradise, and led a captive with him to Hell,
12a	Sanguine proprio quem redemisti deo Illuc et provehis, unde prima corruit paradisi gaudia.	and whom You have redeemed by Your own blood, O God: Bring the human back to the first joys of paradise from whence he fell.
12b	Judex cum veneris judicare saeculum Da nobis petimus sempiternam requiem in sanctorum patria.	When You, the Judge, will come to judge the world. Grant us, we pray You, everlasting rest in the home land of saints,
13	In qua tibi cantemus omnes "alleluia."*	where we all shall sing to You, "Alleluia."

*For the scriptural source of the text, see Acts 1:1–11, read at Mass as the Epistle on the feast day, as well as the Gospel of the day, Matthew 25:14–30, which provides the source for lines 9b–10b.

Rex omnipotens is a late-ninth-century West Frankish text that circulated to the *Occidentana* melody in France, England, and Italy. This texted version was created for a particular feast, Ascension, and offers a narrative of the celebration. The story is told in the couplets that are characteristic of the sequence, whether early, middle, or late. Sequences are through-composed, that is, the music for each strophe is different. However, except for individual lines at the beginning and end, every strophe is divided into couplets; these are paired by use of the same music. Thus the musical form of *Rex omnipotens* is

ABBCCDDEEFFGGHHIIJJKKLLM

In early sequences, the couplets are of very different lengths. There are, however, many very small repeating musical cells that give a powerful sense of organization to what might otherwise seem like a somewhat chaotic form. The most important of these are the cadential phrases that punctuate every line, whether it ends on G, the final of mode 7, or on D, the fifth above. Both of these cadential formulas are five notes long, and the many ways of approaching this group of notes give the piece great variety and musical interest. Two different ways have been used by the editors to lay out these sequence melodies: pairing lines (Crocker, in score 7.1) or writing out each line (Bower, in score 7.2).

7.2 *SANCTI SPIRITUS*

St. Gall, Stiftsbibliothek 484, p. 281, in consultation with St. Gall, Stiftsbibliothek 366, p. 27; Aachen, Bischöfliche Diözesanbibliothek 13, f. 132v; *Le prosaire d'Aix-la Chapelle: Manuscrit 13 du chapitre d'Aix-la-Chapelle (XIIIe siècle, début)* (Rouen: Imprimerie rouennaise, 1961); and Munich, Bayerische Staatsbibliothek Clm 10075, f. 235v. From Calvin Bower, *Editing Notker: Challenges and Discovery.* Reprinted with permission of Calvin M. Bower.

5 Hor - ri - das no-strae men-tis pur - ga te - ne-bras.

6 A - ma-tor san-cte sen-sa - to-rum

sem-per co - gi - ta - tu - um:

7 In - fun - de un - cti - o - nem tu - am,

cle-mens, no-stris sen - si - bus.

8 Tu pu - ri - fi - ca - tor om - ni - um

fla-gi - ti - o-rum, spi-ri-tus

9 Pu - ri - fi - ca no-stri o - cu-lum

in - te - ri - or - is ho-mi-nis,

10 Ut vi - der - i sup - re-mus ge - ni - tor

pos-sit a no-bis,

11 Mun - di cor-dis quem so - li cer - ne - re

pos-sunt o - cu - li.

19 I - do - la - tras ad cul - tum De - i

re - vo - cans, ma - gi - stro - rum op - ti - me.

20 Er - go nos sup - pli - can - tes ti - bi

ex - au - di pro - pi - ti - us, San - cte Spi - ri - tus,

21 Si - ne quo pre - ces om - nes cas - sae

cre - dun - tur et in - dig - nae De - i au - ri - bus.

22 Tu qui om - ni - um sae - cu - lor - um san - ctos

22+ Tu - i nu - min - is doc - u - i - sti in - stin - ctu

am - plec - ten - do, Spi - ri - tus,

23 Ip - se ho - di - e a - po - sto - los Chri - sti

23+ Don - ans mu - ne - re in - so - li - to

et cunc - tis in - au - di - to sae - cu - lis

24 Hunc di - em glo - ri - o - sum fe - ci - sti.

1	Sancti Spiritus assit nobis gratia,	May the grace of the Holy Spirit be with us,
2	Quae corda nostra sibi faciat habitaculum,	To make our hearts its dwelling place,
3	Expulsis inde cunctis vitiis spiritalibus.	After having expelled all spiritual vices.
4	Spiritus alme, illustrator hominum:	O life-giving Spirit, source of light for humankind:
5	Horridas nostrae mentis purga tenebras.	Dispel the frightful darkness of our soul.
6	Amator sancte sensatorum semper cogitatuum:	O holy one, lover of the thoughts of sensate beings:
7	Infunde unctionem tuam, clemens, nostris sensibus.	Mercifully pour your balm over our senses.
8	Tu purificator omnium flagitiorum, spiritus	You, O spirit, purifier of all shameful thoughts and deeds,
9	Purifica nostri oculum interioris hominis,	Purify the eye of our interior being,
10	Ut videri supremus genitor possit a nobis,	That the supreme source of being might be seen by us,
11	Mundi cordis quem soli cernere possunt oculi.	The source whom only eyes of a pure heart can discern.
12	Prophetas tu inspirasti, ut praeconia Christi praecinuissent inclita;	You inspired the prophets, so that they chanted the glorious announcement of Christ;
13	Apostolos confortasti, uti tropheum Christi per totum mundum veherent.	You strengthened the apostles to carry the sign of Christ through the whole world.
14	Quando machinam per verbum suum fecit Deus caeli terrae marium,	When God through his word made the edifice of heaven, of earth, of the seas,
15	Tu super aquas foturus eas numen tuum expandisti, Spiritus.	You, O Spirit, to give it warmth, spread out your divine breath.
16	Tu animabus vivificandis aquas foecundas;	You seeded the waters to bring forth living beings;
17	Tu aspirando das spiritales esse homines.	You, in exhaling, enable humankind to be spiritual.
18	Tu divisum per linguas mundum et ritus adunasti, Domine,	You, O Lord, united the world, divided through tongues and religious rites,
19	Idolatras ad cultum Dei revocans, magistrorum optime.	Calling idolators back to the worship of God, O greatest of all teachers.
20	Ergo nos supplicantes tibi exaudi propitius, Sancte Spiritus,	Therefore, O Holy Spirit, graciously give ear to us as we beseech you,
21	Sine quo preces omnes cassae creduntur et indignae Dei auribus.	You without whom all prayers are empty and unworthy for the ears of God.
22	Tu qui omnium saeculorum sanctos	You who embracing them taught the saints in all times
22+	Tui numinis docuisti instinctu amplectendo, Spiritus,	Through the impulse of your divine breath, O Spirit,
23	Ipse hodie apostolos Christi	Today you yourself—
23+	Donans munere insolito et cunctis inaudito saeculis	Endowing the apostles of Christ with a gift exceptional and incredible to all ages—
24	Hunc diem gloriosum fecisti.	Have made this a day glorious.

Notker the Stammerer, a monk at the Abbey of St. Gall in what is now Switzerland, wrote new texts for West Frankish melodies that were brought east of the Rhine in the late ninth century; one of them was *Occidentana* (also known as *Cithara*). *Sancti Spiritus*, the text he wrote for this melody, is for the feast of

Pentecost and celebrates the descent of the Holy Spirit upon the Virgin Mary and the Apostles, an event described in the Bible. The text is not a narrative, but rather a catalogue of attributes of the Spirit, and a list of the seven gifts of the Spirit, adapted in Christian theology from Isaiah 11:2–3.

Notker tells us that he started early in his career to set words to the preexisting long melodies (also called *sequelae* in modern scholarship), but that his early experiments were not up to the expectations of his teachers. So he tried again, this time wishing to fit the motions of the melody to individual syllables of the words he was writing. A more detailed look at the relationships between text and music in *Sancti Spiritus* gives a sense of Notker's ideas about how to write new works based on preexisting melodies. The first line of *Occidentana* can be thought of as sung to the word "Alleluia." If you then put Notker's words to this melismatic phrase, you can notice the ways in which he allows the text to suit the small cells of the music. "Alle-" parallels "Sancti"; "Spiritus" fits the phrase A–G–C and then finishes out the line with its descent to an ornamented G; and the "-tia" of "gratia" rhymes with "-luia." The sequence in this early stage is a skillful prosula. Many other lines hold similar delights, and each of them pushes toward the powerful cadential formula of a slight dip followed by two repeated notes. The text always is suited to this feature of the music, with an accent on the antepenult. *Sancti Spiritus*, Notker's masterful setting of *Occidentana*, is one of a handful of his sequences that also became popular in France and England. His sequences were also widely copied in Italian regions, as of course they were east of the Rhine.

The glories of the medieval trope and sequence repertories are too rarely sampled in modern recordings. One of the most outstanding efforts is that of Dominique Vellard and the Ensemble Gilles Binchois, *Music and Poetry in St. Gallen*, which contains Notker's *Sancti Spiritus*. The album *1000: A Mass for the End of Time*, recorded by Anonymous 4, also features tropes and sequences. Anonymous 4 sings *Rex omnipotens* with an introductory trope and long melismas at the ends of lines, while improvising a polyphonic elaboration of the parent melody.

These two recordings allow us to compare the two ninth-century settings of *Occidentana*. Many people would have known both *Rex omnipotens* and *Sancti Spiritus* from their local liturgies. They may have noticed the musical relationships between these two widely circulating settings of the same melody, even though the West Frankish and East Frankish versions of *Occidentana* can be quite different. The "composition" performed by the Ensemble Gilles Binchois is a Latin version from a French tradition with more smoothed-out accentuation in the setting of the melody. Anonymous 4 offers a Latin setting of the melody from a German tradition, and here the Latin is more accentual. These performances contrast the flexible "prose" of the French tradition, which is more speechlike in its rendering, with the accentual symmetry of Notker's setting of *Occidentana*.

ANONYMOUS AND ADÉMAR OF
CHABANNES (C. 988–C. 1034)

Tropes for the Introit *Resurrexi*
Early 11th century

8.1 *EGO AUTEM* AND OTHER TROPES

Paris, BN lat. 1121, f. 11v; from Paul Evans, *The Early Trope Repertory of Saint Martial de Limoges* (Princeton: Princeton University Press, 1970), 155–56. © 1970 Princeton University Press, 1998 renewed PUP. Reprinted by permission of Princeton University Press.

Ego autem constitutus sum rex, praedicans preceptum tuum, et morte devicta.

For I have been established as king, proclaiming Your command, and with death having been conquered.

Resurrexi.

Resurrexi.

Dormivi, pater, and surgam diluculo, et somnus meus dulcis est michi.

I slept, Father, and at dawn I rise, and my slumber is sweet.

Posuisti.

Posuisti.

Ita, pater, sic placuit ante te, ut moriendo mortis mors fuissem, morsus inferni, et mundo vita.

So, Father, it was pleasing to you that I by dying might be the death of death, a sting for Hell, and life for the world.

Mirabilis.

Mirabilis.

Qui abscondisti haec sapientibus, et revelasti parvulis, alleluia.

You who concealed these things from the wise and revealed them to the weak, alleluia.

Alleluia.

Alleluia.

8.2 *QUEM QUAERITIS*

Quem quę - ri - tis in se - pul - chro, o Chris-ti - co - lę?

Hie - sum Na - za - re - num cru - ci - fi - xum, o Cae - li - co - lae.

Non est hic, sur - re - xit, sic - ut prae - di - xe - rat; i - te

nun - ti - a - te qui - a sur - re - xit. Al - le - lu - ia.

Ad se - pul - chrum re - si - dens an - ge - lus nun - ti - at

re - sur - re - xis - se Xpis - tum. En ec - ce

com - ple-tum est il - lud quod o - lim ip - se

per pro - phe - tam di - xe - rat ad pa-trem, ta - li - ter in - qui - ens: Resurrexi.

Paris, BN lat. 1121, f. 11v; from Paul Evans, *The Early Trope Repertory of Saint Martial de Limoges* (Princeton: Princeton University Press, 1970), 155–56. © 1970 Princeton University Press, 1998 renewed PUP. Reprinted by permission of Princeton University Press.

Quem quęritis in sepulchro, o christicolę?   "Whom do you seek in the tomb, O Christian women?"

Hiesum Nazarenum crucifixum, o Caelicolae.   "Jesus the Nazarean, who was crucified, O heavenly beings."

Non est hic, surrexit, sicut praedixerat;   "He is not here, but He has risen, just as He foretold.

ite, nuntiate quia surrexit, Alleluia;   Go! Say that He is risen! Alleluia."

Ad sepulchrum residens angelus nuntiat resurrexisse Xpistum.   The angel encamped at the tomb reports that Christ has risen.

En ecce completum est illud quod olim ipse per prophetam dixerat ad patrem, taliter inquiens: *Resurrexi.*   And behold that is fulfilled which He himself had said before to the Father through the prophet, singing, "*Resurrexi.*"

The Introits of the Mass liturgy were provided with tropes in the ninth and tenth centuries, glossing the meanings of the original texts. Tropes for the Introit are additions of both texts and music, sung lines that may or may not be poetic. The monk Adémar of Chabannes, sometimes in residence at the Abbey of St. Martial in Limoges, copied a number of trope sets for the Easter Introit *Resurrexi* (see Anthology 3.1). All but one of them work interlinearly. The set beginning with *Ego autem* (Anthology 8.1), for example, shows that the Introit was divided into phrases, each of which was glossed or commented upon by a trope verse. The ways in which poetic strategies not found in the original psalmodic text of the Introit have been adopted in the new piece can be seen in line 3 of the trope set *Ego autem*. Notice the play upon the words *mors*, meaning death, *morior*, to die, and *morsus*, which means bite or sting. The English translation, here and in most places, simply cannot do justice to the wordplay in the original.

The ways in which *Resurrexi* was divided and commented upon were traditional, and in the score only the textual cues are provided for the Introit. Even when the trope elements themselves were different, conventions for how to divide the parent text would be followed. It is difficult to know how trope elements themselves were chosen, and there was a great deal of variety from region to region. Tracing the relationships between sets of tropes is fascinating work, and allows for speculation about regional and interregional relationships.

The purpose of the textual elements is to comment on the meanings of the psalm text, relating it more profoundly to the feast. As can be seen in *Ego autem*, the melodies of the tropes both establish and comment on the characters of the phrases of the parent chant *Resurrexi*. The first trope element, for example, plays with the interval of a third that opens the Introit. The element *Dormivi* places much emphasis on D and F, pitches that are of major importance to the phrase of the Introit that begins with "posuisti." And the trope elements help establish the tricky deuterus maneria by cadencing on E, just before the chant element to be decorated launches into another tonal realm.

Adémar copied several tropes for the Introit *Resurrexi*. The first of these stands alone; it is an introductory rather than an interlinear trope. Its opening lines are famous as the *Quem quaeritis* trope (Anthology 8.2), although, as will be seen, they are expanded upon here. These opening four lines, frequently anthologized in collections of medieval texts, need to be sung for full dramatic impact. The music proclaims the words in elegant, lofty gestures and links the angels (*caelicolae*) to the Maries (*christicolę*) through repetition on the cadences for "O Christian women" and "O heavenly beings." The leap up a fifth in this mode 1 melody, from D to A, is well suited to the central message of this musical play: "He is not here, but He has risen."

Adémar may have been responsible for adding two further lines (the second very long) to this playlet; they are rare in the sources, and the way they function musically is sophisticated. It seems Adémar wished to connect the well-known four-line trope *Quem quaeritis*, established in tradition as a mode 1 piece, to a mode 4 Introit melody, *Resurrexi*, preparing the singer to shift gears and readying the choir to sing the Introit antiphon. The opening of the added two lines beginning "Ad sepulchrum" places a good deal of emphasis on the pitch E, and cadences on it as well. What is probably unfolding before our ears is the work of an early-eleventh-century musician joining two musical pieces and their traditions, and wishing to move smoothly from one mode to another and one kind of piece to another.

One of the things a cantor had to do in the long and complicated musical extravaganzas of the Mass and Office was to set the pitch for every chant by intoning the opening few notes. There was no A = 440 in the Middle Ages. All pitch was relative, and the cantor decided not only the pitch appropriate for every chant, but also the relationships between the pieces. In addition to being related musically to the parent chant, Introit tropes offered commentaries on the liturgical meanings of the psalmodic texts. Introductory tropes helped the cantor establish the pitch, but as he did so, he needed to think ahead to the chant that would follow, sung by the choir.

Our anthology follows the varied editorial practices of many scholars so students will have exposure to the many styles of edited medieval music encountered in the sources. Paul Evans used bars to indicate ligatures. He indicated liquescence using small noteheads with a slash through the stem, and he indicated the *quilisma* (see Primer II.1) by a squiggle beneath the note. His practice is very different from those of Richard Crocker and Calvin Bower (see Anthology 7), although each is legitimate.

9

ANONYMOUS

Congaudentes exsultemus

Sequence for St. Nicholas

Second half of the 11th century

1a. Con - gau - den - tes ex - sul - te - mus vo - ca - li con - cor - di - a

1b. Ad be - a - ti Ni - co - la - i fes - ti - va so - le - mni - a.

2a. Qui in cu - nis ad - huc ia - cens ser - van - do ie - iu - ni - a,

2b. Ad pa - pil - las coe - pit sum - ma pro - me - re - ri gau - di - a.

3a. A - do - le - scens am - ple - cta - tur lit - te - ra - rum stu - di - a,

3b. A - li - e - nis et im - mu - nis ab om - ni la - sci - vi - a.

4a. Fe - lix con - fes - sor, cu - ius fu - it dig - ni - ta - tis vox de cae - lo nun - ti -

4b. Per quam pro - ve - ctus, prae - su - la - tus sub - li - ma - tur ad sum - ma fa - sti - gi - a.

5a. E - rat in e - ius a - ni - mo pi - e - tas ex - i - mi - a, et op - pres - sis im - pen -

de - bat mul - ta be - ne - fi - ci - a.

5b. Au - ro per e - um vir - gi - num tol - li - tur in - fa - mi - a, at - que pa - tris e - a -

rum - dem le - va - tur in - o - pi - a.

Utrecht University Library MS 417; N. de Goede, ed., *The Utrecht Prosarium: Liber sequentiarum ecclesiae capitularis Sanctae Mariae ultraiectensis saeculi XIII: Codex Ultraiectensis*, Universitatis Bibliotheca 417, Monumenta Musica Neerlandica (Amsterdam: Vereniging voor nederlandse Muziiekgeschiedenis, 1965), 111–13; text follows edition.

6a. Qui - dam nau - tae na - vi - gan - tes et con - tra flu - ctu - um sae - vi - ti - am

lu - ctan - tes na - vi pe - ne dis - so - lu - ta,

6b. Nam de vi - ta de - spe - ran - tes, in tan - to po - si - ti pe - ri - cu - lo

cla - man - tes, vo - ce di - cunt om - nes u - na:

7a. O, be - a - te Ni - co - la - e, nos ad por - tum ma - ris tra - he de mor - tis an - gu - sti - a.

7b. Tra - he nos ad por - tum ma - ris, tu qui tot au - xi - li - a - ris pi - e - ta - tis gra - ti - a.

8a. Dum cla - ma - rent nec in - cas - sum, ec - ce qui - dam di - cit: as - sum ad ve - stra prae - si - di - a.

8b. Sta - tim au - ra da - tur gra - ta et tem - pe - stas fit se - da - ta, qui e - ve - runt ma - ri - a.

9a. Ex i - psi - us tum - ba ma - nat un - cti - o - nis co - pi - a,

9b. Quae in - fir - mos o - mnes sa - nat per e - ius suf - fra - gi - a.

10a. Nos, qui su - mus in hoc mun - do, vi - ti - o - rum in pro - fun - do iam pas - si nau - fra - gi - a,

10b. Glo - ri - o - se Ni - co - la - e, ad sa - lu - tis por - tum tra - he, u - bi pax et glo - ri - a.

11a. I - psam no - bis un - cti - o - nem im - pe - tres a do - mi - no, pre - ce pi - a,

11b. Qua sa - na - vit lae - si - o - nem mul - to - rum pec - ca - mi - num in ma - ri - a.

12a. Cu - ius fe - stum ce - le - bran - tes gau - de - ant per sae - cu - la,

12b. Ut co - ro - net e - os Chri - stus post vi - tae cur - ri - cu - la. A - men.

1a	Congaudentes exsultemus vocali concordia	Rejoicing together, let us exult with tuneful harmony
1b	Ad beati Nicolai festiva solemnia.	on the sacred feast of St. Nicholas,
2a	Qui in cunis adhuc iacens servando ieiunia,	who, by observing fasts at his mother's breasts,
2b	Ad papillas coepit* summa promereri gaudia.	though still lying in the cradle, already began to merit heavenly joys.
3a	Adolescens amplectatur litterarum studia,	As an adolescent he is drawn to the study of letters,
3b	Alienis et immunis ab omni lascivia.	averse and immune to every sinful passion.
4a	Felix confessor, cuius fuit dignitatis vox de caelo nuntia.	Blessed confessor, whose worth was announced by a voice from heaven.
4b	Per quam provectus, praesulatus sublimatur ad summa fastigia.	Thereby exalted, this bishop is elevated to the highest honors.
5a	Erat in eius animo pietas eximia, et oppressis impendebat multa beneficia.	In his soul there was exceeding compassion, and he did many kind deeds for the oppressed:
5b	Auro per eum virginum tollitur infamia, atque patris earumdem levatur inopia.	with gold he prevented the disgrace of virgins, and lifted their father from poverty.
6a	Quidam nautae navigantes et contra fluctuum saevitiam luctantes navi pene dissoluta,	Certain sailors traversing the sea, struggling against the raging waves, and nearly shipwrecked,
6b	Nam de vita desperantes, in tanto positi periculo clamantes, voce dicunt omnes una:	despairing of their lives in such great danger, cry out with one voice:
7a	O, beate Nicolae, nos ad portum maris trahe de mortis angustia.	"O blessed Nicholas, steer us away from the straits of death and into the seaport,
7b	Trahe nos ad portum maris, tu qui tot auxiliaris pietatis gratia.	draw us into the seaport, you who help so many by the grace of compassion!"
8a	Dum clamarent nec incassum, ecce quidam dicit: assum ad vestra praesidia.	While they were crying out—and not in vain—behold! Someone says, "I am here to protect you."
8b	Statim aura datur grata et tempestas fit sedata, qui everunt maria.	Immediately, there is a favorable breeze, the tempest calms, and the seas become quiet.
9a	Ex ipsius tumba manat unctionis copia,	From his tomb flows an abundance of oil,
9b	Quae infirmos omnes sanat per eius suffragia.	which heals all those who are ill, through his prayerful intercession.
10a	Nos, qui sumus in hoc mundo, vitiorum in profundo iam passi naufragia,	We, who live in this world, have already been shipwrecked in the abyss of our sins.
10b	Gloriose Nicolae, ad salutis portum trahe, ubi pax et gloria.	Glorious Nicholas, steer us to the port of salvation, where there is peace and glory.
11a	Ipsam nobis unctionem impetres a domino, prece pia,	Procure from the Lord that oil for us, by your pious prayer,
11b	Qua sanavit laesionem multorum peccaminum in maria.	by which He healed the wound of Mary's many sins.
12a	Cuius festum celebrantes gaudeant per saecula,	Let those celebrating His feast rejoice for all time,
12b	Ut coronet eos Christus post vitae curricula. Amen.	so that Christ might crown them after this life has run its course. Amen.

* Correction from the original "caepit."

In order to discuss medieval music, much of which is set to verse, a simple vocabulary is essential. *Congaudentes exsultemus*, like all sequences, unfolds in double versicles, but in this piece the versicles are musically paired half-strophes of accentual poetry. Sequences are the matrix of medieval melodic style, and their characteristics are reflected in many other genres of music, secular as well as sacred. The sequence is the only genre that continued to grow and develop from the ninth through the fourteenth century. Comparing an eleventh-century sequence with its ninth-century ancestors studied in Anthology 7 highlights some of the most important ways that music was changing in the eleventh century.

Congaudentes exsultemus is an example of the *cantica nova* (new song), a song set to sharply accentual, rhyming Latin poetry. The opening half-strophe, "Congaudentes exultémus // vocali concórdia," consists of 15 syllables divided by a caesura, or pause, in the middle (marked by //). The first eight-syllable unit closes with a *paroxytone*, a word whose accent falls on the next-to-last (penultimate) syllable, commonly represented by 8p. The following seven-syllable unit ends with a *proparoxytone*, a word with the accent on the antepenultimate syllable (two from the end); it is commonly labeled 7pp. The whole line is expressed as 8p + 7pp, a very common rhythm for many genres in the style.

The lines of *Congaudentes exsultemus* are not completely consistent in the number of syllables (as they will be in the Victorine sequences studied in Anthology 19), but two- or three-line half-strophes—8p + 7pp or 8p + 8p + 7pp— have come to prevail for most sequences in the style. Also, most of the 7pp lines cadence not only with the formula described below that occupies three notes, but also with a three-syllable rhyme. The ends of lines are heavily weighted, both textually and musically. (The spirited performance by Schola Hungarica features a division of the choir, with children singing the first of every pair of lines and the whole choir joining in for the second line.) An accentual sequence like *Congaudentes* makes a grid of beats through the repeating accentual patterns of the poetic lines. Upon this grid, melodic phrases are displayed and manipulated, offering composers their first large-scale design for motivic development. As the grid became more predictable, as in the twelfth-century Parisian or Victorine sequence, composers would gain even more opportunities to explore relationships between many phrases of melody, interrelated on the grid created by the text through position, yet free to be altered as a piece unfolded.

A closer look at the melodic phrases of *Congaudentes exsultemus* reveals the varied interplay between text and melody that makes such music delightful to sing and to hear. The clipped textual phrases that begin each couplet are rendered by short, cell-like musical phrases, mostly four notes long, that match them accentually. Note, for example, how the pitch rises on the accented syllables "congaudéntes" and "exsultémus." The pitch rises on the first syllable of "vocáli," but falls on the second syllable of "concórdia" to accommodate the cadential formula. The contrast is striking: in the first half of the line, before the caesura, the pitch rise underscores word accent, but in the powerful cadential phrase, the lowered pitch marks the word accent. Each pair of lines offers a fresh interplay between text and music.

A piece such as *Congaudentes exsultemus* would have stood out in the Mass liturgy for St. Nicholas as something very new and different, distinguished from ancient layers of Proper chants, and even from its nearer cousins in the Mass Ordinary. In addition to its musical and poetic newness, such a hagiographic work fulfilled a function different from that of any other piece of chant in the Mass liturgy. The sequence text presents a narrative outlining the saint's life and his major miracles, including that of the healing oil said to exude from the sacred stones of his tomb in Bari, in southern Italy. Music associated with shrines and their miracles allowed for a kind of pilgrimage through song to a particular famous place, and an attempt to share in the powers of association. These connections with saints' cults help to explain the great popularity of later sequences written for saints. In the Eucharist, celebrated upon an altar that represented a tomb to medieval Christians, the rhythms of action in the liturgy offered contexts for the lesser yet connected powers of the saints.

In this particular edition, the Latin has been altered to follow classical orthography, and the ways of dividing syllables are different from those encountered in several other editions we have seen. The editor has also marked off the lines for the sake of clarity.

The Three Daughters (opening scenes)

Saint's play from the Fleury Playbook
Late 12th century

Orléans, Bibliothèque Municipale MS 201, ff. 176–243; G. Tintori and R. Monterosso, *Sacre rappresentazioni nel manoscritto 201 della Bibliothèque municipale di Orléans IMa*, 1st ser., vol. 2 (Cremona, 1958), 3–5.

(Pater conquerens ad filias):

Ca - ra mi - chi pi - gno - ra fi - li - e
o - pes pa - tris i - no - pis u - ni - ce
et so - la - men me - e mi - se - ri - e mi - chi mes - to
tan - dem con - su - li - te me mi - se - rum O - lim
di - ves et nunc pau - per - ri - mus lu - ce fru - or et noc -
te an - xi - us et quam fer - re non con - su - e - vi - mus
pau - per - ta - tem gra - vi - ter fe - ri - mus Me mi - se - rum
Nec me me - a tan - tum i - no - pi - a quan - tum ves - tra
ve - xit pe - nu - ri - a qua - rum pri - mus la - ci - va cor - po - ra
lon - ga mo - do damp - nat ie - iu - ni - a. [M]e mi - se - rum

(Prima filia ad patrem):

Ca - re pa - ter lu - ge - re de - si - ne
nec nos lu - gens lu - gen - dum pro - mo - ve et quod ti - bi
va - le - o di - ce - re con - si - li - um hoc a me re - ci - pe
Ca - re pa - ter u - num no - bis res - tat au - xi - li - um
per de - de - cus et per ob - pro - bri - um ut nos - tro - rum spe - ci -
es cor - po - rum no - bis vic - tum lu - cre - tur pu - bli - cum

ca - re   pa - ter Et me   pri-mam pa - ter si iu - be - as

de - de - - co - ri sub - mit - tet   pi - e - tas   ut sen - - ci - at pri -

ma an - xi - e - tas   quam con - - tu - lit pri - ma na - - ti - - vi - tas

Ca - re   pa - - ter

FATHER

a	In lamentum et merorem	Into lamenting and sorrowing
	versa est leticia	our joy is now transformed,
b	quam prebebat olim nobis	a joy which an abundance of possessions
	rerum habundancia.	once gave us.
C	O rerum inopia!	O the lack of things!
d	Heu! Heu! perierunt	Alas! Alas!
	huius vite gaudia!	The joys of this life have perished!
a	Forma, genus, morum, splendor,	Style, rank, fashion,
	iuventutis gloria,	youthful ambition,
b	comprobatur nichil esse,	good is nothing
	dum desit pecunia.	if money is lacking.
C	O rerum inopia!	O the lack of things!
d	Heu! Heu! perierunt	Alas! Alas!
	huius vitae gaudia!	The joys of this life have perished!

THREE DAUGHTERS

a	Finis opum dum recedunt	Finished now is his work,
	luctus et suspiria.	now it gives way to sorrow and sighing.
b	Eia! pater ipse lugens	Alas! Our father, himself mourning
	opes lapsas predia	lost wealth, ponders his estates
d	tractat secum ut speramus	as we expect, with the companionship of
	dampnorum socia	his losses.
C	O rerum inopia!	O the lack of things!
D	Heu! Heu! perierunt	Alas! Alas!
	huius vite gaudia!	The joys of this life have perished!
d	Adeamus, audiamus	Let us go and hear
	que capit consilia.	what his advice is.

FATHER

(*Pater conquerens ad filias*)
Cara michi pignora, filie,
opes patris inopis unice
et solamen mee miserie,
michi mesto tandem consulite.
Me miserum!
Olim dives et nunc pauperrimus,
luce fruor et nocte anxius,
et quam ferre non consuevimus
paupertatem graviter ferimus.
Me miserum!
Nec me mea tantum inopia
quantum vestra vexit penuria,
quarum primus laciva corpora
longa modo dampnant ieiunia
[Me] miserum!

(*Lamenting Father to Daughters*)
Dear to me you pledges of love, Daughters,
the comfort of your father's singular poverty,
and solace of my misfortunes,
in the end, you console me, dejected.
O wretched me!
Formerly rich and now destitute,
enjoying daylight but fearing nightfall,
and though we are not accustomed to bear it,
we must bear poverty with dignity.
O wretched me!
Nor does my own hardship vex me
so much as your poverty.
You, whose bodies, once flourishing,
presently require long fasts.
O wretched me!

FIRST DAUGHTER

(*Prima filia ad patrem*)
Care Pater, lugere desine,
nec nos lugens lugendum promove,
et quod tibi valeo dicere
consilium, hoc a me recipe,
Care Pater.
unum nobis restat auxilium,
per dedecus et per obprobrium
ut nostrorum species corporum
nobis victum lucretur publicum
Care Pater.
Et me primam, Pater, si iubeas
dedecori submittet pietas
ut senciat prima anxietas
quam contulit prima nativitas
Care Pater.

(*First Daughter to Father*)
Dear Father, lament no more,
and do not by deploring your misfortune increase ours.
And because I am so bold as to give you
advice, take it from me,
dear Father:
One way remains available to us,
through disgrace and through infamy: that
the beauty of our bodies
should gain us a prostitute's life,
dear Father.
And if you ask me, Father, as the eldest,
piety will submit to dishonor,
that worry may first concern
what belongs to the first-born,
dear Father.

(*St. Nicholas throws a bag of gold in among them.*)

The Three Daughters is a play celebrating a miracle performed by St. Nicholas,
one of four plays for this saint in the so-called Fleury Playbook, a twelfth-
century collection of dramatic works set to music. The text exists in an

earlier version from the eleventh century. In the twelfth-century play, a well-known saint's miracle story comes to life, a story that circulated in an earlier eleventh-century version, but without music. The father—apparently a widower—has lost his fortune and his livelihood, and he and his three daughters must now rethink their lives. He laments their coming poverty and the realization that he will not have the money to provide dowries for them. They say that they will take to the streets, selling their bodies to make ends meet. One by one, they are ransomed with sacks of gold coming through the window. At the end, the father discovers their patron: St. Nicholas!

The first scene (ending on "consilia") has music that is different from the repeating melody used for the rest of the work, and this is the section not found in the eleventh-century play. If small letters represent lines with the same music, and capital letters represent lines with the same text and music, the structure of the opening is as follows:

a (8p + 7pp) **b** (8p + 7pp) **C** (7pp) **D** (8p + 7pp) (twice by the father)

a (8p + 7pp) **b** (8p + 7pp) **d** (8p + 7pp) **C** (7pp) **D** (8p + 7pp) **d** (8p + 7pp) (once by the daughters)

The structure allows for the father to say something and the daughters to provide a comment on his circumstances, which he apparently does not hear, when they sing to the same music. Line **C**, "O rerum inopia" (O the lack of things), is repeated in each of the three sections, forming a lamenting refrain in this third-mode opening act of the play. The six-note melisma on "O" is a striking dramatic touch. The melody as a whole is exceedingly simple, consisting of an ornamented fifth (D, A) and a contrasting fifth (C, G). The final, E, is the third of the chain of thirds between C and G, and in each case the music circles around it before coming to rest.

The text is set syllabically for the most part, except at the ends of some lines, which are marked by decorative melismas. There are some dramatic touches that depend on contrafactum technique (besides the large-scale repetitions themselves) and that come out quite well when the play is staged. For example, the father sings "heu heu perierunt // huius vite gaudia" (Alas! Alas! The joys of this life have perished), but the daughters also sing this crisp phrase to different words: "Adeamus audiamus // que capit consilia" (Let us go and hear what his advice is). So the father sings of the loss of life's joys, while they sing of going to get his advice. The music makes the point that they are offering two versions of the same feelings; moreover, their common sorrow is about to climax in a need for action.

The rest of the play (of which only a portion is given here) has a text that is very like its eleventh-century source, or the tradition to which it belonged. The poetry is strophic and rhythmic, with the same melody repeating for each four-line strophe. Each line is made up of ten syllables (4p // 6pp) followed by a four-syllable refrain, the text of which varies according to the dramatic action, moving steadily from sorrow to joy in each scene. Although the lamenting music of the first part of the play does not return, the new music is related to it. The descent that characterizes the lamenting cadence of the opening scene on page 47 is transformed into a new melody consisting of short interconnected cells in the form **1-2-1-3-1'-2-1-3'-1'** and so on, as can be seen in the Father's speech to his Daughters on page 48. Cell 1 (or a variant of it) always falls on the four-syllable phrases, creating a tightly organized, rounded musical structure that is readily adaptable to a variety of emphases.

The notation in the Fleury Playbook does not express the rhythms of the music, giving contemporary singers freedom in their interpretations of the characters. *The Three Daughters* employs music like a foundation to give voice to the text, suggests action (much of which would have been mimed), and aids in the development of the characters. Although the characters would all have been played by males, still the work points to the problems that women in urban settings, dependent for their livings on men, could face when a father or spouse was no longer able to provide for them. The recording by Schola Hungarica is of this work, but somewhat truncated. The graceful lines are shaped by treating the short melismas like ornaments.

The edition of the play we have followed was made in 1958, and the music was expressed in rhythmic values not found in the manuscript. Another edition made by Fletcher Collins in 1976 uses the rhythmic modes, which were commonly adopted for monophonic settings of accentual poetry in the mid-twentieth century. We have ignored those rhythmicizations in our adoption of these earlier editions as there is little historical justification for them.

11

ANONYMOUS

Surrexit Dominus vere

Polyphonic Alleluia from the Winchester Troper
1020s–1030s

Cambridge, Corpus Christi College MS 473, ff. and 166r. From Susan Rankin, *The Winchester Troper: Facsimile Edition and Introduction* (London: Stainer and Bell, 2007), p. 71. Reprinted with permission.

Alleluia.   Alleluia.
Surrexit dominus vere   The Lord is risen indeed
et apparuit Petro.   and appeared to Peter.

In the tenth and eleventh centuries, polyphonic singing was created ex tempore, and because there was little need to record the music in writing, very little of it survives. The Winchester Troper, compiled in England in the early eleventh century, demonstrates how various techniques of making polyphonic music had changed since *Musica Enchiriadis* and *Scolica Enchiriadis* were written in the ninth century (see Chapter 3 of *Music in the Medieval West*).

The repertory found in the Winchester Troper marks a significant transition in the development of polyphonic settings of liturgical chants. No longer exclusively improvised, the practice had become a written one as well. Organum, as this early polyphony was called, was being transformed from an essentially pedagogical tool into an artistic repertory. As such, it was deemed worthy not only of transcription but also of organization into a liturgically ordered collection. The Winchester Troper is the first such collection of polyphonic music known to us. It seems to have been created because musicians believed so powerfully in the beauty and importance of their practice and its results.

Our score of the opening section of the Easter Alleluia *Surrexit Dominus vere* has been transcribed from single lines of nonheightened notation (that is, the neumes are not precisely arrayed above the words to indicate pitch; see Primer II.1). Once each line has been interpreted, it must be fitted to the chant for which it was conceived. The transcription involves editorial conjecture informed by years of study. In addition, the editor, Susan Rankin, has used the rules set forth in early theory treatises to read the pitches expressed in the notation. The lower or organal voice (*vox organalis,* labeled OV) serves to adorn the chant or principal voice (*vox principalis,* CV) and as a result is closely tied to it, creating an artful rhetoric that emphasizes phrases and words in particular ways. The notations of the parent chant and the organal chants are also interdependent. The musician who notated *Surrexit Dominus vere* in the eleventh century worked with a chant manuscript at his elbow and consulted it as he did his work. He knew the improvised practice of organum well and was able to write it down from memory, although some of the time he may have been "composing."

The musician-scribe thought in terms of boundaries for the added voice: in general it should not exceed a distance of a fourth below the chant, and it should arrive at a unison pitch at the end of a phrase, creating a meeting (or *occursus*, as later named by Guido of Arezzo; see Chapter 5 of *Music in the Medieval West*). But this was not a mechanical process; in places where the plainchant leaped, the transcriber had decisions to make, and sometimes chose to exceed the boundaries. Also, to make the music flow as he desired, he often held a note until he found it judicious to move again. The musician-scribe was sophisticated beyond the Carolingian theoretical understanding as expressed in the *Enchiriadis* treatises. Using the idea of occursus, he might delay joining with the cadential note of a phrase until the singing of the plainsong had arrived at it, and then complete the sense of finality by moving to the unison. If the chant moves upward to the final note of a phrase, the organal voice might rush ahead, so once again the aesthetic of prolonging the meeting of the two can be obeyed. The acceptance of dissonance is far greater in the early eleventh century than in the ninth century. It is exploited, especially at cadences, but must be resolved.

Surrexit Dominus vere has the advantage for us of being a chant that, like many Alleluias, repeats long sections of music. This gives us an opportunity to consider three different settings of the same musical phrase, and see how both medieval singers and the modern editor have worked. For example, the setting of the word "alleluia" shows observance of the boundary note in the organum: at no time is it more than a fourth away from the chant. The composer-scribe also shows a desire to observe the range of the chant. The organal voice leaps up a third to the syllable "-lu-" of "alleluia" in line 1, to A, higher than the plainchant, artfully anticipating the motion from F to A in the principal voice.

The variety of solutions for ornamenting an occursus can be seen in many places: in the second group of neumes fitted to the "-le-" of "alleluia" (line 1), the OV remains on F as a kind of anticipation. However, on the "-re" of "vere" (line 2), in the third group of neumes, the OV remains on F after the CV cadences on G, and then itself moves to G. This same kind of dissonance, resolved by the motion of the OV, can be seen on the antepenultimate group of neumes (on the word "Pe-tro"), a nearly identical repetition of the neumation in line 1 of the score (on "-lu-ia").

It has been said that the history of Western harmonic practice can best be studied by examining changes in understandings of the cadence over the centuries. If that is the case, we can see a milestone in the Winchester Troper, and in the early eleventh century more broadly.

12

ANONYMOUS

Annus novus

Polyphonic versus or conductus

c. 1100

Paris, BN lat. 1139, f. 36v; B. Gillingham, ed., *Paris Bibliothèque Nationale, Fonds Latin 1139* (Ottawa: Institute of Mediaeval Music, 1987); from Sarah Fuller, "Aquitanian Polyphony of the Eleventh and Twelfth Centuries," Vol. III (Ph.D. diss., University of California, Berkeley, 1976), 2, with some notes supplied from other sources. Revised and © 2013. Reprinted with permission.

1

Annus novus in gaudio agatur in principio magna fit exultatio in cantoris tripudio.	Let the new year begin in joy; let there be great leaps in the cantor's dance.

REFRAIN

Ad hec sollemnia *concurrent omnia* *voce sonantia* *cantoris gratia* *et vite spatia* *per quem letitia* *fit in ecclesia.*	*Let everything unite in this solemn festival—harmonious voices, a singer's gift, and a spacious life—and through him let there be joy in the church!*

2

Anni novi principium vox celebret psallentium et cantorem egregium hymnus extollat omnium.	May our singers' voices celebrate the beginning of the new year, and may the hymn of all extol our most distinguished cantor.
Ad hec sollemnia, etc.	*Let everything unite, etc.*

3

Anno novo in cantica recitentur organica tota sonet ars musica in cantoris presentia.	Let songs in organum be sung at the new year; let the entire art of music sound forth in the presence of our cantor.
Ad hec sollemnia, etc.	*Let everything unite, etc.*

4

Annum novum celebrantes exultantes et letantes et cantorem venerantes gaudeamus congaudentes.	Celebrating the new year, rejoicing, being glad, and venerating our cantor, let us all rejoice together.

REFRAIN

Ad hec sollemnia, etc.	*Let everything unite, etc.*

5

Anne nove fit titulis   O new year! Today your cantor becomes
hodie ineffabilis   ineffable and wondrous with glory; be steadfast
tui cantor mirabilis   forever!
esto per saecla stabilis.

REFRAIN

Ad hec sollemnia, etc.   *Let everything unite, etc.*

Annus novus can be called either a versus or a conductus; the former term was used more generally in the south of France, the latter in the north. In the twelfth century, both terms referred to a short strophic work with a text in accentual verse, often used for times in the service when people had to move from one area of the church to another. Such works are usually monophonic in this period, but there are polyphonic settings as well (such as the double-texted *Benedicamus Domino* presented in Anthology 13). We often think of polyphonic settings as being of traditional liturgical chants, but *Annus novus* is as new in its text as in its music. Moreover, it lacks a specific role to play in the liturgy. It is also written in an experimental form of notation in Paris, BN lat. 1139, sometimes called successive notation: first one voice is completely written out, and then another. The modern editor has the difficult task of lining up the parts.

Annus novus was sung for some sort of stylized clerical procession or dance performed on New Year's Day. On January 1, the Feast of the Circumcision, the youth in a cathedral school sometimes enacted ritual role reversals, which might include stealing liturgical vessels and other furnishings and using them for parodied action (see Chapters 6 and 9 of *Music in the Medieval West*). The cantor (with his assistant, the succentor) was in charge of the musical and liturgical work of a monastery or cathedral school. The symbols of the cantor's authority, the cape and rod (*baculus*), would sometimes be stolen and the position itself taken over by one of the boys, who might function as musical leader for the day. *Annus novus* may have been written to honor the substitute boy cantor, and doubtless would have been sung at the close of an Office on New Year's Day. If this was the case, the boys were praising one of their own and wishing his "rule" could endure.

The text takes the form of a schoolroom exercise designed to demonstrate the student's knowledge of the cases of the Latin word *annus* (year). It also illustrates the love of the new song, or cantica nova, the accentual style of poetry that was beginning to catch on in the late eleventh and early twelfth centuries, as represented by *Congaudentes exsultemus* (see Anthology 9). In pieces such as these, poetic and musical understandings fuse with polyphonic strategies to make something doubly "new."

The text of the monophonic verse of *Annus novus* is rhyming, accentual, and strophic, with the form 8pp + 8pp + 8pp + 8pp (although in the next-to-last strophe the accentual ending shifts to 8p). A caesura after the first four syllables of each line adds emphasis to the shifting cases of the word *annus*. There is no indication of rhythm offered either in the notation itself or in the transcription. The repeating strophic verses are not musically identical, but the differences between them are so small that they are not notated in our transcription. The melodic line grows ever more ornate, beginning syllabically, with phrases closely matched to the text, and then transforming the last line with a descent from B to an ornamented cadential D. The descending chain of thirds from C–A to F–D (see, for example, "hec sollemnia"), so important in the D authentic mode, is emphasized through several strategies, including ornamentation of the pitches, neighbor notes, and artful delays.

The polyphonic refrain ("Ad hec sollemnia," etc.) has a text made up of seven rhyming lines of six syllables each, and every line closes with a proparoxytone. The musical scheme is **abcabc′d**. The texture of the music is very different from that found in the Winchester Troper (see Anthology 11). It can be seen that the intervals between the two voices are sometimes wider than the boundary of a fourth or fifth. In particular, the **a** lines begin with an octave, and in the final florid cadence of **d** the wide span of a seventh is filled in. Each line is a small arc of motion from one perfect interval to another: octave to fifth (**a**); unison to unison (**b**); fourth to unison (**c**); octave to fifth (**a**); unison to unison (**b**); fifth to unison (**c′**; the bottom line is the same, the top not); unison to (delayed) unison (**d**).

Contrary motion from an octave to a unison or fifth is highly favored, and this causes the voices to cross frequently. Oblique motion is common as well, perhaps to avoid what might be heard as awkward parallels. (Parallel motion was apparently considered undesirable in this repertory.) The cadence of the refrain offers a new texture as well: the top voice becomes a true "upper" voice and takes flight with a series of staggered descending melismas that unfold above the slower-moving bottom voice. The transcription given here, by Sarah Ann Fuller, shows dissonances on the openings of several phrases that immediately slide to perfect intervals. The most striking instance is the B against C in the next-to-last phrase, which does not resolve until the final cadence on D, an anticipated unison that gives an especially strong sense of closure. Because the refrain was expressed in successive notation in the original source, the editor has to choose how to align the two voices.

13

ANONYMOUS

Stirps Jesse florigeram

Double-texted *Benedicamus Domino*

Mid-12th century

/ ce - lo - rum   Do - mi - no

UPPER VOICE

Stirps Jesse florigeram
germinavit virgulam
et in flore spiritus
quiescit paraclitus

The shoot of Jesse germinates a flowering
small rod, and on the flower rests the Spirit,
the Paraclete.

fructum profert virgula*
per quem vivunt secula
stirpis ex Davitice
virga dicta mistice
que sic que sic floruit
et que florem protulit (o)

The small rod brings forth this fruit
through which the ages survive.
Mystically, the rod is called of the Davidic
shoot, for it, like it, bloomed and brought
forth its flower.

virga Jesse virgo est dei mater
flos filius eius est cuius pater (o)
huic flori preter morem edito
canunt chori sanctorum ex debito

The rod of Jesse is the virgin Mother of God;
the flower is her Son, and her Father.
To this lofty flower, more than usual,
the choir of saints sings for our debt.

laus laus et jubilatio
potestas cum imperio
sit sine termino
celorum Domino

Praise, praise and jubilation, let power with
authority be without end to the Lord of the
heavens.

LOWER VOICE

Benedicamus Domino

Praise the Lord.

*"Virgulam" in the manuscript, but this is a mistake, as indicated by both the rhyme and the grammar.

Stirps Jesse florigeram, a double-texted *Benedicamus Domino* closely related to *Annus novus* (see Anthology 12) in time and region, demonstrates some of the beauties offered to the listener—and the problems posed for the scholar—in early polyphonic works from southern France. Such works illustrate the transition between improvised practice and written repertories. Although an earlier version of *Stirps Jesse florigeram* is found in the manuscript that contains *Annus novus,* it cannot be precisely transcribed from that source because of alignment problems between the voices. Even the later version transcribed here presents a range of choices for lining up the two voices. The chant—in this case, the familiar *Flos Filius eius* melisma (see Anthology 5), a popular melody for the text *Benedicamus Domino*—is placed in the lower voice. The upper voice is a free-flowing soloistic melody set to a text that relates directly to the theme of the original responsory. Hence, *Stirps Jesse florigeram* could have served as a substitute for the *Benedicamus Domino,* which was sung at the end of every liturgical hour of prayer (except Matins; see Primer IV.3).

The first part of the poetic text unfolds in five rhyming couplets of seven syllables each. This pattern breaks when the bottom line reaches the first "o" (after the upper voice's "protulit"; "Do-" of "Domino" is elongated with two indications of "o," taking up most of the composition in the lower voice). It seems there was a desire to quote almost directly from the text of the responsory *Stirps Jesse* at this point: the syllable count is not exact for the lines from the responsory: "virga Jesse virgo est dei mater / flos filius eius est cuius pater." Also at this point, the notes of the melisma in the lower part move more quickly, giving the upper voice less time to develop. Once dues have been paid to the text of the parent chant, the text begins to be rhythmic and regular once again (a ten-syllable couplet, an eight-syllable couplet, and a six-syllable couplet); the chant melody in the lower voice lengthens out into a very few sustained notes. The principle observed here will be crucial for the development of polyphonic textures in northern Europe: when the melody of the plainsong moves more quickly, the upper polyphonic voice moves in shorter phases to stay with the chant, a foreshadowing of the texture known as "discant."

The upper voice of *Stirps Jesse florigeram* is dynamic and free by comparison to any other polyphonic voice seen in earlier sources. This style of writing is encountered in *Annus novus* only at the final cadence; here the florid line moves above a slow-moving chant throughout the piece. This texture would become known as florid organum.

The phrasing of the lower voice is of special interest. The first rhyming couplet in the upper voice unfolds above a sustained low D. The melody in the first poetic line moves down from the upper D to A and back up again on the cadence; the second line of the pair makes a long, arching descent from D to A and then down to an ornamented D on "virgulam." For the next pair of phrases, the music must move to A, which is the next pitch of the lower voice. It does so on the cadence of the first line of the pair ("spiritus"), then returns to low D for the cadence on "paraclitus," the second line of the pair. We can see that a kind of rhythm exists between the changing of pitches in the "Benedicamus" line and the upper line, with its cadences on the ends of rhythmic lines of texts. This is a very carefully integrated piece, one that is attentive to several musical dimensions at one time.

When the *Benedicamus* melisma on "Do-" begins, the upper voice must move more quickly, keeping the piece from growing too long. At this point, the integration breaks down, the cadences coming more quickly and at irregular intervals until the notes of the *Benedicamus* are once again sustained for long periods. The final cadence is exceedingly florid. The phrases of texts in the upper voice are rhymes ending in "o," matching the final "-o" of "Benedicamus Domino." The melisma that marks the last syllable of "termino" is especially striking. It begins with a short descent to F from A and back up again. When the chant moves to E, the melisma glides downward to F, then rises to C, with an upper neighbor note of D, resulting a a great deal of dissonance, before the melisma ends on B, a fifth above the E in the lower voice.

Congaudeant catholici

Polyphonic conductus

Mid-12th century

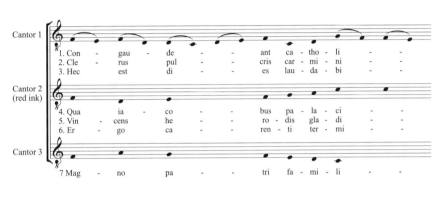

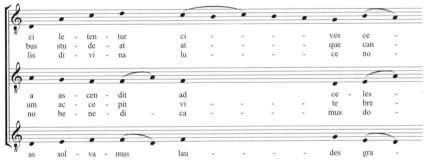

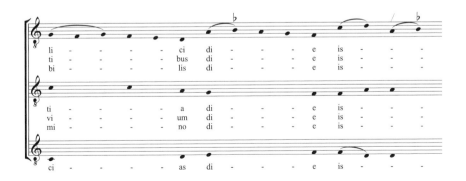

Santiago de Compostela, Biblioteca de la Catedral Metropolitana s.s. f. 185; from Paul Helmer, ed., *The Mass of Saint James* (Ottawa, Canada: Institute of Mediaeval Music, 1988), 243–45. Reprinted with permission.

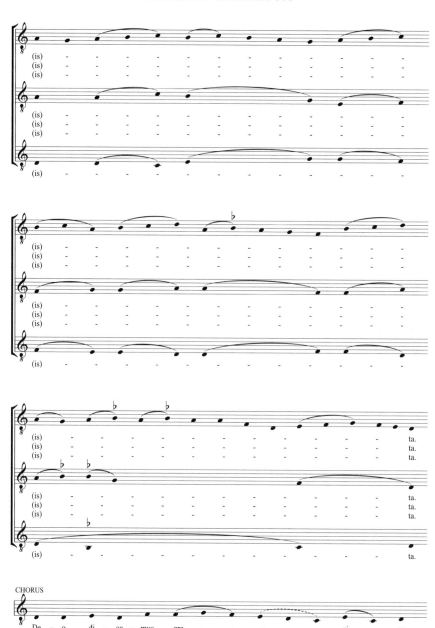

(is) - - - - - - - - - - - - ta.
(is) - - - - - - - - - - - - ta.
(is) - - - - - - - - - - - - ta.
(is) - - - - - - - - - - - - ta.
(is) - - - - - - - - - - - - ta.
(is) - - - - - - - - - - - - ta.
(is) - - - - - - - - - - - - ta.

CHORUS

De - o di - ca - mus gra - - - - - ci - as.

1

Congaudeant catholici
letentur cives celici die ista.

Let all Christian people rejoice together; let
the citizens of heaven delight on this day.

2

Clerus pulcris carminibus
studeat atque cantibus die ista.

May the clergy busy themselves with lovely
songs and melodies on this day.

3

Hec est dies laudabilis
divina luce nobilis die ista

Here is the praiseworthy day, ennobled
with divine light on this day

4

qua iacobus palacia
ascendit ad celestia die ista.

on which James ascends to heavenly
palaces on this day.

5

Vincens herodis gladium
accepit vite brevium die ista.

Conquering the sword of Herod, he
received the shortness of life on this day.

6

Ergo carenti termino
benedicamus domino die ista.

Therefore, for one free from end, let us
praise the Lord on this day.

7

Magno patri familias
solvamus laudes gracias die ista.
Deo dicamus gracias.

To the great paterfamilias we render
gracious praises on this day.
To God we sing thanks.

Congaudeant catholici is found in the Codex Calixtinus, part of a supplement
of polyphonic works apparently planned during a time of revision in the
third quarter of the twelfth century. It is a conductus, a *Benedicamus* substitute, attributed in the manuscript to Albertus Parisiensis (Master Albert of
Paris). It has long been considered the first known notated piece of three-voice

polyphony, although this cannot be conclusively demonstrated. The recording by Anonymous 4 has been influential in its interpretative power, shaping a
fairly unruly piece into something that sounds carefully planned.

As the original notation would show, and the transcription indicates, one of
the three voices—that of Cantor 2—is an addition in red ink to a two-voice piece.
The use of red ink was an innovative idea, allowing two voices that occupy the
same space on the staff to be distinguished one from the other. The notational
style of this added voice is different from that of the main scribe who wrote the
polyphonic fascicle of the Codex Calixtinus and the two original voices of the
piece. The red-ink scribe is contemporary, however, so the fact that this voice
was added in the twelfth century does not in itself alter the status of the work as
a three-voice polyphonic piece (as opposed to a two-voice piece in two alternative versions).

Each of the seven strophes of *Congaudeant catholici* is made up of two eight-
syllable lines, followed by the four-syllable refrain "die ista" (on this day);
the piece as a whole ends with a monophonic statement playing upon the "Deo
gratias" that closes out the *Benedicamus Domino*. The refrain includes a long
melisma on the "i-" of "ista," balancing the texted and untexted sections. Of
the two original voices, the bottom voice is the melody of the conductus, with
the upper voice forming an ornamented addition, usually moving in lofty arcs
that cadence with main arrivals as follows):

Congaudeant catholici: unison

letentur cives celici : unison

die ista (melisma): octave; octave; unison

This can be compared to the relationship of the red-ink voice to the conductus
voice at the main cadences:

Congaudeant catholici: fifth

letentur cives celici : fifth

die ista (melisma): fifth; fifth; unison

The upper voice is florid and explores the higher part of the range. The red-
ink voice is more pedestrian, closely tied to the motion of the lower voice. Does
this mean that we have two two-voice works, with the red line offering a choice
for less skilled singers? Or was the simpler voice added without the upper voice
in mind? Does the midrange voice written in red ink duplicate the upper voice
in ways that would make it seem unlikely that they were meant to be sounded
simultaneously? Or does it indeed show that a twelfth-century musician
desired a three-part work that explored the midrange?

There are no conclusive answers to these questions. About half the time, the middle voice duplicates (although never exactly) the basic motion of the upper voice, but the rest of the time it doesn't, adding instead a new dimension to the music. What about dissonance? Are there places where the middle voice doesn't fit at all with the upper voice (and so was conceived to be sung independently of it)? There are dissonant intervals between the upper voices—for example, the seconds between the upper voices on "(Congau)de(ant)"—but the passing tritones on "ci(ves)" are present with or without the middle voice. Each performing group must decide for itself which mode of performance is correct, recognizing that our ears may enjoy *Congaudeant catholici* so much in its three-voice state because we are accustomed to dissonance.

15

PETER ABELARD (?) (1079–1142)

Epithalamica
Easter sequence
After 1131

A
1a. E - pi - tha - la - mi - ca dic, Spon - sa, can - ti - ca,
1b. In - tus quae con - spi - cis dic for - ris gau - di - a,
1c. et nos lae - ti - fi - cans, de Spon - so nun - ti - a,
1d. cu - ius te re - fo - vet sem - per prae - sen - ti - a.

B
2a. A - du - le - scen - tu - lae, vos cho - rum du - ci - te;
2b. cum haec prae - ci - ne - rit, et vos suc - ci - ni - te.
2c. A - mi - ci Spon - si vos vo - ca - runt nu - pti - ae,
2d. et no - vae mo - du - los o - pta - mus Do - mi - nae.

C
3a. In mon - ti - bus hic ec - ce sa - li - ens
4a. Hor-rens e - nim hi - ems iam trans - i - it,

D
3b. ec - ce ve - nit, col - les trans - i - li - ens;
4b. gra - vis im - ber re - ce - dens ab - i - it;

C
3c. per fe - ne - stras ad me re - spi - ci - ens,
4c. ver a - moe - num ter - ras a - pe - ru - it;

D
3d. per can - cel - los di - cit, pro - spi - ci - ens:
4d. pa - rent flo - res, et tur - tur ce - ci - nit:

E
3e. "A - mi - ca, sur - ge, pro - pe - ra!
4e. co - lum - ba ni - tens, ad - vo - la!"

F
5a. Rex in ac - cu - bi - tum iam se con - tu - le - rat,
6a. Per no - ctem i - gi - tur hunc quae - rens ex - e - o;

Paris, BN n.a. lat. 3126, ff. 90v-91v; and Le Puy, Bibliothèque du Grand Seminaire, *Prosolarium Ecclesiae Aniciensis* (no shelf number), ff. 54r–57r; Chrysoganus Waddell, "*Epithalamica:* An Easter Sequence by Peter Abelard," *Musical Quarterly* 72 (1986): 239–71, at 248–53.

G
5b. et me - a re - do - lens nar - dus spi - ra - ver - at;
6b. huc, il - luc, an - xi - a quae - ren - do cur - si - to;

H
5c. in hor - tum ve - ne - ram, in quem de - scen - de - rat,
6c. oc - cur - runt vi - gi - les; ar - den - ti stu - di - o,

G
5d. at il - le trans - i - ens iam de - cli - na - ver - at.
6d. quos cum trans - i - e - rim, Spon - sum in - ve - ni - o.

I
7a. Iam vi - de - o quod o - pta - ve - ram,
7b. iam te - ne - o quod a - ma - ve - ram;
7c. iam ri - de - o quae sic fle - ve - ram,
7d. plus gau - de - o quam do - lu - e - ram:

J
7e. Ri - si ma - ne, fle - vi no - cte;
7f. ma - ne ri - si, no - cte fle - vi.

I'
8a. No - ctem in - so - mnem do - lor du - xe - rat
8b. quem ve - he - men - tem a - mor fe - ce - rat;
8c. di - la - ti - o - ne vo - tum cre - ve - rat,
8d. do - nec a - man - tem a - mans vi - si - tat.

J'
8e. Plau - sus di - e, plan - ctus no - cte;
8f. di - e plau - sus, no - cte plan - ctus.

K
9a. E - ia nunc, co - mi - tes et Si - on fi - li - ae,
9b. ad Spon - sae can - ti - ca psal - mum ad - ne - cti - te,
9c. quo moe - stis red - di - ta Spon - si prae - sen - ti - a
9d. con - ver - tit e - le - gos nos - tros in can - ti - ca!

L
10a. Quam fe - cit Do - mi - nus
11a. Quae nos e - ri - pu - it
12a. Quae Spon - sum su - sci - tat
13a. Ve - ris a - moe - ni - tas

M
HAEC EST DI - ES!

N
10b. Quam ex - spe - cta - vi - mus
11b. Ho - stes quae sub - ru - it
12b. Quae Spon - sam su - sci - tat
13b. Mun - di iu - cun - di - tas

O
HAEC EST [DI - ES!]

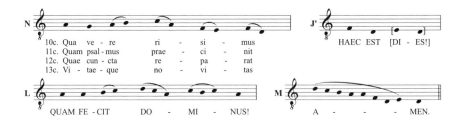

Verses

		Music	
1a	Epithalamica dic, Sponsa, cantica,	**A**	O Bride, sing your wedding song! Sing
1b	intus quae conspicis dic foris gaudia,	**A**	aloud the joys you experience within
1c	et nos laetificans, de Sponso nuntia,	**A**	and, making us glad, sing news of your
1d	cuius te refovet semper praesentia.	**A**	Bridegroom, whose presence ever warms you again.
2a	Adulescentulae, vos chorum ducite;	**B**	Young maidens, lead the choral dance:
2b	cum haec praecinerit, et vos succinite.	**B**	when she begins, then you join in. The
2c	Amici Sponsi vos vocarunt nuptiae,	**B**	friends of the bridegroom have called
2d	et novae modulos optamus Dominae.	**B**	you to the wedding, and we desire songs for the new wife.
3a	In montibus hic ecce saliens	**C**	Behold, the bridegroom is leaping
3b	ecce venit, colles transiliens;	**D**	upon the mountains; behold, he comes
3c	per fenestras ad me respiciens,	**C**	skipping over the hills; gazing at me
3d	per cancellos dicit, prospiciens:	**D**	through the windows, looking in through
3e	"Amica, surge, propera!	**E**	the lattices, he says, "Rise, Love, be quick!
4a	Horrens enim hiems iam transiit,	**C**	For rough winter now has gone;
4b	gravis imber recedens abiit;	**D**	the heavy rain, receding, is over;
4c	ver amoenum terras aperuit;	**C**	charming spring has uncovered our land;
4d	parent flores, et turtur cecinit:	**D**	the flowers appear and the turtle dove sings:
4e	columba nitens, advola!"	**E**	'Come away, shining dove!'"
5a	Rex in accubitum iam se contulerat,	**F**	The king in his chamber already has
5b	et mea redolens nardus spiraverat;	**G**	collected himself and my aromatic
5c	in hortum veneram, in quem descenderat,	**H**	nard [ointment] exhaled fragrance;
5d	at ille transiens iam declinaverat.	**G**	I come into the garden into which he has descended, but he, crossing over, already has turned aside.
6a	Per noctem igitur hunc quaerens exeo;	**F**	Therefore all night I go out seeking
6b	huc, illuc, anxia quaerendo cursito;	**G**	him; here, there, anxious, I run about
6c	occurrunt vigiles; ardenti studio,	**H**	seeking; the watchmen run up, and when
6d	quos cum transierim, Sponsum invenio.	**F**	I pass them I find my Bridegroom with burning zeal.

7a	Iam video quod optaveram,	I	I now see what I had desired,
7b	iam teneo quod amaveram;	I	I now hold what I had loved,
7c	iam rideo quae sic fleveram,	I	I now laugh when before I had cried,
7d	plus gaudeo quam dolueram:	I	and I rejoice more than I mourned.
7e	Risi mane, flevi nocte;	J	I laughed in the morning; I wept in the
7f	mane risi, nocte flevi.	J	evening. At morning I laughed; in the evening I wept.

8a	Noctem insomnem dolor duxerat	I'	Pain created a sleepless night
8b	quem vehementem amor fecerat;	I'	that love had made severe;
8c	dilatione votum creverat,	I'	the pledge increased with the delay
8d	donec amantem amans visitat.	I'	until the lover came to the beloved.
8e	Plausus die, planctus nocte;	J'	Clapping by day; a lament by night;
8f	die plausus, nocte planctus.	J'	by day, clapping; by night, a lament.

9a	Eia nunc, comites et Sion filiae,	K	Rejoice now, companions and daughters
9b	ad Sponsae cantica psalmum adnectite	K	of Sion! Join a psalm to the song of the
9c	quo moestis reddita Sponsi praesentia	K	Bride, by which the presence of the
9d	convertit elegos nostros in cantica!	K	Bridegroom offered to the grieving transforms our elegies into songs!

10a	Quam fecit Dominus HAEC EST DIES!	L/M	Which the Lord has made THIS IS THE DAY!
10b	Quam exspectavimus HAEC EST DIES!	N/O	Which we have awaited THIS IS THE DAY!
10c	Qua vere risimus HAEC EST DIES!	N/J'	On which truly we have laughed THIS IS THE DAY!

11a	Quae nos eripuit HAEC EST DIES!	L/M	Which has lifted us up THIS IS THE DAY!
11b	Hostes quae subruit HAEC EST DIES!	N/O	Which has subdued the enemy THIS IS THE DAY!
11c	Quam psalmus praecinit HAEC EST DIES!	N/J'	Which the psalm foretells THIS IS THE DAY!

12a	Quae Sponsum suscitat HAEC EST DIES!	L/M	Which wakes up the bridegroom THIS IS THE DAY!
12b	Quae Sponsam suscitat HAEC EST DIES!	N/O	Which wakes up the bride THIS IS THE DAY!
12c	Quae cuncta reparat HAEC EST DIES!	N/J'	Which restores all things THIS IS THE DAY!

13a	Veris amoenitas HAEC EST DIES!	L/M	The delight of spring THIS IS THE DAY!
13b	Mundi iucunditas HAEC EST DIES!	N/O	The joyfulness of the world THIS IS THE DAY!
13c	Vitaeque novitas HAEC EST DIES!	N/J'	And the newness of life THIS IS THE DAY!
	QUAM FECIT DOMINUS! AMEN.	L/M	WHICH THE LORD HAS MADE! AMEN.

Epithalamica (Love Songs) is a massive work, a kind of sequence cast in the guise of a miniature Easter play. This highly innovative piece actually combines several genres into a work unlike anything else encountered in the twelfth century. It works intertextually with the Easter Gradual *Haec dies* (Psalm 118 [117]), especially in the final strophe; with an eleventh-century Easter sequence *Victimae paschali laudes* (both text and music are referenced); and with several biblical narratives, most prominently the *Song of Songs*.

Peter Abelard, to whom *Epithalamica* has been attributed, was one of the foremost scholars of his day. If the piece is indeed by Abelard, his ill-fated marriage to his pupil Heloise provides a poignant subtext to this theological love song, in which human and divine love are fused. With such a complex work, Abelard was able to make his music resonate on several levels at one time, an aesthetic especially prized in the later Middle Ages. We do know that the sequence was sung at the Paraclete, the monastery for women founded by Abelard and Heloise; the version of the text and music found here were reconstructed by Chrysoganus Waddell, using two manuscripts and consulting others.

Epithalamica is a free adaptation of the double-versicle form used for sequences and, like other works in this genre, is through-composed. It can be seen that each major block of text is set to new music (indicated by letters), but not in the usual way for sequences. Although it is called a sequence, this work is really very different in form. The first poetic strophe has the same music for each of its four lines; the second strophe also is set to the same melody for each of its four lines, but the music is different from that used for strophe 1. Strophes 3 and 4 do have the same music (**CDCDE**) for their five lines, and so look more like the half-strophes of a more normal sequence. Unlike most other sequences of this era, Abelard's also makes use of a refrain at the end of the piece. But the words of the refrain—"Haec est dies!" (This is the day!)—are set to different music at each appearance (**M/O/J'**). At the very end, the last line completes the well-known Easter text, and also is set to the same music found for the first line of strophes 10–13, conveying a magnificent sense of closure in both text and music.

This large-scale work shows complete control of both its musical and textual dimensions, including a sophisticatedly creative understanding of form and genre. But the small details receive great care as well. Each poetic line is set to a musical phrase that suits its rhyme and rhythm. Rhyme saturates the piece in several ways. Rhyming is often multisyllabic, involving two or more syllables. In the first line, for example, "tha-la-mi-ca" rhymes with "–sa, can-ti-ca." The last two syllables of every line in the strophe rhyme as well. The accents of cadential words in every strophe match precisely.

Epithalamica also includes a fine example of chiasmus, or criss-cross structure, in the last two lines of strophes 7 and 8.

risi mane   flevi nocte
mane risi   nocte flevi

The overall theme of the piece is reversals: death to life, sorrow to joy, absence to presence, longing to fulfillment. To sing this wordplay is delightful, as it embodies the idea of reversal. The little musical formula that sustains both cells (marked **J**), F–D–E–D, is highly significant structurally, as its cadence is found in many places throughout the piece.

Much like the cadential formulas of the sequences studied in earlier commentaries, the formulas in this sequence ground the piece formally. The tiny cadential phrase D–E–D closes out melodic units **D**, **G**, and **J**, and all four refrain statements (transposed up a fifth in **O**). By the time the refrains occur, accompanying the final strophes, the ear is well prepared to receive them. Through this art, the song of the bride is joined to the final exultation of her maidens, and early sorrow is recast in Easter joy.

16

MARCABRU (FL. C. 1129–C. 1150)

L'autrięr jost'una sebissa
Pastorela
First half of the 12th century

1. L'au-trięr jost'-u-na se-bis - sa 2. Tro-bęi pas-to-ra mes-tis - sa,
3. De jǫi e de sen mas-sis - sa, 4. Si cum fil-la de vi-la - na,
5. Cap' e go-nęl' e pe-lis - sa 6. Vęst e ca-mi-za tres-lis - sa,
7. Sot-lars e caus-sas de la - na.

1

L'autrięr jost'una sebissa	The other day beside a hedge
Trobęi pastora mestissa,	I found a humble shepherdess,
De jǫi e de sen massissa,	full of joy and good sense,
Si cum filla de vilana,	like the daughter of a peasant girl;
Cap' e gonęl' e pelissa	a cape, a coat, and fur
Vęst e camiza treslissa,	she wore, and a shirt of rough cloth,
Sotlars e caussas de lana.	shoes and woolen stockings.

2

Ves lięis vinc per la planissa:	I came to her across the plain.
"Toza, fi·m ieu, res faitissa,	"Young girl," I said, "charming creature,
Dǫl ai car lo freitz vos fissa."	I am pained because the cold pierces you."
"Séigner, sǫ·m dis la vilana,	"Sir," said to me the peasant girl,
Merce Dięu è ma noirissa,	"Thanks to God and my nurse,
Pauc m'o pretz si·l vens m'erissa,	it does not concern me if the wind ruffles my hair,
Qu'alegreta sui e sana."	for I am cheerful and healthy."

Paris, BN fr. 22543, f. 5r; from Margaret Switten, *The Medieval Lyric, Anthology I*, 2nd ed. (NEH and Mount Holyoke College, 2001), p. 51. Reprinted with permission.

3

"Toza, fi·m ieu, cauza pia,
Destors me sui de la via
Per far a vos compaignia;
Quar aitals toza vilana
No deu ses pareill paria
Pastorgar tanta bestia
En aital terra, soldana."

"Young girl," I said, "sweet thing,
I have turned out of my way
to keep you company,
for such a young peasant girl
should not, without a comrade,
pasture so many beasts
in such a place, alone."

4

"Don fetz ela, qui que·m sia,
Ben conosc sen e folia,
La vostra pareillaria,
Séigner, so·m dis la vilana,
Lai on se tang si s'estia,
Qua tals la cuid' en bailia
Tener, no·n a mas l'ufana."

"Sir," she said, "be what I am,
I know common sense from folly;
your company,
sir," so said to me the peasant girl,
"should be offered where it is fitting,
for one who thinks she can hold it
in her power has nothing but the illusion."

5

"Toza de gentil afaire,
Cavaliers fon vostre paire
Que·us engenret en la maire,
Car fon corteza vilana.
Con plus vos gart, m'etz belaire,
E per vostre joi m'esclaire,
Si·m fossetz un pauc humana!"

"Young girl of noble condition,
your father was a knight
who got your mother with child,
for she was a courtly peasant girl.
The more I look at you, the prettier you seem,
and by your joy I am gladdened.
If only toward me you were more human!"

6

"Don, tot mon ling e mon aire
Vei revertir e retraire,
Al vezoig et a l'araire,
Séigner, so·m dis la vilana;
Mas tals se fai cavalgaire
C'atrestal deuria faire
Los seis jorns de la setmana."

"Sir, all my lineage and my family
I see returning and going back
to sickle and plow,
sir," so said to me the peasant girl.
"But some pass themselves off as knights
who should be doing likewise
six days of the week."

7

"Toza, fi·m ieu, gentils fada,
Vos adastret, quan fos nada,
D'una beutat esmerada

"Young girl," said I, "a noble fairy
blessed you, when you were born,
with perfect beauty

Sobre tot' autra vilana;	above any other peasant girl;
E seria·us ben doblada,	and it would be doubled
Si·m vezí' una vegada,	if I saw myself just once
Sobira e vos sotrana."	above and you below."

8

"Séigner, tan m'avętz lauzada,	"Sir, you have praised me so much
Que tota·n sui enojada;	that I am quite annoyed;
Pois en pretz m'avętz levada,	since you have raised me in worth,
Séigner, sǫ·m dis la vilana,	sir," so said to me the peasant girl,
Per sǫ n'auretz per soudada	"you will have for recompense
Al partir: bada, fǫls, bada	on departure: gape, fool, gape,
E la muz a meliana."	vainly waiting at noonday."

9

"Toz' estraing cǫr e salvatge	"Young girl, a wild and skittish heart
Adomęsg' om per uzatge.	one can tame by using it.
Ben conosc al trespassatge	I certainly realize on passing by here
Qu'ab aital toza vilana	that with such a young peasant girl
Pǫt hom far ric compaignatge	a man can find noble company
Ab amistat de coratge,	with heartfelt friendship,
Si l'us l'autre non engana."	if neither deceives the other."

10

"Don, hom coitatz de follatge	"Sir, a man pressed by madness
Jur' e pliu e promet gatge:	swears and pledges and guarantees:
Si·m fariatz homenatge,	thus you would do me homage,
Séigner, sǫ·m dis la vilana;	sir," so said to me the peasant girl.
Mas ieu, per un pauc d'intratge,	"But I, for a cheap entrance fee,
Non vuǫil ges mon piucellatge	do not want to exchange my virginity
Camjar per nom de putana."	for the name of whore."

11

"Toza, tota creatura	"Young girl, every creature
Revertis a sa natura:	reverts to its nature;
Pareillar pareilladura	we should prepare to form a couple,
Devem, ieu e vos, vilana,	you and I, peasant girl,
A l'abric lonc la pastura,	under cover beside the pasture,
Car plus n'estaretz segura	for you will be in greater safety there
Per far la cauza doussana."	to do the sweet thing."

12

"Don, oc; mas segon dreitura   "Sir, yes; but according to what is right,
Cerca fols sa follatura,   the fool seeks his foolishness,
Cortes cortez' aventura,   the courtly, courtly adventures,
E·il vilans ab la vilana;   and the peasant boy, the peasant girl;
En tal loc fai sens fraitura   wisdom is lacking in any place [circumstance]
On hom non garda mezura,   where moderation is not observed,
So ditz la gens anciana."   so say the ancients."

13

"Toza, de vostra figura   "Young girl, about your face,
Non vi autra plus tafura   I never saw one more dishonest,
Ni de son cor plus trefana."   nor a heart more deceitful."

14

"Don, lo cavecs vos ahura,   "Sir, the owl promises you
Que tals bad' en la peintura   that one man gapes before the painting
Qu'autre n'espera la mana."   while the other expects reward."

L'autrier jost'una sebissa, the first known pastorela, is written in Old Occitan by the troubadour Marcabru, who was known for his moralizing tone. The genre of the pastorela, meaning "little shepherdess" and typically involving an amorous encounter with a knight, signified a particular rustic setting and a range of topics that would be central to medieval songs, both monophonic and polyphonic. A courtly parody of lust and the bucolic world of the shepherdess, L'autrier jost'una sebissa also hints at the darker specter of rape and immorality, a characteristic of the high-minded style, of which Marcabru is an early representative.

The seven-line coblas doblas (stanzas paired with respect to rhyme sound) feature the same rhyme for every two stanzas, but the fourth line invariably ends with "vilana" (peasant girl), creating a kind of refrain, as the music for this word is always the same as well. The seventh line follows the refrain in its rhyme, always ending in "-ana." So it is that the refrain exerts a tight control over the entire poem, both as the ending of the first pair of lines in each stanza and by determining the rhyme of the final line of every strophe.

Each strophe divides in two both textually and musically, with lines 1–4 (abab) forming the front end, or frons, and lines 5–7 (ccd) the cauda, or back end. The frons is often divided into two equal sections known as feet (pedes). The musical form of each cobla (**ababccd**) mirrors the poetic structure. Although the final pitch is A, much of the music explores the fifth above and the fourth below C, the pitch that actually forms the tonal center of the piece. The first line cadences on D and is clearly unstable, pushing toward the next phrase, ending on C. These two make a balanced pair. Lines 5 and 6, both set to the same music, end on an unstable note as well, and the last line provides a kind of ending, making the ear welcome another strophe of the song. With its many twists and turns, Marcabru's music is well suited for an ongoing narrative. The melodic ornamentation on the next-to-last syllable of every eight-syllable line fits the accents of the text, and the five-note melisma on the last syllable of each strophe prepares us for more of the story.

The poem begins with the knight revealing his baseness as he insults the shepherdess. She is located near a "sebissa," usually translated as "hedge" but more accurately a pen or other enclosure for animals. (The description of the shepherdess as "mestissa," or half-breed, reinforces the bestial imagery.) He appeals to her by saying that her own mother was seduced by a knight, making her a bastard. It is the vilana who speaks for the poet, taking a high tone and exposing the knight's immorality.

The double tornadas at the end of the poem, one spoken by the knight and the other by the shepherdess, underscore the learned sophistication of the work as whole. The knight, having been rejected, insults the girl, but she responds with a philosophical comment about the difference between real and superficial understanding, quoting a literary passage, or refrain (in this case, meaning a citation, a short text borrowed from another work or from an oral tradition). The sense of her retort is as follows: "Sir, the owl [cryptically] augurs to [the two of] us that such a person [as you] gapes at the [mere] painted [surface], while another [one of us, namely, me] hopes for the [genuine] manna [hidden underneath]." The final six lines of the pastorela are the first time we have not had the word "vilana" anchoring the whole. But the shepherdess's rhyme ("-ana") occurs at the end of both three-line units, symbolizing her triumph and singing in tune with the moralizing owl, Marcabru himself. Although the genre is "low style" on the surface, the content is clearly "high," the song demonstrating the ways in which poet-composers played with tradition.

17

BERNART DE VENTADORN (C. 1145–1180)

Can vei la lauzeta mover

Canso

Mid-12th century

Can vei la lau-ze-ta   mo - ver   De joi sas a-las   con - tra·l rai

Que s'o-bli - d'e·s lais - sa   cha - zer   Per la dous-sor   c'al cor li   vai,

Ai,   tan grans en - ve-ya m'en ve   De cui qu'eu ve-ya   jau - zi - on,

G: Milan, Biblioteca Ambrosiana R 71 sup., f. 10r; R: Paris, BN fr. 22543, f. 56v; W: Paris, BN fr. 844, f. 190v; Switten: from Margaret Switten, *The Medieval Lyric, Anthology I*, 2nd ed. (NEH and Mount Holyoke College, 2001), pp. 68–70. Reprinted with permission.

Me-ra-vi-lhas   ai, car   des-sé   Lo cọr de   de - zi - rẹr   noˑm fon.

1

Can vei la lauzeta mover
De jọi sas alas contraˑl rai
Que s'oblid' eˑs laissa chazer
Per la doussor c'al cọr li vai,
Ai, tan grans enveya m'en ve
De cui qu'eu veya jauzion,
Meravilhas ai, car dessé
Lo cọr de dezirẹr noˑm fon.

When I see the lark beating
his wings, for joy, against the sun's ray
until he forgets to fly and lets himself fall
for the sweetness which goes to his heart,
alas! such great envy comes over me
of those whom I see rejoicing,
I marvel that at once
my heart does not melt from desire.

2

Ai las! tan cuidava saber
D'amor, e tan petit en sai!
Car eu d'amar noˑm pọsc tener
Celẹis don ja pro non aurai.
Tọut m'a mo cọr e tọut m'a me
E se mezeis e tot lo mon;
E can seˑm tọlc, noˑm laissẹt re
Ma dezirẹr e cọr volon.

Alas! I thought I knew so much
about love, and I know so little!
For I cannot keep myself from loving
the one from whom I shall have no good.
She has stolen my heart from me, and stolen my self,
and her self and all the world;
and when she took herself away, she left me nothing
except desire and a longing heart.

3

Anc non aguí de me poder
Ni no fui meus de l' ọr' en sai
Queˑm laissẹt en sos ọlhs vezer
En un miralh que mout me plai.
Miralhs, pus me mirẹi en te,
M'an mọrt li sospir de preon,
C'aissiˑm perdẹi com perdẹt se
Lo bẹls Narcisus en la fon.

Never have I had power over myself
or belonged to myself from the very hour
that she let me see into her eyes,
into a mirror that pleases me greatly.
Mirror, since I mirrored myself in you,
deep sighs have slain me;
I have destroyed myself just as the beautiful
Narcissus destroyed himself in the fountain.

4

De las domnas me dezesper;
Ja mais en lor no·m fiarai;
C'aissí com las solh chaptener,
Enaissí las deschaptenrai.
Pois vei c'una pro no m'en te
Vas leis que·m destrui e·m cofon,
Totas las dopt' e las mescré,
Car be sai c'atretals se son.

I despair of ladies;
no more will I trust them;
and just as I used to defend them,
now I shall abandon them.
Since I see that none aids me
against her who destroys and confounds me,
I fear and distrust them all,
for well I know that they are all alike.

5

D'aisso·s fa be femna parer
Ma domna, per qu'e·lh o retrai,
Car no vol so c'om deu voler
E so c'om li devéda fai.
Chazutz sui en mala mercé
Et ai be faih co·l fols en pon,
E no sai per que m'esdevé
Mas car trop puyei contra mon.

In this, she surely shows herself to be a woman,
my lady; that is why I reproach her;
for she does not want what one ought to want,
and what one forbids her, she does.
I have fallen into ill favor,
and I have acted like the fool on the bridge,
and I do not know why this happens to me,
unless I tried to climb too high.

6

Mercés es perduda, per ver,
Et eu non o saubi anc mai,
Car cilh qui plus en degr'aver,
No·n a ges, et on la querrai?
A! can mal sembla, qui la ve,
Qued aquest chaitiu deziron,
Que ja ses leis non aurá be,
Laisse morir, que no l'aon.

Mercy is lost, truly,
and I never knew it,
for she, who ought to have most of it,
has none, and where shall I seek it?
Ah! how terrible it appears, to one looking at her,
that this poor, lovesick wretch,
who will never have good without her,
she allows to perish, without helping him.

7

Pus ab midons no·m pot valer
Precs ni mercés ni·l dreihz qu'eu ai,
Ni a leis no ven a plazer
Qu'eu l'am, ja mais no·lh o dirai.
Aissí·m part de leis e·m recré;
Mort m'a e per mort li respon,
E vau m'en pus ilh no·m reté
Chaitius, en issilh, no sai on.

Since with my lady nothing can help,
neither prayers nor pity nor the rights I have,
and since to her it is no pleasure
that I love her, never shall I tell her again.
Thus I leave her and give up.
She has slain me, and by death I shall answer,
and I go away, since she does not retain me,
wretched, into exile, I know not where.

8

Tristans, ges no·n auretz de me,   Tristan, you will have nothing more from me,
Qu'eu m'en vau, chaitius, no sai on.   for I depart, wretched, I know not where.
De chantar me gic e·m recré,   I forsake and give up singing,
E de joi e d'amor m'escon.   and I hide myself from joy and love.

Can (or *Quan*) *vei la lauzeta mover* is perhaps the most famous of all troubadour songs, and surely the most anthologized. Its several versions reveal
discrepancies in melody, text, and ordering of stanzas. A standard modern
edition of the poem is provided here, along with a version of what has become
the best known of the surviving melodies (as followed by Margaret Switten,
whose translation we have also adapted). What we use—both of text and melody—belong to a range of possibilities. Still, both words and music testify to
the extraordinary skill of Bernart de Ventadorn, who was among the best of the
troubadour poet-composers, and a major witness to the culture of song from
which he came.

In this affecting *canso*, or love song, the love-sick poet identifies himself
with a lark. Trapped by the memory of previous soaring and broken by the loss
of his lady's favor, the bird rises, drops, and rises again as the poet comes to
despise the woman who has left him in despair. Like Narcissus, he sees himself
reflected in the pool of his lady's eyes and ventures too close, tumbling over the
edge. In similar fashion, the poet overflies social boundaries: his noble patron
is of lofty estate, and he recalls his lowly stature as he plummets to the earth.

Can vei consists of several strophes, each of which is composed of eight
eight-syllable lines. Each strophe has the same rhyme scheme, **ababcdcd**, until
we reach the closing four-line tornada, which is rhymed **cdcd**. The form of the
D-mode melody is **ABCDEFGH**, although there is some similarity between
the **D** and **G** sections. Note the interplay between the two competing chains of
thirds, D–F–A–C and C–E–G–B, in the construction of this melody.

There are very few large intervallic leaps in the music, and each line is a
discrete entity, fitting the ongoing poetic scheme very well. The twittering
ornaments at the ends of lines give the work great expressiveness, while the
dramatic rises and falls in the melody allow skilled singers to convey the sense
of gliding described in the poem. As with all strophic songs that offer both
narrative and thematic shifts, the melody can be adapted by the performer to
suit the affect of the text. The cadences of the lines are telling: the fourth and
eighth lines of each strophe cadence on D, the final. All the other cadences
push the music onward, most especially the G cadence at the end of line 1 and
the striking leap down a fifth to G in line 5. The melodic descent fits strophe 3

particularly well, with the dramatic drop on "en te" (in you). The idea of losing oneself in a mirror, like Narcissus, is one of the great themes of all love poetry. The poet is a lark who "forgets to fly," not from instinct, but from sorrow.

The circumstances behind troubadour songs are often described in two distinct but related types of literature: the *vida*, or short life of the poet, mostly written long after the poet's death, and incorporating various legends about him or her, and the *razo*, a short introduction to a piece that pretends to describe real-life experiences connected with a particular song. Many razos are ascribed to the thirteenth-century troubadour Uc de Saint Circ. In the razo for *Can vei*, we read that the poet-knight called his lady "Lark" because of her love for him, while she called him "Ray." The playful relationship between the bird and the sun in the song's opening takes on new meaning in this context, as the lark tumbles and turns in the sun's warmth. Bernart's vida does not mention a lark, but it does tell of love lost and of wandering. As the razo draws the listener into the opening of the poem, the vida provides a context for the final strophes and the ultimate capture of the exiled poet by his new mistress, Sorrow. "Tristan" here is a *senhal*, a fanciful name created to designate a patron.

18

GUIRAUT DE BORNEHL (C. 1140–C. 1200)

Reis gloriós
Alba
Late 12th century

Reis glo-ri-ós, ve-rais lums e clar-tatz, Dẹus po-de-rós, Sé-nher, si a vos platz,

Al meu com-panh sï-atz fi-zẹls a-iu-da, Qu'eu non lo vi pọs la nọchs fo ven-gu-da,

Et a-dẹs se-rá l'al-ba.

1

Reis gloriós, verais lums e clartatz,
Dẹus poderós, Sénher, si a vos platz,
Al meu companh sïatz fizẹls aiuda,
Qu'eu non lo vi pọs la nọchs fo venguda,
Et adẹs será l'alba.

Glorious king, true light and clarity,
powerful God, Lord, if it please You,
to my companion be a faithful aid,
for I have not seen him since the night he came,
and soon it will be dawn.

2

Bẹl companhó, si dormẹtz o velhatz,
Non dormatz plus, suau vos ressidatz,
Qu'en orïent vei l'estela creguda
Qu'amena·l jorn, qu'eu l'ai ben conoguda,
Et adẹs será l'alba.

Fine companion, whether you sleep or wake,
sleep no longer, but softly rouse yourself,
for in the East I see the star arisen
which brings the day; I have indeed recognized it,
and soon it will be dawn.

3

Bẹl companhó, en chantan vos apẹl:
Non dormatz plus, qu'eu aug chantar l'auzẹl
Que vai queren lo jorn per lo boscatge,
Et ai paor que·l gilós vos assatge,
Et adẹs será l'alba.

Fine companion, in singing I call you:
sleep no longer, for I hear the bird sing
which goes seeking the day through the woods,
and I fear the jealous one may attack you,
and soon it will be dawn.

Paris, BN fr. 22543, f. 8v; from Margaret Switten, *The Medieval Lyric, Anthology I*, 2nd ed. (NEH and Mount Holyoke College, 2001), p. 77. Reprinted with permission.

4

Bęl companhó, eissętz al fenestręl,	Fine companion, go to the window
E regardatz las estelas del cęl;	and look at the stars in the sky;
Conoisseretz si·us sui fizęls messatge:	you will know if I am your faithful messenger;
Si non o faitz, vǫstres n'ęr lo damnatge,	if you don't do this, yours will be the harm,
Et adęs será l'alba.	and soon it will be dawn.

5

Bęl companhó, pǫs mi partí de vos,	Fine companion, since I left you
Eu non dormi ni·m mǫc de ginolhós,	I have not slept nor moved from my knees;
Ans pręguęi Dęu, lo filh Santa Maria,	rather I prayed to God, the Son of St. Mary,
Que·us mi rendés per leial companhia,	that he might give you back to me in loyal friendship,
Et adęs será l'alba.	and soon it will be dawn.

6

Bęl companhó, la fǫras als peirós	Fine companion, out here on the steps
Me preiavatz qu'eu no fos dormilhós,	you begged me that I not be sleepy,
Enans velhęs tota nǫch tro al dia;	but rather keep watch all night until the day;
Era no·us platz mos chans ni ma paria.	now neither my song nor my company pleases you,
Et adęs será l'alba.	and soon it will be dawn.

7

Bęl dous companh, tan sui en ric sojorn	Fair, sweet companion, I am in so rich a dwelling
Qu'eu no vǫlgra mais fos alba ni jorn,	that I would it were never dawn nor day,
Car la gensor que anc nasqués de maire	for the noblest [lady] ever born of mother
Tenc et abras, per qu'eu non pręzi gaire	I hold and embrace; therefore I heed not at all
Lo fǫl gilós ni l'alba.	the jealous fool or the dawn.

No study of medieval music would be complete without an *alba*, or dawn song, and this simple work is one of the greatest in the genre. In this kind of piece, the singer-narrator is a watchman, one who stands outside the door, often braving dangers and cold, both to protect the illicit lovers inside and to wake them at dawn so they can part unobserved. The text of Guiraut de Bornehl's *Reis gloriós* is strophic, consisting of five lines rhyming **aabbc**, with the last line serving as a refrain, which is slightly modified in the final strophe. The strophes are *coblas doblas*, that is, the rhymes are the same for pairs of strophes (1 and 2, 3 and 4, and 5 and 6). Strophe 7 stands alone, just as the watchman does, hearing the angry rejection of his deeply engaged lord.

The music follows the scheme **AABCD**. It is a D-mode melody, with cadences on pitches A, A, C, E, and D. The first two lines are stunning, with the stark ascent of a fifth sounding out a warning like a trumpet blast, first to Christ and then to the watcher's lord. In the last strophe, the lord talks back, berating the faithful watcher and insisting that he will not heed the dawn. In this tradition, the watcher-poet is often despised for his service; in this case, he is accused of being jealous. Each stanza is anchored both at the opening, by a direct address, and at the end, by the refrain. The meanings of these repeating gestures are transformed through the middle lines of each strophe.

The melody requires a closer look, especially the **B** and **C** phrases, which set lines 3 and 4 of every strophe. These lines of text not only rhyme but are related musically as well. Both are tonally unstable, as the *cauda* often is when compared to the *frons* (see Anthology 16 for an explanation of these terms): one line cadences on C, the other on E, that is, on the two notes surrounding the final. Together, these lines make a strong contrast with the bold opening that emphasizes the interval of a fifth above the final. The cluster of notes that opens line 3 reappears midway in line 4, providing another link between the two segments and pairing them musically. Further musical continuity is provided by the opening notes of line 4, which are the same as the opening of the refrain. Lines 3 and 4 of the text are frequently qualifying clauses that challenge the bold messages of the opening lines, and their musical interrelationships and unstable cadences are crucial to the song's power.

Yet another, more subtle range of thematic possibilities comes to mind with this piece. The text resounds with images akin to those studied in our analysis of the hymn *Ave maris stella*; in it, the star of the sea is the guiding light for those in trouble (see Anthology 1). The author of the poem may have had this famous text in mind as he created a suffering character who gazes into the nighttime skies. The melody, too, with its stark opening, may be a gesture recalling the hymn tune (at least the famous version we have studied, which we know was in circulation in southern France). Intertextuality in the complex web of medieval song ranges from the apparent to the subtle. And, of course, correspondences may also be unconscious, hidden deeply in creative minds filled with texts and their melodies.

19

ADAM OF ST. VICTOR (?) (C. 1080–C. 1146)

Zima vetus

Sequence for the Easter season
Second quarter of the 12th century

*"LC" indicates phrases from the sequence *Laudes crucis.*

Paris, BN lat. 14819, ff. 71v–73v; from Margot Fassler, *Gothic Song: Victorine Sequences and Augustinian Reform in Twelfth-Century Paris*, 2nd ed. (Cambridge [England]; New York, NY, USA: Cambridge University Press, 1993). Copyright © 2011 by University of Notre Dame, Notre Dame, Indiana 46556, pp. 421–24. underpress.nd.edu. All rights reserved.

X.1

10A Ihe-su vic-tor ihe-su ui-ta 10B ihe-su ui-te ui-a tri-ta 10C cu-ius mor-te mors so-pi-ta

10D ad pas-ca-lem nos in-vi-ta 10E men-sam cum fi-du-ci-a.

X.2

10a Vi-ue pa-nis ui-uax un-da 10b ue-ra ui-tis et fe-cun-da 10c tu nos pas-ce tu nos mun-da

10d ut a mor-te nos se-cun-da 10e tu-a sal-uet gra-ti-a.

I.1	Zima uetus expurgetur ut sincere celebretur noua resurrectio.	Let the old leaven be purged so that the new resurrection may be celebrated freely.
I.2	Hec est dies nostre spei huius mira uis diei legis testimonio.	This is the day of our hope: the power of this day is marvelous by the testimony of the law.
II.1	Hec egyptum spoliauit et hebreos liberauit de forace ferea.	This day despoiled Egypt and freed the Hebrews from the cruel kiln.
II.2	Hiis in arto constitutis opus erat seruitutis lutum later palea.	When they were established in the labor of their servitude, there were mud, brick, and straw.
III.1	Iam diuine laus uirtutis iam triumphi iam salutis uox erumpat libera: Hec est dies quam fecit dominus dies nostri doloris terminus dies salutifera.	Now the praise of divine virtue, now of triumph, now of salvation, an unimpeded voice breaks out: This is the day which the Lord has made; this day is the end of our pain, the healing day.
III.2	Lex est umbra futurorum christus finis promisorum qui consummat omnia. Christi sanguis igneam hebetauit rumpheam amota custodia.	The law is the shadow of future things: Christ is the end of promises who fulfills all things: Christ's blood has dulled the fiery sword; the watchmen are driven away.
IV.1	Puer nostri forma risus pro quo ueruex est occisus uite signat gaudium.	The boy, form of our laughter, for whom the wether [castrated male sheep] was slain, represents the joy of life.
IV.2	Ioseph exit de cisterna ihesus redit ad superna post mortis supplicium.	Joseph went out from the well; Christ returned on high after the pain of death.
V.1	Hic drachones pharaonis dracho uorat a drachonis immunis malicia. Quos ignitus uulnerat hos serpentis liberat enei presentia.	This serpent devours the serpents of Pharaoh, immune from the evil of the serpent: the presence of the brazen snake makes free those whom the fiery one wounds.
V.2	Anguem forat in maxilla christus hamus et armilla in cauernam reguli. Manum mittit ablactatus et sic fugit exturbatus uetus hospes seculi.	Christ, the hook and buckle, pierces the serpent in its jaw; the weaned child puts his hand in the basilisk's den, and thus the ancient guest of this world flees in confusion.

VI.1	Irrisores helysei dum conscendit domum dei zelum calui sentiunt. Dauid arepticius hyrcus emissarius et passer effugiunt.	The mockers of Elisha, when he goes up to the House of God, feel the anger of the bald one: David is inspired, the scapegoat sent, and the sparrow flees away.
VI.2	In maxilla mille sternit et de tribu sua spernit samson matrimonium. Samson gaze seras pandit et asportans portas scandit montis supercilium.	Samson levels a thousand with a jawbone and rejects marriage from his own tribe; Samson throws open the doorbars of Gaza and, lifting up the city gates, climbs the summit of the mountain.
VII.1	Sic de iuda leo fortis fractis portis dire mortis die surgens tercia.	Thus from Judah the strong lion, with gates of dire death broken, rising on the third day,
VII.2	Rugiente uoce patris ad superne sinum matris tot reuexit spolia.	as the voice of the father roared, carried back so many spoils to the bosom of the celestial mother.
VIII.1	Cetus ionam fugitiuum ueri ione signatiuum post tres dies reddit uiuum de uentris angustia.	The whale restores the fugitive Jonah, significant of the true Jonah, alive after three days, from the narrow straits of his stomach;
VIII.2	Botrus cypri reflorescit dilatatur et excrescit synagoge flos marescit et floret ecclesia.	the cluster of henna blooms again, it is enlarged and swells; the flower of the synagogue droops and the church flourishes.
IX.1	Mors et uita conflixere resurrexit christus uere et cum christo surrexere multi testes glorie.	Life and death have fought, Christ has risen truly, and with Christ many witnesses to the glory have risen. (Paraphrase from *Victime paschali laudes*)
IX.2	Mane nouum mane letum uespertinum tergat fletum quia uita uicit letum tempus est leticie.	Let the new morning, the joyful morning, wipe away the evening weeping: because life conquered death, it is time for joy.
X.1	Ihesu victor ihesu uita ihesu uite uia trita cuius morte mors sopita ad pascalem nos inuita mensam cum fiducia.	Jesus victor, Jesus life, Jesus common way of life, by whose death, death is put to sleep, invite us to the paschal table with confidence.
X.2	Viue panis uiuax unda uera uitis et fecunda tu nos pasce tu nos munda ut a morte nos secunda tua saluet gratia.	Living bread, living water, true and fertile vine, feed us, cleanse us, so that your grace may save us from the second death.

The regular, rhyming sequence associated with the Abbey of St. Victor in Paris is a long, through-composed piece of music that unfolds within a predictable rhythmic grid. The grid is made up of a series of tightly controlled patterns, including a certain number of notes, arranged in particular groupings, and with formulaic cadences. This structure is exemplified by the Easter sequence *Zima vetus*, probably by Adam of St. Victor, the first in a long line of great Parisian poet-composers who laid the foundation for the polyphonic repertories of the thirteenth century (see, for example, Anthology 14, attributed to Albertus, Adam's successor at the Cathedral of Notre Dame). As can be seen in the score, *Zima vetus* is composed as a transformation of the earlier sequence *Laudes crucis* (marked "LC" in the score), for feasts of the Cross. The composer has found another way to change sorrow to joy, through musical restatement (compare to Anthology 15). Both these texts were also sung at the Cathedral of Notre Dame, where the poem *Zima vetus* was set to the melody of *Laudes crucis*.

As the following outline of the first five strophes shows, there is some variation in the formal arrangement of lines of the sequence, but the underlying pattern of rhyming two-line versicles remains essentially undisturbed:

I.1	4//4p + 4//4p + 7pp (**a**)
I.2	4//4p + 4//4p + 7pp (**a**)
II.1	4//4p + 4//4p + 7pp (**b**)
II.2	4//4p + 4//4p + 7pp (**b**)
III.1	4//4p + 4//4p + 7pp + 4//4p + 4//4p + 7pp (**c**)
III.2	4//4p + 4//4p + 7pp + 4//4p + 4//4p + 7pp (**c**)
IV.1	4//4p + 4//4p + 7pp (**d**)
IV.2	4//4p + 4//4p + 7pp (**d**)
V.1	4//4p + 4//4p + 7pp + 7pp + 7pp + 7pp (**e**)
V.2	4//4p + 4//4p + 7pp + 4//4p + 4//4p + 7pp (**e**)

Zima vetus has a musical form of **AABBCC** (etc.) and a corresponding rhyme scheme of **aabbcc** (etc.). In many Parisian sequences written in the twelfth century, this pattern persists for 12 or more strophes of poetry, as it does here. Musicians creating works of such enormous scale knew that the first two phrases of every half-strophe would contain caesurae, and that virtually every line would end with movement from the lower neighbor note to a repeated final. The caesura also divides the eight-syllable lines in half, and this constant dividing begets tiny cells of melody. It is clear that Parisian sequence composers thought of music in terms of small melodic and rhythmic cells that could be decorated, inverted, reversed, transposed, and combined in a variety of ways. Examples occur in almost every strophe of *Zima vetus*, with melodic cells getting kicked around the field (the rhythmic grid created by the poetry) like little footballs of sound.

Related sets of pitches occur at various places on the grid formed by the syllable count and accentual patterns. Strophe 1 alone provides several examples: the D–D–C figure on the syllable "-ge-" of "expurgetur" is transposed in the next phrase to B–B–A and G–G–F; it falls on an accented syllable the first time, but on unaccented syllables in the setting of "sincere." In strophe 2, the many approaches to G are wonderful to sing and to hear. In the cell B–G–A–G (later ornamented as B–A–G–F–G–G), the pitch G occurs on both accented and unaccented parts of words, and is variously approached by a descending leap, a stepwise descent, and a lower neighbor. In the cadential phrase there is a leap of a fifth down to G and a stepwise descent, both placing G on an accented syllable.

Zima vetus also raises a complex group of issues surrounding the use of Old Testament characters and themes in Christian texts. Throughout the Middle Ages exegetes interpreted older texts as containing types of what was to come. In such a manner, Christian ideas are presented as the fulfillment of past developments, as can be seen clearly in this text. On one level, the work is about Passover and many characters found in the Hebrew Bible; but it is also about Easter, a day made powerful "by the testimony of the law." The biblical scholar Andrew of St. Victor (c. 1110–1175) had learned Hebrew and worked closely with rabbis in Paris, producing many learned commentaries on the Bible. In the thirteenth century, this collaborative mood changed. The French king Philip Augustus expelled all Jews from his lands in 1182, and readmitted some in 1198 under severe restrictions. The Talmud was burned publicly in Paris in 1242, and one can imagine that a text like *Zima vetus* might have been interpreted as justification for hateful "purging," which, although it is triumphalist in tone, was not its original intent. It does, however, juxtapose synagogue and church at a time when the parallel began to appear frequently in figural sculpture.*

The music of *Zima vetus* constantly "rhymes" through the use of cadential formulas that match the 7pp rhyming endings of textual lines. In addition to end rhymes, there are internal rhymes of many sorts. Other poetic devices include frequent use of polyptoton, the repeating of words derived from the same root, as in "Viue panis uiuax unda" (X.2) and "asportans portas" (VI.2). Words are frequently repeated within lines and assonance abounds. By means of such poetic, rhythmic, and melodic devices, Adam of St. Victor (or another Parisian poet-composer) created a large-scale structure that echoes the repeating elements of twelfth-century Gothic art and architecture.

---

*See Nina Rowe, *The Jew, the Cathedral and the Medieval City: Synagoga and Ecclesia in the Thirteenth Century* (Cambridge: Cambridge University Press, 2011).

Mathias sanctus

Sequence

1150s

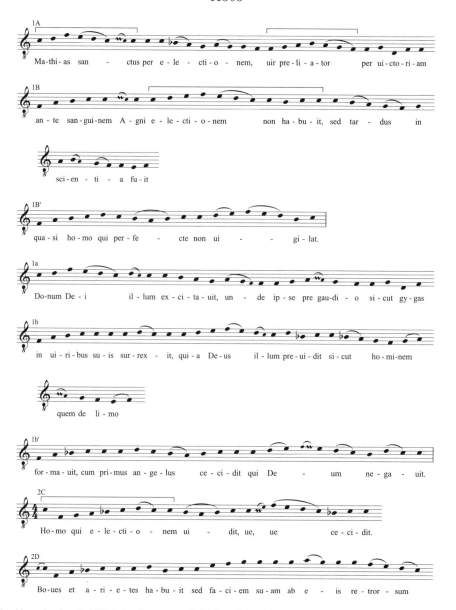

Wiesbaden, Hessischen Landesbibliothek 2, ff. 474v–475r; L. Welker, ed., and M. Klaper, comm., *Hildegard von Bingen Lieder: Faksimile Riesencodex*, ff. 466–481v (Wiesbaden, 1998); Margot E. Fassler, "Volmar, Hildegard, and St. Mathias," in Judith A. Peraino, ed., *Medieval Music in Practice: Studies in Honor of Richard Crocker* (Münster: American Institute of Musiology, 2013), 85–109.

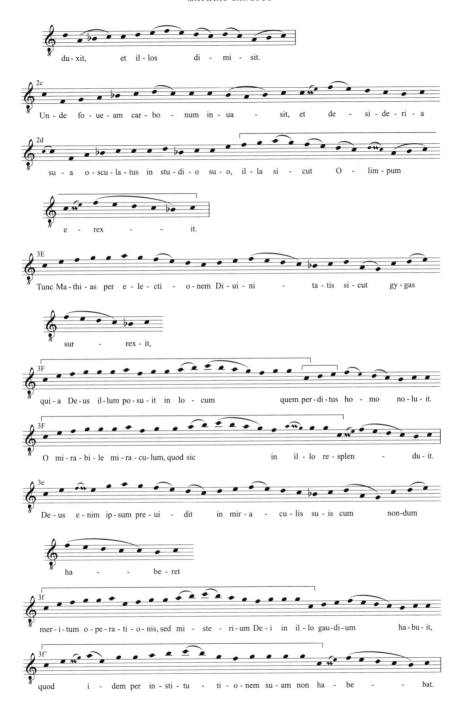

du - xit, et il - los di - mi - sit.

2c
Un - de fo - ue - am car - bo - num in - ua - sit, et de - si - de - ri - a

2d
su - a o - scu - la - tus in stu - di - o su - o, il - la si - cut O - lim - pum

e - rex - - it.

3E
Tunc Ma - thi - as per e - le - cti - o - nem Di - ui - ni - ta - tis si - cut gy - gas

sur - rex - it,

3F
qui - a De - us il - lum po - su - it in lo - cum quem per - di - tus ho - mo no - lu - it.

3F
O mi - ra - bi - le mi - ra - cu - lum, quod sic in il - lo re - splen - - du - it.

3e
De - us e - nim ip - sum pre - ui - dit in mir - a - cu - lis su - is cum non - dum

ha - - be - ret

3f
mer - i - tum o - pe - ra - ti - o - nis, sed mi - ste - ri - um De - i in il - lo gau - di - um ha - bu - it,

3f'
quod i - dem per in - sti - tu - ti - o - nem su - am non ha - be - - bat.

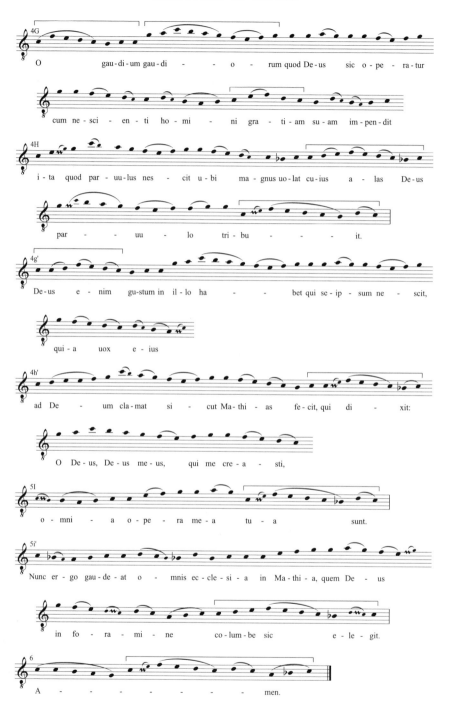

O gau-di-um gau-di - - o - rum quod De-us sic o-pe-ra-tur

cum ne-sci - en-ti ho-mi - ni gra - ti-am su-am im-pen-dit

i-ta quod par - uu-lus nes - cit u-bi ma-gnus uo-lat cu-ius a-las De-us

par - uu - lo tri-bu - - it.

De-us e - nim gu-stum in il-lo ha - - bet qui se-ip-sum ne - scit,

qui - a uox e - ius

ad De - um cla-mat si - cut Ma-thi - as fe-cit, qui di - xit:

O De-us, De-us me-us, qui me cre-a - sti,

o-mni - a o-pe-ra me-a tu-a sunt.

Nunc er-go gau-de-at o - mnis ec-cle-si-a in Ma-thi-a, quem De - us

in fo - ra - mi - ne co-lum-be sic e - le - git.

A - - - - - - men.

1A Mathias sanctus per electionem,
    uir preliator per uictoriam

1B ante sanguinem Agni
    electionem non habuit,
    sed tardus in scientia fuit,

1B′ quasi homo qui perfecte
    non uigilat.

1a Donum Dei illum excitauit,
    unde ipse pre gaudio sicut gygas

1b in uiribus suis surrexit,
    quia Deus illum preuidit
    sicut hominem quem de limo

1b′ formauit, cum primus angelus cecidit
    qui Deum negauit.

2C Homo qui electionem uidit,
    ue, ue cecidit.

2D Boues et arietes habuit
    sed faciem suam ab eis retrorsum duxit,
    et illos dimisit.

2c Unde foueam carbonum inuasit,
    et desideria

2d sua osculatus in studio suo, illa
    sicut Olimpum erexit.

3E Tunc Mathias per electionem Diuinitatis
    sicut gygas surrexit,

3F quia Deus illum posuit in locum
    quem perditus homo noluit.

3F O mirabile miraculum,
    quod sic in illo resplenduit.

3e Deus enim ipsum preuidit
    in miraculis suis
    cum nondum haberet

3f meritum operationis,
    sed misterium Dei
    in illo gaudium habuit,

3f′ quod idem per institutionem suam
    non habebat.

4G O gaudium gaudiorum
    quod Deus sic operatur
    cum nescienti homini
    gratiam suam impendit

---

1 Matthias, saint through election,
warrior through victory,
was not chosen before the slaughter of the
Lamb;
rather, he was late in knowing,
like a human not quite awake.

God's gift stirred him up
and he came forth for joy like a giant
rising in full strengths.
For God foreknew him, just as He did
the person whom He made from mud
when the first angel fell
who denied God.

2 The man who saw his election,
woe, woe, he fell!
He had oxen and goats,
but he turned his face back from them
and sent them away.
Whence he took possession of the pit of
coals
and, embracing his desires with
enthusiasm, raised them up just like Olympus.

3 Then Matthias through the election of
the Divine rose up like a giant,
for God put him in the place
that the lost one denied.
O wondrous miracle that so shines in him.

For God knew him beforehand
in His miraculous ways.
Although Matthias did not yet have the due
reward of divine service,
still the mystery of God held a joy in him

that he did not have through his own
works.

4 O joy of joys that God works thus:
when God assigns divine grace to an
ignorant person

4H	ita quod paruulus nescit	so that the little one does not understand
	ubi magnus uolat	where the great person flies, whose wings
	cuius alas Deus paruulo tribuit.	God assigns to the little one.
4g′	Deus enim gustum in illo habet	For God takes delight in that person
	qui seipsum nescit,	who forgets himself
	quia uox eius	because his voice
4h′	ad Deum clamat sicut Mathias fecit,	cries out to God, just as Matthias did
	qui dixit:	when he said:
	O Deus, Deus meus, qui me creasti,	"O God, my God, you who created me,
5I	omnia opera mea tua sunt.	5　all my efforts are yours."
5i′	Nunc ergo gaudeat omnis ecclesia in Mathia	So now let the entire church take delight in Matthias,
	quem Deus in foramine columbe sic elegit.	whom God thus elected in the cleft of the dove.
6	Amen.	6　Amen.

The nun Hildegard of Bingen was a composer and visionary whose fame spread far beyond the Benedictine monastery she founded in southwestern Germany around 1150. In her treatise *Scivias*, she recorded the revelations she claimed to have received from God, including 14 poems that she set for the Office; the play *Ordo virtutum* (The Order of Virtues) is also directly tied to the visions described in *Scivias*. Hildegard's *Scivias* songs were created for commons of the saints, that is, repertories of chants designated for particular categories of saints—for example, virgins, martyrs, or bishops. But Hildegard also wrote music to commemorate particular saints, most of them local saints to whom religious establishments were dedicated. When she was in her sixties, she traveled to Trier and preached in a monastery where St. Matthias, the last apostle, elected in the place of Judas, was especially revered. The sequence she wrote for him, *Mathias sanctus*, may have been sung by the monks there, and perhaps even on one of the days she was present.

Although Hildegard was attentive to tradition, she was also free in her adaptations of genres. She knew both kinds of sequences we have been studying: the Notkerian sequence, with its heightened prose (see Anthology 7), and the rhythmic sequence, which was popular in her era, especially in Augustinian monasteries both east and west of the Rhine (see Anthology 19 for an example from Paris). *Mathias sanctus* contains elements of each in its shifting alignment of poetry and music. Because of the double-versicle structure of sequences in combination with Hildegard's inventiveness, we chart the course of this sequence using capital and lowercase letters in a somewhat different way than for many other pieces. In the text above, the music for each line is marked with capital letters for the first statements of melodies and lowercase letters for repetitions, with prime signs indicating variants. Hence the musical form of the piece is as follows:

1 **ABB'** 1 **abb'**
2 **CD** 2 **cd**
3 **EFF** 3 **eff'**
4 **GH** 4 **g'h'**
5 **I** 5 **i'**
6 Amen

Perhaps because the melodic units are fairly long, and often melismatic and complex, the text of *Mathias sanctus* is relatively short (as are most of Hildegard's other sequences). Unlike Parisian sequences, the poem is not expressed in regular, syllable-counting accentual verse; nor is it organized around simple, recurring cadential formulas. There is a great deal of rhyme in the text, but it doesn't work in the closely patterned ways familiar to us from Parisian sequences. The first strophe is permeated with words that either rhyme or end with the same consonant; these create a chain of sounds that continues throughout the entire piece.

In similar fashion, Hildegard begins with simple musical phrases and then slowly elaborates upon them, not only by adding notes but also by repeating them at different pitch levels. For example, the opening phrase at **1A** is a small arc that moves from C up to F, and back again to an ornamented C. We see this phrase on "Mathias sanctus" in **1A**, the opening of a line; on "electionem" in **1B**, in the middle of a line; and on "vigilat" in **1B'**, at the end of a line. This arc is balanced by a second similar melodic gesture, from F to B♭, on "vir pre-liator" in **1B**. These two melodic cells are repeated constantly throughout the piece, sometimes ornamented and sometimes not. They contain the same whole step–half step relationships, t–t–s (C–F and F–B♭), thus sounding like transpositions of each other. Hildegard delights in melodic phrases that work in this way; she seems to have been able to work with the Guidonian hand and to have possessed a rudimentary understanding of hexachords (see Chapter 5 of *Music in the Medieval West*). The scribe often indicates B♭, but it is not possible to tell for how many notes the flat applies, and so editors and performers have to make a choice. We have not added editorial B♭s to this piece; it seems that once a flat sign is used, it continues throughout the phrase.

Hildegard is a generative composer: her music often sounds as if it were improvised by a singer who started with a basic set of phrases and then worked forward with increasingly expanded treatment of the material. If we take the little melodic arcs found at the opening of the piece, we can see how she stretches them and plays with them. Each statement of **3F** is essentially a long melodic arc from C up the octave to a peak at high C and back down again, finishing the arc on "perditus homo noluit." The same thing happens in both **4G** and **4H**—long, stretched-out motion from low C up to high C and back again. Taking **4G** as an example, the melody begins with motion from C up to F and back to C on "O gaudium." The next arc is another "transposition," in this case from G up to C and back to G (on "gaudiorum"). A long decorated G ("quod Deus sic operatur") is followed by a descent back to C and a repeat of the familiar C–F melodic arc to close out the line, once on "gratiam," with a circling around C to close the phrase on "suam impendit." Some of the other repeats of the C-to-F arc are bracketed in the score. And the end, after the most expansive stretching on the basic melodic arcs, Hildegard returns to the simplest shape, both to close out the **5I/5i** line and also on the final notes of the "Amen."

Hildegard was a visual thinker, and her taste for the graphic shows up in many of her compositions, the Matthias sequence included. She transforms the character of the music for the second strophe of the poem, in which the Devil is described. Everywhere else in the sequence she works with the upward-arching melody described above, transposing it to several pitch levels and expanding it as the piece goes on. In the Devil's strophe (no. 2), however, the downward-tending melody begins with a descent of a fifth, foreshadowing Satan's fall to the underworld. As a receiver of prophetic visions, Hildegard often composed music that expresses the meaning of the poetic texts through what can only be called tone painting (musical description of the words).

Laude novella

Lauda
13th century

REFRAIN

Laude novella sia cantata   *Let a new song of praise be sung*
A l'alta donna encoronata.   *to the noble crowned lady.*

1

Fresca vergene donçella,   *Fresh virgin maid,*
Primo fior, rosa novella,   *first flower, new rose,*

Biblioteca Comunale di Cortona MS 91, f. 3v; from Hans Tischler, ed., *The Earliest Laude: The Cortona Hymnal* (Ottawa: Institute of Medieval Music, 2002). Reprinted with permission.

Tutto'l mondo a te s'apella;   the whole world appeals to you,
Nella bonor fosti nata.   who were born in happiness.
Laude novella, etc.   *Let a new song, etc.*

2

Fonte se' d'aqqa surgente,   You are a fountain of spring water,
Madre de Dio vivente;   mother of the living God;
Tu se' luce de la gente,   you are the light of the people,
Sovra li angeli exalta.   exalted above the angels.
Laude novella, etc.   *Let a new song, etc.*

3

Tu se' verga, tu se' fiore,   You are the branch, you are the flower,
Tu se' luna de splendore;   you are the moon of splendor;
Voluntà avemo e core   we have the will and the heart
De venir a te, ornata.   to come to you, adorned one.
Laude novella, etc.   *Let a new song, etc.*

4

Tu se' rosa, tu se' gillio,   You are the rose, you are the lily,
Tu portasti el dolce fillio;   you bore the sweetest son;
Però, donna, sì m'enpillio   therefore, I set to work
De laudar te, honorata.   to praise you, distinguished lady.
Laude novella, etc.   *Let a new song, etc.*

5

Archa se' d'umulitade,   You are the ark of humility,
Vaso d'ogne sanctitade;   vessel of all sanctity;
En te venne deitade;   into you came the deity;
D'angel foste salutata.   you were hailed by the angel.
Laude novella, etc.   *Let a new song, etc.*

6

De le vergin' se' verdore,   Of virgins you are the verdure,
De le spose se' honore;   of wives you are the honor;
A tutt[a] gente port' amore,   to all people you bring love,
Tanto se' ingratiata.   so much are you full of grace.
Laude novella, etc.   *Let a new song, etc.*

7

Nulla lingua pò contare	No tongue can tell
Come tu se' da laudare;	how you are to be praised;
Lo tuo nome fa tremare	your name makes Satan
Sathanas a mille fiata.	tremble a thousand times.
Laude novella, etc.	*Let a new song, etc.*

8

Pregot', avocata mia,	I pray you, my advocate,
Ke ne metti en bona via;	to put us on the good path;
Questa nostra compania	may this our company
Siate sempre commendata.	always be commended to you.
Laude novella, etc.	*Let a new song, etc.*

9

Commendan te questa terra	They commend to you this land,
Che la guardi d'ogne guerra;	that you keep it from all war;
Ben s'enganna e trop' erra	he much deceives himself and too much errs
Ki t'afende, O beata.	who vexes you, O Blessed One.
Laude novella, etc.	*Let a new song, etc.*

Laude novella is a *lauda*, an Italian strophic spiritual song with a refrain (*ripresa*). Its clear and fresh melody with a text in the vernacular belongs to the thirteenth century, but emerges naturally from twelfth-century poetic and musical ideals. This is the type of song the Franciscans used to follow a preaching session, in hopes that through singing in the vernacular they might further inspire and teach the people. Such songs had to be simple but memorable, and the texts could not be too "deep," as might be the case with an intellectual troubadour song.

Laude novella is representative of thirteenth-century attempts to organize secular songs into formal patterns; the syllable-counting and rhythmic style that was so popular in Latin religious and secular songs of the twelfth century (perhaps themselves influenced by vernacular works that don't survive) has been taken into the vernacular wholesale, where each language and culture was adapted to unique poetic and musical formulas. The song's refrain consists of two rhyming lines of ten syllables each, while the verses contain four lines of eight syllables each. The first three verse lines rhyme with each other, but the last line rhymes with the refrain, producing a formal scheme of **aabbbaaa**. This turning back toward the repeat of the refrain can also be seen in the music of the last verse line, which is the same as the second line of the refrain: **ABacdbAB**. This structure would help a song leader encourage participation in the refrain, introducing it through text and music.

The piece is in D, and the first line of the refrain seems to reference the famous melody of the hymn *Ave maris stella* (see Anthology 1), also in D. Indeed, *Laude novella* offers a parade of images found in the most beloved Marian chants and miracles of the time: Mary as the rose, Mary as the queen of heaven, Mary as the branch, Mary as the lily, Mary as the ark of the Church, Mary as the model of women, Mary as the scourge of the Devil, Mary as advocate, and Mary as protector of country and home. It is an imagistic sermon in song, whose refrain praising "the noble crowned lady" crowns the work as a whole.

The featured performance by the Freiburger Spielleyt offers only four of the song's nine verses (1, 2, 5, and 9). The performance is highly idiosyncratic: in works created for vernacular use, singers often feel free from the constraints of ideas about sacred repertory. The singer, Regina Kabis, has chosen a rhythmically free style of interpretation. She treats the melismas like ornaments and decorates the melodic line in a variety of other ways, making this simple little piece sound extremely virtuosic. The addition of other voices and instrumental accompaniment in the refrain is questionable on historical grounds, but contributes to the wonderfully musical display.

The recording is far different rhythmically from the score, here as edited by Hans Tischler. The Cortona manuscript, dated to the last quarter of the thirteenth century, does not provide secure indications of rhythmic values. Yet nearly all contemporary performers use some sort of blending of longer and shorter note values, although rarely with the regularity of Tischler. We include his transcription as an example of the superimposition of the rhythmic modes on vernacular song. His rendition of the refrain has become standard.

Bache bene venies

Drinking song from *Carmina burana*
Early 13th century

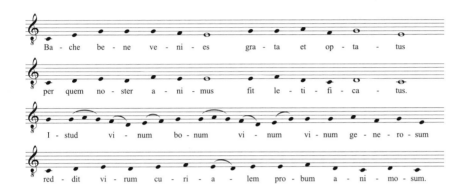

1

Bache bene venies gratus et optatus
per quem noster animus fit letificatus.

Bacchus, be welcome, dear esteemed guest,
through whom our heart is cheered.

REFRAIN

Istud vinum bonum vinum
vinum generosum
reddit virum curialem
probum animosum.

Such a wine, a wine so fine,
exquisite wine,
makes every man of the curia
honest and valiant.

2

Iste cyphus concavus de bono mero profluus
siquis bibit sepius satur fit et ebrius.
Istud vinum, etc.

This deep cup, flowing with good pure wine,
whoever sips from it often is quickly full and drunk.
Such a wine, etc.

Text from *Carmina Burana: lateinisch-deutsch: Gesamtausgabe der mittelalterlichen Melodien mit den dazugehörigen Texten.*
Ed. René Clemencic et al. (Munich: Heimeran, 1979), pp. 131–32. Music for the text has been adapted from *The Play of Daniel*
(*Danielis ludus*), as found in British Library, Egerton 2615, fols. 95–108.

3

Hec sunt vasa regia quibus spoliatur
jerusalem et regalis babilon ditatur.
Istud vinum, etc.

Behold the splendid vessels twinkling, of which
Jerusalem was despoiled and royal Babylon enriched.
Such a wine, etc.

4

Ex hoc cypho conscii bibent sui domini
bibent sui socii bibent et amici.
Istud vinum, etc.

From this cup its penitent owners drink,
its companions drink, and its friends drink.
Such a wine, etc.

5

Bachus forte superans pectora virorum
in amorem concitat animos eorum.
Istud vinum, etc.

Bacchus, stirring up the hearts of men,
hurls their spirits into love.
Such a wine, etc.

6

Bachus sepe visitans mulierum genus
facit eas subditas tibi o tu venus.
Istud vinum, etc.

Bacchus, often visiting womankind,
makes them subject to you, O Venus.
Such a wine, etc.

7

Bachus venas penetrans calido liquore
facit eas igneas veneris ardore.
Istud vinum, etc.

Bacchus, penetrating the veins with hot liquid,
makes them burn with the flame of Venus.
Such a wine, etc.

8

Bachus lenis leniens curas et dolores
confert iocum gaudia risus et amores.
Istud vinum, etc.

Calm Bacchus, calming cares and pains,
bestows joking, delight, laughter, and love.
Such a wine, etc.

9

Bachus mentem femine solet hic lenire
cogit eam citius viro consentire.
Istud vinum, etc.

Bacchus tends to ease the mind of a woman,
and compels her to consent more quickly to man.
Such a wine, etc.

10

Aqua prorsus coitum nequit impetrare
bachus illam facile solet expugnare.
Istud vinum, etc.

Water certainly cannot attain coitus,
but Bacchus is accustomed to conquer her easily.
Such a wine, etc.

11

Bachus numen faciens hominem iocundum
reddit eum pariter doctum et facundum.
Istud vinum, etc.

Bacchus, spirit who makes man jovial,
renders him equally learned and eloquent.
Such a wine, etc.

12

Bache deus inclite omnes hic astantes
leti sumus munera tua prelibantes.
Istud vinum, etc.

Bacchus, illustrious god, all of us standing here
are happy blessing and drinking your gifts.
Such a wine, etc.

13

Omnes tibi canimus maxima preconia
te laudantes merito tempora per omnia.
Istud vinum, etc.

We all sing the greatest commendations to you,
praising you deservedly for all time.
Such a wine, etc.

Carmina burana (Songs of Benediktbeuern) is the greatest collection of student song that survives from medieval Europe. The deluxe illustrated manuscript, now housed in the Bavarian State Library, was found in the early 1800s in the library of the monastery of Benediktbeuern, near Munich. Copied around 1230, primarily by a pair of anonymous scribes, the anthology includes music that would appeal to or was written by students, who often saw themselves as members of a tribe of wandering scholars and ecclesiastics known as goliards (named after the mythical Bishop Golias, a parody of the ideal clerical leader). *Carmina burana* contains more than 250 lyrics (mostly in Latin) representing the full range of Latin secular poetry: moral and satirical songs, love songs, religious plays, and gambling and drinking songs.

Anyone who had mastered accentual Latin poetic and musical conventions—monks, clerics, students in minor orders—could write in the goliardic style, criticizing abuses in the Church, praising the wandering life (imagined or otherwise), or conjuring up male fantasies of sex and seduction. Just as there was a pretend world of courtly love and lovers, the imagined loud and lascivious space occupied by goliardic song—with its mixture of learning and longing, the Bible, the liturgy, and the low life—was a distorted reflection rather than an accurate mirror of life. The parallels between contemporary rap and this repertory are many, including the wordplay and the rhythmic, in-your-face thrust of the songs.

Bache bene venies is a lively song in praise of the power of wine as an aphrodisiac. It is found in the *Carmina burana* without musical notation, but the verse form matches very closely with music found in the early-thirteenth-century *Ludus Danielis* (The Play of Daniel); in addition, as can by seen by comparison between the text of the refrain and of a stanza of this processional song for the King of Babylon, the text of the refrain is related to text from the play (see also *Music in the Medieval West*, Chapter 8). As a result, it is possible to reconstruct the music for this drinking song by using the pitches from the possible contrafactum in the *Ludus Danielis* (Ex. A2). The goliardic character is present in both works. There are several ways to adapt music from the Daniel play for *Bache bene venies*, and the first choice is based on what seem to be parallels in both text and music; also included is the way of taking music from this chant in the Daniel play and adapting the text of *Bache bene* to it, as found in the featured recording. Either choice works well.

The most common form for goliardic verse is the 13-syllable line (7pp + 6p), but 14-syllable lines (8p + 6p) are associated with the goliardic tradition as well. Here we find both: the verses are 7pp + 6p and the refrain is 8p + 6p. The utter saturation with rhyme of all kinds exceeds anything found in the Victorine sequence repertory (see Anthology 19); this is a game, played with language, in which one can imagine all kinds of one-upmanship going on: the more one could find rhyming words that made sense and kept to the form, the closer one would be to winning the prize. Halves of lines rhyme, words within lines rhyme, and the rhymes used in cadences are the most outrageous of all. In the 11-word refrain, for example, all but two of the words rhyme.

Example A2: Excerpt from *The Play of Daniel*

Let the joyous throng resound with magnificent poems!
Let them play the cithara, let hands clap, let them sound out with one thousand measures!

The punchy and memorable tunes encourage singers to sound the refrain in lusty unison and then for soloists to work through many verses, adding as many new texts as desired. As transcribed here, the verse is essentially a decorated triad (F–A–C). The first half of the refrain explores a higher range of pitches, but is linked to the verse through the cadential third that ends the first lines of both the refrain and the verses.

The featured performance, which joins the Oni Wytars Ensemble and the Unicorn Ensemble, is a musical reverie on medieval debauchery, employing many tempi and textures. *Bache bene venies* in this performance is filled with churchly intonations and dramatic pauses, placing the work in a mock-liturgical context. The strophes are sung by a variety of characters, male and female, introducing the idea of barmaids or some sort of female presence. Several instruments—a drum, a bagpipe, a hurdy-gurdy, fiddles, and a recorder—are played in this medieval hoedown, and the entire work ends with a grandiose phrase sung in parallel organum.

Chançon ferai que talenz

Chanson with refrain
Second quarter of the 13th century

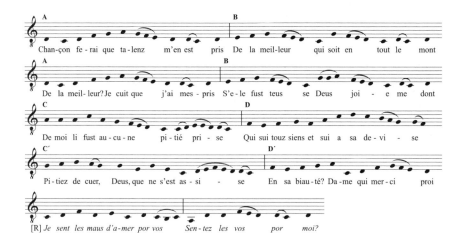

1

Chançon ferai que talenz m'en est pris,	I shall make a song, since the desire has overtaken me,
De la meilleur qui soit en tout le mont.	about the best one in the world.
De la meilleur? Je cuit que j'ai mespris.	About the best? I think I've made a mistake.
S'ele fust teus, se Deus joie me dont,	If she were such, so may God grant me joy,
De moi li fust aucune pitié prise,	some pity would have taken hold in her
Qui sui touz siens et sui a sa devise.	for me—I am all hers and at her will.
Pitiez de cuer, Deus! que ne s'est assise	Pity of the heart—God! Why is it not seated
En sa biauté? Dame, qui merci proi,	in her beauty? Lady, from whom I beg mercy,
Je sent les maus d'amer por vos.	*I feel the pains of love for you.*
Sentez les vos por moi?	*Do you feel them for me?*

2

Douce dame, sanz amor fui jadis,	Sweet lady, formerly I was without love,
Quant je choisi vostre gente façon;	at the moment I chose your gentle manner;
Et quant je vi vostre tres biau cler vis,	and when I saw your beautiful, bright face,
Si me raprist mes cuer autre reson:	my heart changed its attitude:

Paris, Arsenal MS 5198, f. 12r; P. Aubrey, ed., *Le chansonnier de l'Arsenal* (Paris: P. Geuthner, 1909–1912); from Margaret Switten, *The Medieval Lyric, Anthology I*, 2nd ed. (NEH and Mount Holyoke College, 2001), p. 142. Reprinted with permission.

De vos amer me semont et justise,
A vos en est a vostre conmandise.
Li cors remaint, qui sent felon juïse,
Se n'en avez merci de vostre gré.
Li douz mal dont j'atent joie
M'ont si grevé
Morz sui, s'ele m'i delaie.

it summons and orders me to love you,
it is within your command.
The body remains [to perish], feeling cruel justice
if you have no pity on it of your free will.
The sweet sorrows from which I await joy
have so tormented me
that I am dead if she makes me wait.

3

Mult a Amors grant force et grant pouoir,
Qui sanz reson fet choisir a son gré,
Sanz reson? Deus! je ne di pas savoir,
Car a mes euz en set mes cuers bon gré,
Qui choisirent si tres bele senblance,
Dont jamès jor me ferai desevrance,
Ainz sousfrirai por li grief penitance,
Tant que pitiez et merciz l'en prendra.
Diré vos qui mon cuer enblé m'a?
Li douz ris et li bel oeil qu'ele a.

Love has great force and power
to make you choose her will without reason.
Without reason? God! I am not saying I know,
for my heart is grateful to my eyes,
which chose a countenance so beautiful
that I will never part from it;
to the contrary, I will suffer grievous penance for her,
so much that pity and mercy will overcome her.
Shall I tell you who stole my heart?
Her sweet smile and beautiful eyes.

4

Douce dame, s'il vos plesoit un soir,
M'avrïez vos plus de joie doné
C'onques Tristans, qui en fist non pouoir,
N'en pout avoir nul jor de son aé;
La moie joie est tornee a pesance.
Hé, cors sanz cuer! de vos fet grant venjance
Cele qui m'a navré sanz defiance,
Et ne por quant je ne la lerai ja.
L'en doit bien bele dame amer
Et s'amor garder, qui l'a.

Sweet lady, if it pleased you one evening,
you would give me more joy
than ever Tristan—who did all he could—
was able to win a day of his life;
my joy has turned to pain.
Ah! Body without heart! She's taken vengeance on you,
the one who cut me to the quick without challenge,
and yet I'll never leave her.
One must love a beautiful lady
and keep her love, if one has it.

5

Dame, por vos vueil aler foloiant,
Que je en aim mes maus et ma dolor,
Qu'après les maus la grant joie en atent
Que je avrai, se Deu plest, a brief jor.
Amors, merci! ne soiez oublïee!
S'or me failliez, c'iert traïson doublee,
Que mes granz maus por vos si fort m'agree.
Ne me metez longuement en oubli!
Se la bele n'a de moi merci,
Je ne vivrai mie longuement ensi.

Lady, for you I want to follow folly,
for you I love, my suffering and sadness,
since after my sufferings I expect the great joy
I shall have, God willing, very shortly.
Love, help! Don't forget!
If you fail me now, it will be double treason
that my sufferings for you please me so much.
Don't let me be long forgotten!
If the fair one does not take pity on me,
I will not live long like this.

6

La grant biautez qui m'esprent et agree,	The great beauty that sets me aflame and pleases me,
Qui seur toutes est la plus desirree,	that is desired above all others,
M'a si lacié mon cuer en sa prison.	has bound up my heart in her prison.
Deus! je ne pense s'a li non.	*God! I think only of her.*
A moi que ne pense ele donc?	*Why doesn't she think of me?*

The modern performers of *Bache bene venies* (Oni Wytars Ensemble and the Unicorn Ensemble; see Anthology 22), with its boisterous Latin wordplay, place the song in the context of an imaginary tavern scene. But how did thirteenth-century audiences listen to songs composed in the high courtly style, such as *Chançon ferai que talenz* by the trouvère Thibaut, count of Champagne, king of Navarre, and scion of one of the oldest noble families in France? Such complex songs required close attention on the part of their hearers and a minimum of extraneous noise. At the same time, the rapt silence that accompanies modern concert performances was probably not expected. Trouvère songs were written, for the most part, by and for men, and dealt with male themes and sensibilities. When poet-composers did write for women, the songs may have been sung in the women's chambers rather than in the masculine domain of the hall; and when they were commissioned by women, we can assume that their wishes were respected and their interests engaged: the compositions of women reflect their points of view. If instrumental accompaniment was employed, it most likely would have been a stringed instrument, and at times aristocratic women may well have both sung and accompanied the songs.

Chançon ferai que talenz is cast in the usual form for a *grand chant courtois*, the most refined and complex type of French song: its text consists of five stanzas, each made up of eight lines with ten syllables each, and a three-line *envoi* (a short final stanza). The rhyme scheme for each stanza is **ababcccd**, and the musical phrases are as follows, with their cadential pitches in parentheses: **A** (D) **B** (D) **A** (D) **B** (D) **C** (C) **D** (F) **C'** (C) **D'** (D). As in many chansons of the troubadours (see Anthology 16–18), there may be close formal correspondence between text and music in the first half of the piece, not in the second half, and the opening is often tonally more stable as well. The first four stanzas are a pair of *coblas doblas* (two stanzas employing the same rhyme sounds), with the fifth stanza standing alone.

At the same time, *Chançon ferai que talenz* differs from many trouvère songs in that it has multiple refrains (meaning, in this case, citations, borrowed from other sources), one for each stanza. (The refrains are printed in italics above.) The refrains are a kind of glue for the entire piece, for they drive the rhyme: the last line of each stanza rhymes with the last line of the refrain. The text and music of the different refrains are drawn from other well-known thirteenth-century songs, showing how poet-composers linked their songs to popular culture.

As we know, it is typical of chansonniers to supply the melody for the first stanza alone; part of the work of the performer is to fit the rest of the text to the melody. But *Chançon ferai* offers special difficulties because of the refrains. Only the first refrain is supplied with music in the Chansonnier de l'Arsenal, but it is clear that each subsequent refrain is a quotation from another song, and that music from that song should be supplied when the text triggers the memory of the performer. Scholars have identified the refrains for stanzas 4 and 5 in other sources, and so their music, but what to do about those borrowed texts whose music cannot be located? On our featured recording, Paul Hillier improvises music for the citations for stanzas 2 and 3 based on his deep knowledge of the trouvère repertory. In the thirteenth century, performance of this chanson was dependent upon an art of memory; today its performance depends on deep immersion in the repertory.

Although each line of music forms a well-constructed melodic "sentence," a variety of small musical motives are employed throughout the piece to create a sense of unity. The most important motive is D–C–D, which opens and closes phrase **A** of the melody, closes phrase **B**, and recurs at the end of the first refrain. Overall, the melody is very contained: phrases **A** and **B** move only the distance of a sixth, and phrase **D** is the only one to move up to the octave above the final. The first refrain is striking not only for its sheer loveliness, but also because it explores the tetrachord below the final.

Rosa das rosas

Cantiga de loor
Second half of the 13th century

[R] Ro - sa das ro - sas e Fror das fro - res,

Do - na das do - nas, Se - nnor das se - nno - res. Ro - sa de

bel - dad' e de pa - re - cer, e Fror d'a - le - gri - a

e de pra - zer, Do - na en mui pi - a - do - sa se -

er, Se - nnor en to - ller coi - tas e do - o - res.

Madrid, Biblioteca Nacional, MS 10069, f. 20 [To]; J. Ribera, ed., *La musica de las Cantigas: Estudio sobre su origen y naturaleza, con reproducciones fotograficas del texto y transcripcion moderna* (Madrid, 1922); San Lorenzo de El Escorial, Biblioteca del Real Monasterio, T.I.1, f. 17 [E2]; M. L. Serrano et al., eds., *El "Códice Rico" de las Cantigas de Alfonso el Sabio: Ms. T.I.1 de la Biblioteca de El Escorial* (Madrid, 1979); San Lorenzo de El Escorial, Biblioteca del Real Monasterio, b.I.2, f. 39 [E1]; H. Anglès, ed., *La música de las Cantigas de Santa María del Rey Alfonso el Sabio*, vol. 1 (Barcelona, 1943), 18; Alfonso X El Sabio, *Cantigas de Loor*, ed. Martin Cunningham (Dublin: University College Dublin, 2000), 90–92 (text).

Rosa das rosas e Fror das frores,   *Rose of roses, flower of flowers,*
Dona das donas, Sennor das sennores.   *lady of ladies, liege of lieges.*

1

(*mundanza*)
Rosa de beldad' e de parecer,   Rose of beauty and seemliness,
e Fror d'alegria e de prazer,   and flower of joy and delight,
Dona en mui piadosa seer,   lady, in your great compassion,
(*vuelta*)
Sennor en toller coitas e doores.   liege, in taking away troubles and sorrows.
Rosa das rosas, etc.   *Rose of roses, etc.*

2

Atal Sennor dev' ome muit' amar,   Such a liege must love man greatly,
que de todo mal o pode guardar,   that she can guard him from all evil
e pode-ll' os pecados perdõar   and can forgive him his sins,
que faz no mundo per maos sabores.   which he commits in the world by his evil desires.
Rosa das rosas, etc.   *Rose of roses, etc.*

3

Devemo-la muit' amar e servir   We must love and serve her greatly,
ca punna de nos guardar de falir;   since she endeavors to keep us from failing;
des i, dos erros nos faz repentir   likewise she makes us repent our errors,
que nós fazemos come pecadores.   which we commit, sinners that we are.
Rosa das rosas, etc.   *Rose of roses, etc.*

4

Esta Dona que tenno por Sennor,   This lady whom I hold as my liege,
e de que quero seer trobador: and whose troubadour I desire to be:
se eu per ren poss' aver seu amor,   if I can only have her love,
dou ao demo os outros amores.   I will give to the Devil those other loves.
Rosa das rosas, etc.   *Rose of roses, etc.*

The *Cantigas de Santa María* is the central collection of *cantigas* (songs) recounting the miracles of the Virgin Mary. In each of the three major surviving manuscripts, the songs are organized into groups of nine miracle-narrations, each followed by a *cantiga de loor*, or song of praise. Each loor has three dimensions: the theological, the troubadour-courtly, and the personal—the passion of the king for his Lady, the Virgin Mary. In *Rosa das rosas*, the king swears that he is a servant to this woman, in a feudal relationship. Whether the learned Spanish king known as Alfonso the Wise composed the *Cantigas de Santa María*, or merely had a hand in the compilation of the original collection, his voice can clearly be heard in each of the songs found in the collections that bear his name. The texts are written in Galician-Portuguese, the literary language of his court.

Rosa das rosas, the first loor in all three manuscripts, is a D-mode piece with the poetic form **aa** (the *estribillo*, or refrain) **bbb** (the *mundanza*) **a** (the *vuelta*, or "turn" to the rhyme of the opening) **aa**. The musical structure is **ABccdbAB**, with capital letters indicating lines in which text and music constitute a refrain, both elements repeated throughout the unfolding of the song. Text and music exist in a kind of interplay, and in many cantigas de loor the music anticipates the refrain in the last line of the mundanza. Here, however, both words and music "turn" toward the refrain on the same line. Although there is a good deal of slight variation in the genre, the estribillo always brackets the mundanza and its vuelta, providing a powerful sense of structure, as the refrain does in other sacred and secular song repertories of the twelfth and thirteenth centuries (see Anthology 15, 18, 21, 22, and 25).

As with so much thirteenth-century song, rhythm remains a problem in the *Cantigas*. The highly influential transcriptions of Higini Anglès, published in 1943—an example of which is followed here—provide the neumation and also show that there is disagreement in the medieval sources. Modern scholars surely disagree about the realization of the rhythms and the extent to which the rhythmic modes come into play (see Primer II.3 and Chapter 9 of *Music in the Medieval West*). It is best to work closely with the sources and make decisions on a case-by-case basis; in general, the notation of the *Cantigas* is neither modal nor mensural, but something in between.

The question of Arabic (or Andalusian) influence on this repertory looms large. A wide range of performing musicians gathered at the court of Alfonso the Wise, including some women—singers as well as instrumentalists—and a host of poets, some of whom are depicted as Moors. The Arabic *muwashshah* and *zajal* are strophic forms with refrains that may have originated in Andalusian Spain (the southern part of the country, where the Arabic, or Moorish, influence was strongest); both forms have schemes that relate to the loor. Certain rhythmic patterns found in some cantigas may also be related to Andalusian music. The ways in which the instrumentalists at Alfonso's court—Moorish, Christian, and Jewish—mingled their playing styles and techniques cannot be known; nor do we know how, if, or when the cantigas were accompanied. Nevertheless, many modern performers have been inspired to reconstruct the music in light of their understanding of the medieval Arabic tradition.

Ondas do mare de Vigo

Cantiga de amigo
Late 13th century

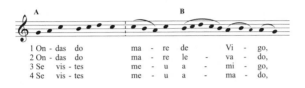

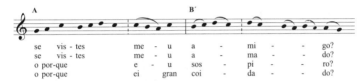

1

| Ondas do mare de Vigo, | O waves of the sea of Vigo, |
| se vistes meu amigo? | have you seen my friend? |

REFRAIN

| *E ai Deus! Se verrá cedo?* | *And oh God! Will he come soon?* |

2

Ondas do mare levado,	O waves of the swelling sea,
se vistes meu amado?	have you seen my beloved?
E ai Deus! Se verrá cedo?	*And oh God! Will he come soon?*

New York, Pierpont Morgan Library MS M979; P. Vindel, ed., *Las siete canciones de amor: Poema musical del siglo XII* (Madrid, 1915). From M. P. Ferreira, *The Sound of Martin Codax: On the Musical Dimension of the Galician-Portuguese Lyric* (Lisbon, 1986), p. 129. Reprinted with permission.

3

Se vistes meu amigo,	Have you seen my friend,
o porque eu sospiro?	the one for whom I sigh?
E ai Deus! Se verrá cedo?	*And oh God! Will he come soon?*

4

Se vistes meu amado,	Have you seen my beloved,
o porque ei gran coidado?	who causes me great care?
E ai Deus! Se verrá cedo?	*And oh God! Will he come soon?*

Ondas do mare de Vigo is a strophic *cantiga de amigo* (friend's song) with a refrain, a very precious testimony to what must have been an extraordinary repertory of song: of more than 1,700 secular poems found in medieval Galician *cancioneiros* (songbooks), only fourteen survive with their music. Seven of these are by Martin Codax and seven are attributed to King Dinis I of Portugal. Like the *Cantigas de Santa María* (see Anthology 24), the songs by Martin Codax are written in Galician-Portuguese. Little is known about Martin except that he was a jongleur who set all of his songs in Vigo, a small coastal village in northwestern Spain, near the Portuguese border.

Ondas do mare has the rhyme scheme **abcb** (verse) **db** (refrain), and the form of the music is **ABAB'CB'**. The stanzas shift with an artful sense of wordplay; like a succession of waves, each line is like what came before it, and yet different. Thus "de Vigo" in stanza 1 becomes "levado" in stanza 2, while "amigo" turns into "amado." Stanzas 3 and 4 both begin with the words "Se vistes."

One can only imagine the musical interplay that must once have existed between the vast secular and sacred repertories in the region of Galicia. Martin's music resembles an ornamented psalm tone (see Anthology 4 and Primer III.3), rising from G to an ornamented C, which repeats throughout the line before the descent to G, a gesture that becomes more melismatic in the **B'** phrase. A musically jarring note occurs in the first phrase of the refrain, when the melody unexpectedly moves down to F, a lower neighbor to the final of G. Since the F is heard only in this very unstable and dramatic refrain, it underscores the speaker's direct and pleading question to God.

Hearing a song by Martin Codax sung well is one of the greatest joys offered by the medieval song repertory. *Ondas do mare de Vigo* is a song of endless longing, striking in its glorious futility. The poetic refrain, a question, is especially poignant. Of course, the ship will never return, the waves will continue to lap, and the heartbroken woman will remain alone, talking to the sea. Yet the poem bespeaks a larger continuity with poetic and musical tradition, and with the hopes of generations of lovers.

Sol oritur in sidere

Monophonic conductus
First third of the 13th century

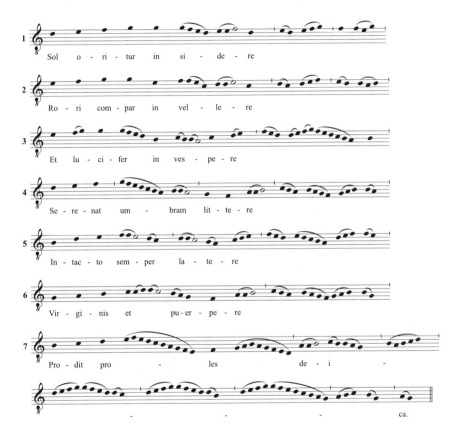

Sol oritur in sidere,	The sun is born in the star,
rori compar in vellere,	like dew in the fleece,
et lucifer in vespere,	and in the evening the morning star
serenat umbram littere;	lightens the shadow of the word;
intacto semper latere	from the ever-chaste loins
Virginis et puerpere	of the Virgin and the childbearer
prodit proles deica.	the divine offspring comes forth.

Florence, Biblioteca Medicea-laurenziana Pluteus 29.1, f. 422r; L. Dittmer, ed., *Faksimile Ausgabe Firenze, Biblioteca medicea-laurenziana, Pluteo 29, I* (Brooklyn, NY: Institute of Medieval Music, 1966–1967); from Susan Rankin, "Some Medieval Songs," *Early Music* 31. 3 (2003): 326–45, at 331. By permission of Oxford University Press.

Divino verbo numinis	By the divine Word of God
supplente vicem seminis	supplying an exchange of seed,
tumescit alvus virginis;	the Virgin's womb begins to swell;
absconsa virtus luminis,	the concealed strength of the light,
quod lucet mundi terminis,	which shines to the ends of the world,
lapsum reformat hominis	reforms the fall of humankind
gratia vivifica.	with life-giving grace.

Quod clamant vaticinia,	What prophecies declare,
quod murmurant misteria,	what mysteries murmur,
iusta produnt indicia:	just signs bring forth:
lactante patrem filia,	with the daughter nursing her father,
inclinantur celestia;	the heavens are bent downward;
indulcans legis gratia	the sweet grace of the law
terris unit celica.	joins heaven with earth.

The context in which polyphonic music of the Notre Dame School of the twelfth and thirteenth centuries developed includes monophonic Parisian sequences (see Anthology 19), secular songs (see Anthology 23), and conductus, many of which were set polyphonically as well (see Anthology 12 and 14). The newly rising Cathedral of Notre Dame was, like many Gothic cathedrals, dedicated to the Virgin Mary. Because she was the patron saint, music for her veneration became supreme and was of great variety.

The monophonic conductus *Sol oritur in sidere* has been attributed to Philip, a poet who was a scholar, composer, and chancellor of the Cathedral of Notre Dame in Paris. He not only composed several conductus, but also provided prosulae for some organa, and wrote both texts and music for motets, early examples of which (although not attributed to Philip) are discussed in Anthology 30. Philip represents the collaboration that must have taken place between various musical forces at the Cathedral of Notre Dame in the early thirteenth century involving performers who could improvise in the practice and try out new pieces—poet-composers like Philip and Pérotin (see Anthology 29)—and those who were notating music in new ways.

Sol oritur has three seven-line strophes written in accentual, rhyming Latin poetry, with the scheme **aaaaaa** (8pp) **b** (7pp). The poet's description of the wonders of the virgin birth focuses on the way light shines into and through the female body—perhaps especially meaningful in a building filled with stained-glass images of the Virgin. The text survives with music only in a deluxe early-thirteenth-century Parisian manuscript preserved in Florence, one of three major sources for the fluid repertory of liturgical music performed at Notre Dame known as the *Magnus liber organi* (Great Book of Organum).

The first six lines (**a**) of each strophe rhyme, and the seventh lines (**b**) of each strophe rhyme with each other, linking the three stanzas together. Although no two musical lines are precisely the same, they share a uniform melodic contour: an initial rise of a third, fourth, or fifth, followed by a dramatic ornamented fall to a pitch that is lower, in most cases, than the pitch that began the line. At this midpoint, a little rising figure in six of the seven lines (on the penultimate or last syllable of the final word) seems to signal that the music is about to take off. The second half of the musical line soars aloft, typically cadencing in a lengthy melisma spanning as much as an octave. These melismatic "tails," or *caude* (singular, *cauda*), also exhibit uniformity of contour, and two, in lines 4 and 6, are almost identical.

Sol oritur in sidere anticipates the decoration deemed appropriate for later medieval Marian veneration, especially in the last line of each strophe, which is twice as long as any other line. The composer artfully manipulates the melismas to create parallels between one phrase and another: in strophe 1, for example, the melismas on the syllables "pro-" and "-les" move in similar ways, but on different pitch levels. Generally speaking, *Sol oritur in sidere* is a mode 7 piece, but the pitches transcend the usual ambitus of the mode. It would not be difficult to improvise such music, as long as a singer had the "destination" pitches in mind, since many common melodic figures are employed throughout. One could also imagine some sort of slow-moving second voice, the addition of which would turn the piece into florid organum. On the featured recording, the ensemble Sequentia treats the melismas like ornaments and demonstrates the vocal virtuosity demanded in this repertory.

27

ANONYMOUS

Stirps Jesse

Organum triplum
First third of the 13th century

Florence, Biblioteca Medicea-laurenziana Pluteus 29.1, f. 26v; L. Dittmer, ed., *Faksimile Ausgabe Firenze, Biblioteca medicea-laurenziana, Pluteo 29, I* (Brooklyn, NY: Institute of Medieval Music, 1966–1967); from Edward H. Roesner, ed., *Les quadrupla et tripla de Paris*, vol. 1 of *Magnus Liber Organi de Notre-Dame de Paris* (Monaco: Éditions de l'Oiseau-Lyre, 2002), pp. 117–19. Reprinted with permission.

Stirps Yesse* [virgam produxit virgaque florem   The shoot of Jesse [produced a rod, and the rod a
Et super hunc florem requiescit spiritus almus.]   flower, and over that flower rests a nurturing spirit.]

*An alternate spelling of the more common *Stirps Iesse* or *Stirps Jesse.*

The three- and four-voice examples of Notre Dame organa are among the most
striking creations of the entire medieval repertory. They are now considered to belong to an earlier rather than a later layer of the *Magnus liber organi*
(Great Book of Organum), which embodies the Parisian repertory as it evolved
from the late twelfth through the mid-thirteenth century. This setting of the
responsory *Stirps Jesse* (there are many spellings of this phrase in medieval
sources) is found in Manuscript W1 (and also in F), in a section containing
three-voice organum, or *organum triplum*, in which two voices move simultaneously above the tenor. (For a discussion of the major manuscript sources of

the Notre Dame repertory, see Chapter 9 of *Music in the Medieval West*.) An especially ornate piece such as this was designated for major feasts, especially during Christmas week, or, as in this case, for the Virgin Mary, the patron saint of the cathedral in Paris.

As Edward Roesner has transcribed them, the two upper voices are completely modal, and mostly in rhythmic mode 1. There were six rhythmic modes, expressed in notes called longs and breves—actually the standard virga and punctum of square notation, but expressed by ligatures. Mode 1 (long-short, or trochaic) is the most important of the rhythmic modes, and the earliest to be notated. As the rhythmic modes evolved in the course of the thirteenth century, terminology changed to reflect more rhythmic variety. At first, a foot in mode 1 was made of a long of two counts followed by a breve, and so the two-count long was standard. But by the time of the theorist Lambertus (who flourished in the third quarter of the thirteenth century), the idea of perfection and of perfect three-count longs had become dominant. Accordingly, each "foot" has a count of three beats and constitutes a "perfection": a perfection might consist of a perfect long, an imperfect (two-beat) long plus a breve; three breves; or two breves, the second of which was altered to have two beats. (See the discussion of the rhythmic modes in Primer II.3.)

The modes are expressed in patterns called *ordines* (singular, *ordo*), and these are separated by rests. In the setting of the opening notes of *Stirps Jesse*, the two upper voices move in short mode 1 ordines. They are completely wedded to each other, both rhythmically and harmonically, with cadences falling on fifths and octaves above the slow-moving tenor notes. Notice how the ordines unfold, with the first and last notes of almost every tightly controlled phrase being worth the same value. The brackets above the notes represent ligatures of the chant notation, and the arrangements of the ligatures express the modes. The practice depends on being able to read the feet of the rhythmic mode, and the values of the notes, the modus (the value of the longs) and tempus (the value of the breves) as found within the carefully arranged ligatures of square notation.

Stirps Jesse introduces the kinds of motion that are characteristic of polyphonic textures in the late medieval and Renaissance periods, with an emphasis on contrary motion. The first phrase is a fine example, with both voices moving inward to the fifth above the tenor and then outward to the octave (and unison). The power of the droning tenor note keeps the harmonies static. But when the tenor moves to C at 20 (the numbers in the score relate to ligatures rather than measures), the upper voices shift gears dramatically; this kind of shifting is what keeps the piece musically alive. The voice occupying the top line (actually, its overall range is lower than that of the middle voice) leaps up a seventh to start on high C (while the middle voice jumps down a sixth). A dissonant leap such as this happens only in places of transition. There are some large leaps within lines that involve perfect intervals, however, such as the octave leap from high to low C in the top line, at 26. There is frequent crossing of the two upper voices as well in this repertory.

Alejandro Enrique Planchart has pointed out that two clausula-like sections are embedded in this part of the setting: two different upper lines unfolding above the melismatic tenor on "Yesse" at 110–59 and 161–90. These parts of the piece may represent a later layer in the work. The skipping-note descents that close out these miniature masterpieces are not to be forgotten, and were found as well near cadences of polyphonic settings in the Codex Calixtinus (see Chapter 6 of *Music in the Medieval West*). The approaches to the tenor's arrival on D at 159 and 190 are highly decorated by upper voices. These cadences that introduce dramatic changes in texture are marked by large-scale musical punctuation points such as the skipping-note descent found in the second voice at 146–52 and 178–84. Both passages are clearly expressed in the recording of the piece by the Schola Hungarica.

As we have said, organa tripla and quadrupla of the *Magnus liber organi* are now thought to belong to an early layer of the Notre Dame repertory. One of the reasons for this has to do with the discant sections of such pieces: it is believed that in earlier layers the use of the rhythmic modes was not fully developed. As can be seen in this setting of *Stirps Jesse*, the word "Yesse" is melismatic in the chant and so is set in discant. The notes in the tenor move more quickly, and as a result the upper voices move differently, sometimes with what seems to be a fracturing of the rhythmic mode; occasionally the voices move freely one against the other, although the ordines still line up exactly and are marked by simultaneous rests. However, the more-quickly-moving tenor notes are not "patterned," but simply unfold in a series of longs, as can be seen at 112–19 and 138–44. When the triplum tenor here is compared with the short discant sections studied in Anthology 28, the difference is clear. The tenor in the discant sections of the organum duplum unfolds in a series of ordines separated by rests.

28

ANONYMOUS

Styrps Yesse

Organum purum and discant

First third of the 13th century

Florence, Biblioteca Medicea-laurenziana Pluteus 29.1, f. 75r; L. Dittmer, ed., *Faksimile Ausgabe Firenze, Biblioteca medicea-laurenziana, Pluteo 29, I* (Brooklyn, NY: Institute of Medieval Music, 1966–1967); transcription by Rebecca A. Baltzer.

DUPLUM AND TENOR

Styrps Yesse   The shoot of Jesse

Thirteenth-century theorists speak of three different kinds of organum: *orga-num purum*, discant, and *copula*. (Copula is a kind of polyphonic texture that is used at the joining of one texture to another; it is a complicated term and will not be discussed here.) Because many of the theorists wrote in the second half of the thirteenth century, when interest in sustained-note organum purum had apparently waned, there is less written about it than one might hope. According to several theorists, the rhythmic modes were not used in organum purum; the rhythm is free. Anthology 28 is taken from the opening of the responsory *Stirps Jesse*, a polyphonic setting of the intonation of the chant. This part would have been sung by a soloist, before the choir sang the rest of this half of the responsory monophonically, followed by a polyphonic rendition of the verse *Virgo Dei genitrix*.

In this edition the opening two notes of the duplum (upper voice), C and D, begin the responsory before the tenor comes in on D. In this excerpt (taken from Manuscript F, one of three major sources of Notre Dame polyphony), the duplum has been transcribed in free rhythm. The kinds of motion manifested in it are common in the upper lines of Parisian organum, and represent the stock in trade of Parisian singers in this period. *Styrps Yesse* illustrates the basic techniques that solo singers at the Cathedral of Notre Dame and elsewhere used to improvise melodies in the new polyphonic style.

Each phrase of the responsory cadences on the unison, fifth, or octave. Between these harmonic goalposts, the duplum is carefully crafted, often in short, crisp phrases that are directional, working to set up the pitch requisite to create the next major cadence, in accordance with the tenor. Phrase 1 (the phrases have been numbered for ease of identification) is an ornamented motion from high D to the fourth below (A), followed by a decorated, leaping ascent back up to D to cadence at the octave. In phrase 2, the duplum must move above the droning C of the tenor, while preparing for it to move back to D. In phrase 2, three short melodic sequences ("sequence" in the sense of a short pattern repeated at different pitch levels) in the duplum join to create a longer melodic descent from C down to D. The first of these moves from C down to an ornamented G; the next from C down to F; and the third moves from A down to D. In each case the contour of the short melodic sequence is the same. In the third and fourth phrases, short melodies above the tenor E and then F create a pair of lines that complement each other. The undulating character of phrases 1–4 changes in phrase 5, which includes two smooth scalar descents, one from E down to E and another from A down to C. Although the duplum is generally higher than the tenor, there is some voice crossing in phrase 6, as the duplum spirals downward repeatedly to the C below the tenor F, and then finally ascends a third to cadence on a unison E.

Although the music for the entire opening section of the piece is transcribed in free rhythm, in places where the transcriber thinks measured rhythms may be indicated by the ligatures of the notation, she has offered alternative modal readings above the staff. The rhythmic modes, patterns that were indicated by the ligatures of square notation, are further discussed in Primer II.3 and Anthology 27.

On the word "Yesse" in the tenor, the texture of the music changes to discant and the two voices move at more nearly the same speed. In this section, the music is nearly in mode 1, but the piece is early and reflects a style that we can think of as pre-modal. The upper voice is another example of how the rhythmic modes work in phrases called ordines, mostly following the rule that an ordo in a particular mode should begin and end with a note (or group of notes) of the same rhythmic value (or values). Here the first ordo (beginning on "Yes-" of "Yesse") is composed of a ternary long, followed by a long of two beats (which was normal in the early stages of modal notation) and a breve to make a three-beat foot, followed by another ternary long. The next ordo consists of a long plus a breve (first foot), three breves (second foot), and a ternary long (last foot). Continuing, every group of notes in the upper voice between the rests is equivalent to three ternary longs. The tenor moves in ordines made up of the value of three ternary longs as well, and the voices always move together, with cadences on octaves. In fact, we can say the tenor is written in rhythmic mode 5 (and tenors often are expressed in this mode in later repertory as well). The little rhythmic figure at the beginning of "-se" (of "Yesse") is a foot in iambic rather than trochaic rhythm, and, to highlight the last syllable, momentarily fractures the rhythmic patterns otherwise found in the duplum.

The ways musicians improvised and notated music in the twelfth and thirteenth centuries in Paris were many and mingled. Although it is possible to date some layers of compositions, those who try to draw timelines too neatly, or insist upon the "progressive" triumph of written versions of music over all other manifestations of the art, will ultimately be thwarted. Even as music was notated in increasingly complex ways, a robust oral tradition persisted. Musicians of all kinds continued to improvise and to be taught to sing and play on the basis of unwritten practices.

We must assume that precious little of the music made in this period was written down, while being infinitely grateful for what was. The works of the Notre Dame School are superb music for listening and singing. Determining exactly how to perform some of them will always prove difficult, especially in the earlier layers of written polyphonic repertories, when many composers and theorists were experimenting with the rhythmic aspects of music and their notation.

Flos Filius eius

Organum duplum and clausulae
Notated in the mid-13th century

The word *clausula* had many meanings in the Middle Ages. Most commonly in music it means a section of either a plainchant or a polyphonic work. (In this sense it is synonymous in some medieval theory with the word *punctum*, borrowed from classical oratory and meaning short section.) But in the *Magnus liber organi*, clausula has an even more specific meaning: a small section that is written in discant. Discant clausulae could sometimes be substituted not only for a large section of organum (as can be seen here), but also for one another, and the practice of writing them took off in a major way in the opening decades of the thirteenth century. There are hundreds of such discant clausulae in Manuscript F, which seems to have been copied around 1248 (see *Music in the Medieval West*, Chapter 9). A substitute clausula has the same tenor as the section it was meant to replace.

29.1 A SECTION OF TWO-VOICE ORGANUM AT THE END OF THE VERSE FOR THE RESPONSORY *STIRPS JESSE*

29.1: Florence, Biblioteca Medicea-laurenziana, Pluteus 29.1, f. 75v; L. Dittmer, ed., *Faksimile Ausgabe Firenze, Biblioteca medicea-laurenziana, Pluteo 29, I* (Brooklyn, NY: Institute of Medieval Music, 1966–1967); transcription by Rebecca A. Baltzer.

29.2 TWO-VOICE SUBSTITUTE CLAUSULA

29. 2: Florence, Biblioteca Medicea-laurenziana, Pluteus 29.1, f. 166r; L. Dittmer, ed., *Faksimile Ausgabe Firenze, Biblioteca medicea-laurenziana, Pluteo 29, I* (Brooklyn, NY: Institute of Medieval Music, 1966–1967); transcription by Rebecca A. Baltzer.

Flos filius eius   The flower, her Son

In general, substitute clausulae are more compact than the sections of discant they replace. The first of our two clausulae on *Flos Filius eius* (Anthology 29.2) fits without a hitch as a substitute for a section of organum (Anthology 29.1) found at the end of the verse of the two-voice *Stirps Jesse*. Yet what a difference there is between the two settings! The compactness of the substitute clausula is immediately evident. The relationship between the two voices in the clausula is not like anything we have seen before. Although both voices in the substitute clausula are modal and fit into a large gridwork of beats, they are also rhythmically independent. The tenor is truly lower in range and unfolds in a series of ordines made of a long followed by a breve rest, two long-breve feet, and another long followed by a breve rest. The chant melody is presented twice, in accordance with the melodic development in the dominant upper voice, or duplum. Still, if one sings through the chant melody in the tenor following the rhythms of the first mode and observing places where there is a cadence with the upper voice, it will be seen that the integrity of the chant melody is respected.

The upper voice of Anthology 29.2 is a little tour de force, providing as it does two very different settings for the repeat of the pitches of the chant melisma. Possibilities are limited in that the duplum must make cadences on perfect intervals with the tenor at the end of every melodic phrase, but the powerful rhythmic dimension of the music makes these restrictions less painful. Various melodic turns are expanded upon and varied; for example, the little phrase from A down to D and back up to A occurs several times in various guises, at the opening of the piece, just before the point where the tenor begins to repeat, and elsewhere. This melodic phrase is characterized by the occasional use of quicker note values, semibreves, here transcribed as sixteenth notes. In the future the semibreve would slowly break down the modes and lead to the expression of a more rhythmically flexible line.

29.3 THREE-VOICE CLAUSULA

29.3 Florence, Biblioteca Medicea-laurenziana, Pluteus 29.1, ff. 11a-11b; L. Dittmer, ed., *Faksimile Ausgabe Firenze, Biblioteca medicea-laurenziana, Pluteo 29, I* (Brooklyn, NY: Institute of Medieval Music, 1966–1967); transcription by Alejandro Enrique Planchart, "The Flower's Children," *Journal of Musicological Research* 22 (2003): 316. Reprinted by permission of the publisher (Taylor & Francis Ltd.; www.tandf.co.uk/journals). A plicated note is indicated by an x.

Flos filius eius   The flower, her Son

Unlike the clausula in score 29.2, this three-voice clausula on *Flos Filius eius* is a freestanding work that was not meant for substitution in a section of organum. Recall that modal notation depended on various shapes of ligatures standing in for the patterns of the rhythmic modes; this worked well when the music was melismatic. But when texts were added, the ligatures were broken to accommodate the syllables of the words. Some clausulae may have been written as guides to singing pieces in modal rhythm when ligatures were no longer present and modal patterns could not be easily understood. There is no simple, straightforward narrative to account for the birth of the motet as a kind of prosula fitted to two- and three-voice clausulae; it was doubtless slow in coming (see Anthology 30).

In our score, the ligatures are shown by brackets; the "measure" numbers above the systems indicate the ternary foot, and the Roman numerals in the tenor show where the pitches repeat. Although the two upper voices (triplum and duplum) are rooted both rhythmically and harmonically in the motion of the tenor, they are independent and there is musical interplay between them; for example, the downward figure of the duplum at 21 is picked up by the triplum at 23, introducing imitation.

The chant melisma (the material for the lower voice) is somewhat different in character from that of the substitute clausula in score 29.2. Here too there is a set of regularly patterned ordines, but the effect in singing through them is not quite the same. It is as if the notes of the chant melody have been poured into this set of ordines, without regard for the integrity of the melodic phrases of the original. The plainsong has become melodic fodder for the rhythmic and harmonic needs of the upper voices, although its rich symbolic meanings remain in play, like old wine in new skins.

30

ANONYMOUS

Plus bele que flor/Quant revient/L'autrier joer/Flos Filius; Castrum pudicicie/Virgo viget/Flos Filius

Polyphonic motets (on *Flos Filius eius* clausula)
Second half of the 13th century

The polyphonic motet (from the French word *mot*, meaning word) was born when words were set to the duplum of a discant clausula; many of the earliest motets, then, are prosulae, and all the earliest ones are two-voice works—a tenor with a texted duplum. Very popular tenors, with their clausulae, often could generate a complex of interrelated motets, as with *Stirps Jesse*. David Rothenberg lists one family of these *Flos Filius eius* motets containing ten pieces in a variety of voicings and with several different texts. The French triple (four-voice) motet *Plus bele que flor/Quant revient/L'autrier joer/Flos Filius* (Anthology 30.1) is just one of many settings. There are two-voice (tenor plus motetus, also called duplum), three-voice (lacking the quadruplum), and four-voice works. The three-voice Latin version *Castrum pudicicie/Virgo viget/ Flos Filius* (Anthology 30.2) exists in only two manuscripts, and seems to be a later rather than an early setting of this popular complex of materials.

30.1 *PLUS BELE QUE FLOR/QUANT REVIENT/L'AUTRIER JOER/FLOS FILIUS*

Montpellier, Bibliothèque Inter-Universitaire, Section Médecine, H 196, f. 26v [Mo]; Y. Rokseth, ed., *Polyphonies du XIIIe siècle: Le manuscrit H196 de la Faculté de médecine de Montpellier* (Paris: Éditions de l'Oiseau-Lyre, 1936), 2: 46–47; text translation by Elizabeth Close, from Gordon Anderson, ed., *Motets of the Manuscript La Clayette: Paris, Bibliothèque nationale, nouv. acq. fr. 13521* (Rome: American Institute of Musicology, 1975); David Rothenberg, *The Flower of Paradise: Marian Devotion and Secular Song in Medieval and Renaissance Music* (Oxford: Oxford University Press, 2011), 42.

QUADRUPLUM

Plus bele que flor	More lovely than a flower,
Est, ce m'est avis,	I believe, is
Cele a qui m'ator.	she to whom I give myself.
Tant com soie vis,	As long as I live,
N'avra de m'amor	no one but this
Joie ne delis	flower of Paradise
Autre mès la flor	will rejoice and
Qu'est de paradis:	delight in my love:
Mere est au Signour	she is the mother of the Lord
Qu'est si noz amis	who put us here
Et nos a retor	and who in return
Veut avoir tot dis.	wants to keep us always.

TRIPLUM

Quant revient et fuelle et flor	When leaf and flower come back
Contre la seison d'esté,	with the approach of the summer,
Deus! adonc me sovient d'amors	Lord! then I remember Love,
Qui toz jors	who has always been
M'a cortois et doz esté.	courtly and gentle with me.
Moult aim ses secors,	I am so grateful for his help,
Car sa volenté	because he lightens my pain
M'alege de mes dolors;	when I desire it.
Moult me vient bien et henors	One gains much good and much honor
D'estre a son gré.	from being his friend.

DUPLUM

L'autrier joer m'en alai	The other day I was wandering
Par un destor;	in a lonely place,

En un vergier m'en entrai	and into an orchard I went
Pour queillir flor.	to pick a flower.
Dame plesant i trovai,	There I found a pleasing lady,
Cointe d'atour,	prettily dressed;
Cuer et gai,	her body was frail and
Si chantoit en grant esmai:	she was singing in great distress:
"Amors ai,	"I am in love,
Qu'en ferai?	what shall I do?
C'est la fin, la fin,	It is the end, the end,
Que que nus die, j'amerai."	whatever anyone says, I will love."

TENOR

Flos [Filius eius]	The flower [her Son]

The French triple motet *Plus bele que flor/Quant revient/L'autrier joer/Flos Filius* is found in this version in the Montpellier Codex, a collection of motets in various styles that was copied in Paris in the late 1200s and early 1300s. It comes from the second fascicle, a gathering that belongs to the earliest layer of this manuscript. The notation is nearly mensural, and it can be seen that the piece is completely dependent upon the three-voice clausula studied in Anthology 29.3. But what a difference it makes to have words set to the music! Words help to differentiate the voices, which in turn allows for dramatic presentation of conflict and character.

The themes are expressed in terms of secular love, with the voices presenting the subject in different registers. The top voice (quadruplum) is elegant and courtly: the speaker will love his lady forever, comparing her to the Virgin Mary. In the triplum, the speaker addresses Love at the approach of summer and offers a text from an adage: "One gains much good and much honor from being his friend." The duplum offers another level of understanding, one based on the pastorela (see Anthology 16): a man goes out to pick a flower (a reference to having sex) and discovers a frail young woman in great distress over love. She is not a paragon of virtue (as in the quadruplum), nor has Lord Love served her well (as in the triplum). We are left to think that the speaker may try to help her, or persuade her to help him! The many layers of meaning created through the juxtaposition of these voices demonstrate the joys of interplay between the sacred and the secular, between Mary and Marian, between the distance of unrequited love and the nearness of sexual encounter.

The use of language in the motet shows that the poet-compilers were well aware of the "flower," mentioned in the original text of the melisma that makes up the tenor. Plays on the word "flor" abound, as do rhymes with this word, saturating the texture with flowers. The quadruplum "plus bele que flor" makes a cross-rhyme with the duplum "Par un destor," and this strategy continues for much of the piece. The triplum "Quant revient et fuelle et flor" adds another singing of the word "flor," falling between that proclaimed by the quadruplum and duplum. The word *flower* itself had many meanings, from the pure Virgin in heaven to female genitalia.

The skills of the vernacular poets (who of course knew Latin and Latin verse) and their interests in rhythm and rhyme first entered the world of polyphonic composition via the motet, the great experimental proving ground for the polyphonic chanson. By the end of the thirteenth century, the trouvère Adam de la Halle had produced the first substantial repertory of polyphonic songs (see Chapter 8 of *Music in the Medieval West*). The editor of our score, Yvonne Rokseth, uses small noteheads to indicate variants found in other sources.

30.2 *CASTRUM PUDICICIE/VIRGO VIGET/FLOS FILIUS*

Burgos, Santa María la Real de Las Huelgas MS IX, f. 116r [Hu]; H. Anglès, ed., *El còdex musical de Las Huelgas* (Barcelona, 1931); from Gordon A. Anderson, ed., *The Las Huelgas Manuscript II*. From the original series (CMM), volume (79–2), and page (35) of the original publication. Reproduced by permission of the American Institute of Musicology, Inc., Middleton, Wisc.

10

bis pro-pi - ci-um,   ut__ re-is__ det ve - ni - e   re-me - di - um.

iu-bi - lo   si - ne ter - mi-no / be-ne - di-ca-mus Do - mi - no.

TRIPLUM

Castrum pudicicie,	Fortress of chastity,
numinis triclinium,	dining chamber of God,
spes tocius leticie,	hope of all joy,
gracie tenens privilegium,	holding the privilege of grace,
regem glorie, virgo,	O Virgin, make the King of glory,
filium fac nobis propicium,	your son, well disposed to us,
ut reis det venie remedium.	that He might give sinners the remedy of His pardon.

DUPLUM

Virgo viget melius dum peperit,	The Virgin is strongest when she bears,
sed nature plenius ius deperit	and the law of nature is destroyed completely
nasci Dei filius dum voluit;	when the Son of God desired to be born.
coluit, qui nobis condoluit	He cared for us, he who suffered with us;
cui cum iubilo sine termino	with endless joy
benedicamus Domino.	let us bless the Lord.

TENOR

Flos Filius [eius]	The flower, [her] son

The Latin double motet *Castrum pudicicie/Virgo viget/Flos Filius* exists also as a two-voice Latin motet with the duplum *Virgo viget*; our score is taken from the Las Huelgas Codex (c. 1300). As discussed in Chapter 12 of *Music in the Medieval West*, this extraordinary collection of polyphonic works was prepared for a convent, but one for noblewomen. It also accepted girls from the nobility as a kind of training ground, including the teaching of music. Some of the pieces in the repertory, including this one, were scrubbed clean of their secularity and turned into religious works. Although the text *Virgo viget* for the duplum is not completely regular in its structure, there is an attempt on the part of the poet to create rhyme and rhythmic regularity:

7pp + 4pp	**a**		Virgo viget melius / dum peperit
7pp + 4pp	**a**		sed nature plenius / ius deperit
7pp + 4pp + 3pp	**a**		nasci Dei filius / dum voluit / coluit
7pp + 5pp	**b**		qui nobis condoluit / cui cum iubilo
5pp + 8pp	**b**		sine termino / benedicamus Domino

The poet is setting a text to preexisting music, and his work is mirrored in the notes. Musical lines are divided into two sections each as well: a short statement, followed by a counterstatement. This happens until the third line, when the short phrase on "coluit" breaks the pattern, but forms a kind of hinge to what will follow. The first part of the fourth line rhymes with coluit, but the second part of the line leads to a new series of rhymes on "o," referencing the *Benedicamus Domino* and making the motet a possible substitute for this piece. The melody of the duplum (found in the three-voice clausula as well as in the French motets) is highly memorable; once you know it, it will be in your head all day, especially when matched with these rhyming Latin phrases. The rhythmic modes can seem like shackles to our modern sensibilities, but in this work they generate a musical aesthetic that is delightful to modern ears.

The triplum, like the duplum, is constructed from short, rhythmic, rhyming phrases, but with even less regularity. The rhymes of the lines are important, however, alternating as they do throughout the piece. With their staggered entrances, the notes and texts of the two upper voices create a sense of linguistic contrast. When one voice is offering its end rhyme, the other voice is in the middle or opening of a statement. The two voices never catch each other until the last phrase, and even there they are at odds. The staggered sense creates a powerful forward motion. Most of the cadences (if so they can be called) are perfect intervals, and all of them occur through the interaction of two lines, rarely all three. The aesthetic of imitation that we saw in our study of clausulae (see Anthology 29) has become more intense, both in the music and in the text.

31

PETRUS DE CRUCE (FL. C. 1290)

S'amours eüst point de poer/Au renouveler/Ecce

French double motet

Late 13th century

Montpellier, Bibliothèque Inter-Universitaire, Section Médecine H 196, ff. 270r–273r [Mo]; from *Polyphonies du XIIIe siècle: Le manuscrit H 196 de la Faculté de médecine de Montpellier*, ed. Yvonne Rokseth (Paris: Éditions de l'Oiseau-lyre/Louis B. M. Dyer, 1936), pp. 77–81; text translation by Isabelle Fabre. Reprinted with permission.

TRIPLUM

S'amours eüst point de poer,	If Love had any power,
Je m'en deüsse bien apercevoir,	I would have noticed, for I have served him
Qui l'ai servie tout mon vivant	my life long with a faithful heart.
De cuer loiaument;	
Mès je croi	But I believe that he will be of no help to
K'aidier ne poet a nului ne valoir.	anyone.
Pour moi	As for me,
Je puis le bien prouver et savoir	I can prove it and I know
Vraiement:	it is true:
En son service m'a fait lonc tans doloir	When I served him, he tormented me so
Et vivre en si grief tourment	much and caused me such a great pain
Que je ne sai mie comment	that I cannot imagine how
Nus amant	a lover
Puist vivre en gregneur; et si l'ai soufert	could bear a greater one. But I endured it

Boinement,
Car par bien soufrir
Cuidai joïr.

Pour ce ai enduré si longuement

Mès or voi bien que ne mi vaut noiant;
Qu'en puis je donc se d'amer me repent?
Quant amours de mon service tel guerredon
me rent?
Que plus ai amé
Et desirré,
Plus l'ai comparé
Chierement.
Si m'acort bien a ce k'en dit sovant,
Que li hons qui mauvais seigneur sert
Mauvais loier atent.
Ne set qu'i[l] fait qui a amer enprent,
Car nus ne porroit penser,
S'i[l] veut amer sanz guiler,
L'ennui qui li apent.
Ne je ne dout mie
Que ja ait amie
Cil qui en bien amer entent:
Que plus est vrais amis,
Tant li fera on pis;
Ja pour prier merci
N'avra alegement.
Assez puet [on] dolouser,
Plaindre et plourer et souspirer:
Il n'iert ja autrement
Car de s'amour donner
A l'houme qui l'aint n'a fame nul talent;
Mès a celui qui point ne la desert,
L'otroie a la fois tout entierement.

all the same,
patiently,
for I assumed that as a reward
    I would get some pleasure.
So although this is why I endured it for so
    long,
now I can see that it is of no use.
Am I to blame if I wish I had not loved,
since Love rewards me so badly for my
service?
The more I loved
and longed,
the higher the price
I had to pay.
So I agree with what people often say:
He who serves a bad master
will only get from him a bad reward.
He does not know what he is doing, he who
sets about loving, for no one would dare
imagine the trouble he will meet
even if he wanted to be fair.
So though I have no doubt
that he who strives to love wholeheartedly
in the end will find a beloved,
the more faithful he is,
the more harassed he will be.
In vain he cries for mercy;
never shall he get relief.
For all his complaining,
his moaning, crying, and yearning,
it won't be otherwise;
for a woman does not feel like giving her
love away to the man who loves her,
but she will give it all at once to the one
who does not deserve her.

DUPLUM

Au renouveler du joli tans
M'estuet commencier chançon;
Car bone amour, de cui servir je sui
    desirrans,
M'en a douné ochoison.
Par uns jeus dous et rians
M'a seurpris, si que ne puis penser

When the merry time returns,
then I have to sing a song,
for Good Love, whom I long to serve,

bade me to do so.
Playing around gently,
he caught me, so that I cannot but think

s'a cele non	about the one and only
A cui j'ai fait de moi don;	to whom I gave myself up:
Tant est avenans,	she is so delightful,
Seur toutes autres bele et plaisans,	most beautiful and charming
Et de si bon renon,	and so well spoken of!
Car sanz traïson	With a faithful heart
L'aim et amerai tant com je iere vivant,	I love and shall love her as long as I live,
En atendant	while expecting
Le douz guerredon	the sweet reward
K'amours rent a finz amans	that Love offers true lovers
Qui a son voloir sunt obeïssans	who obey his commands
Sans mesprison.	unfailingly.

TENOR

Ecce	Behold

The double motet *S'amours eüst point de poer/Au renouveler/Ecce* is the first work in fascicle 7 of the Montpellier Codex, the section copied in the late thirteenth century. A song about the joy and suffering of love, it elaborates on themes expressed in the triple motet *Plus bele que flor* (see Anthology 30.1), found in an earlier fascicle of the same manuscript. The early-fourteenth-century theorist Jacques of Liège attributed the piece to Petrus de Cruce, who was closely associated with Franco of Cologne's innovations in notation and rhythm, especially with smaller divisions of the breve.

S'amours eüst point de poer looks forward to the rhythmic flexibility of the fourteenth-century style of polyphony known as the Ars Nova, or "new art." Smaller note values typify the Petronian motet, with the breve becoming the basic unit of time. The breve (worth a quarter note in Yvonne Rokseth's transcription) can be divided into a variety of semibreves of equal value, most commonly two, three, or four. The dot or "point of division" sometimes supplied in the original notation indicates how to group the semibreves, as does their physical closeness on the page. The opening of the motet sounds different from any music we have studied before: because the triplum moves so rapidly, the modal character of the slower-moving duplum is hard to hear.

The diamond-shaped semibreves take on different values, depending on how many of them are assigned to the value of a breve. In Rokseth's transcription, the first two groupings are worth one breve, but so are the next two groupings, regardless of how many semibreves per grouping. Each semibreve is set to a syllable of text, making it possible to declaim a great amount of text in the upper voice. The lack of formal repetition in the triplum is mirrored by the text, which contains a variety of line lengths and no formal rhyme scheme (although some words recur frequently). A motet with such flexibility in the declamation of text is an important step on the road to the development of the polyphonic chansons of the mid- and late fourteenth century (see especially Anthology 35). This apparent lack of attention to the perfection of the modes displeased theorists such as Jacques, who were used to the Trinitarian ideal of multiples of three established in the thirteenth century (see Chapter 9 of *Music in the Medieval West*).

The three texts of the motet reflect different modes of understanding love. The miniature *dit*, or first-person narrative (Machaut's *Remède de Fortune* is an example; see Anthology 33), in the triplum is a lament: if Love has power, this faithful servant would have been rewarded instead of being consigned to a life of suffering. The duplum is sung by one who does not yet know the inevitable sorrow that will befall him: Love has caught him and he joyfully awaits his reward. In case we have missed the point, the tenor is there to remind us: its pitches are taken from a responsory for St. Stephen, a faithful servant who died for love—in his case, love of Christ.

We have grown accustomed to rhythmically patterned tenors generating foundations for other voices in polyphonic textures. In the third quarter of the thirteenth century, theorists began to express modal rhythms in terms of perfection, and a three-beat long became the norm. The rules for transcribing music in mensural notation found in Primer II.4 are based on this concept. In this piece we witness something even more rhythmically intricate than anything seen before: although the tenor melody repeats, the rhythmic values change from the initial pattern of long-long-long-rest to long-breve-long-breve-long-rest in measures 53–55, providing an early example of diminution. Accordingly, the first statement of the tenor occupies 52 measures, each worth a perfect long of three beats, while the second statement takes up 24 measures; the relationship is 13 to 6, a complexity showing the delight that late-thirteenth- and fourteenth-century composers often took in numbers and proportion. The voices shift to accommodate the newly shortened tenor. When the tenor repeats in its new guise, reaffirming the theme of martyrdom, the triplum voice sings that the truer a lover is, the worse is his fate, while the duplum naively proclaims: "I love and shall love her as long as I live."

The illumination in the Montpellier Codex (see Fig. 10.1 in *Music in the Medieval West*) shows two faithful lovers on the left side of the page, reaching out to each other, while on the right another lover laments alone. One can think of a motet like this as an elaborate weaving of disparate threads, similar to those in the luxurious silk and woolen garments favored by the upper classes in the late thirteenth and fourteenth centuries. The different texts may have been read aloud before the performance so the warp and woof of the upper voices could be better understood.

32

PHILIPPE DE VITRY (1291–1361)

Tribum/Quoniam/Merito

Isorhythmic motet from the *Roman de Fauvel*
1317–1318

Paris, BN fr. 146, ff. 41v–42r; E. Roesner, F. Avril, and N. F. Regalado, eds., *Roman de Fauvel in the Edition of Mesire Chaillou de Pesstain: A Reproduction in Facsimile of the Complete Manuscript, Paris, Bibliothèque Nationale, Fonds Français 146* (New York, 1990); transcription from *The Roman de Fauvel; The Works of Philippe de Vitry; French Cycles of the Ordinarium Missae*, ed. Leo Schrade, Polyphonic Music of the Fourteenth Century, vol. 1 (Monaco: Éditions de l'Oiseau-Lyre, 1956), pp. 54–56. Reprinted with permission.

un - de ni - chil me - li - us quam nil ha - bu - is - se se - cun - dum.

to ca - - - - su que va - lu - e - re ru - unt.

TRIPLUM

Tribum que non abhorruit
indecenter ascendere
furibunda non metuit
Fortuna cito vertere
dum duci prefate tribus
in sempiternum speculum
parare palam omnibus
non pepercit patibulum.
Populus ergo venturus
si trans metam ascenderit,
quidam forsitan casurus,
cum tanta tribus ruerit,
sciat eciam quis fructus
delabi sit in profundum
post zephyros plus ledit hyems, post gaudia luctus;
unde nichil melius quam nil habuisse secundum.

Raging Fortune has not feared to
swiftly invert the tribe that did not
abhor to ascend indecently; while
for the leader of this tribe she
has spared nothing in making ready a
gallows openly before all as an
eternal mirror. Therefore, if a coming
people climb up across the boundary,
let someone who might fall
know, since such a tribe as
this has fallen, what the result might be to
sink into the depths. Winter hurts
more than the west wind, grief
hurts more than joy; wherefore, it is
better to have nothing than to be
reduced to nothing again.

DUPLUM

Quoniam secta latronum
spelunca vispilionum
vulpes que Gallos roderat
tempore quo regnaverat
leo cecatus subito
suo ruere merito
in mortem privatam bonis:
concinat Gallus Nasonis
dicta que dolum acuunt:
omnia sunt hominum tenui pendencia filo
et subito casu que valuere ruunt.

Since a band of thieves, that cave of nighttime
robbers, that fox which chewed
on the cocks [French], in the time
when the blind lion ruled,
suddenly by its own merit has fallen
into a death deprived of good things,
let the cock [Frenchman] sing the words of
Ovid that sharpen the treachery:
"All human affairs hang on a
slender cord; and with a sudden fall
what once flourished comes to ruin."

TENOR

Merito hec patimur.

We suffer these things justly.

Tribum/Quoniam/Merito has been securely attributed to Philippe de Vitry, a composer closely associated with the rhythmic and notational innovations of the Ars Nova in early-fourteenth-century France. This Latin double motet is included in the richly illuminated manuscript Paris, BN fr. 146, which contains poetry and music for the *Roman de Fauvel*, a bitingly satirical allegory written by a circle of chancery clerks and their friends at the Parisian court in the waning years of the Capetian dynasty. *Fauvel* pillories the royal establishment, the Catholic Church, and contemporary society in general. The text of the motet plays upon the Latin word *gallus*, which means both "cock" and "Gaul," or "Frenchman." The many expressions of falling in the piece (both text and music) refer to the demise of Enguerrand de Marigny, the detested head of the royal household, who, along with others of his ilk, is allegorized by the evil horse Fauvel. Enguerrand's public hanging on Ascension Day in 1315 is celebrated in the work as a whole, and in this motet in particular.

Philippe de Vitry's motet, like the *Roman de Fauvel* itself, is not only about a single allegorized figure; it is a deep critique of government, in France and in the Church, and of the vile men—the followers of Fauvel—who besiege it from within. Yet even as *Tribum* decries "the tribe that did not abhor to ascend indecently," it offers hope, for buried in its text and music are themes of sudden fall and comeuppance for real-life evildoers. There is reason to believe that the Ovidian couplet at the end of the duplum voice, with its image of "the slender cord" from which "all human affairs hang" (a powerful reference to Enguerrand's end), was the seed from which Philippe's composition grew.

Tribum is an isorhythmic motet; that is, it features groups of rhythmic patterns that are "equal" or, by extension, the "same" (*iso* in Greek). Such a technique was hardly new in polyphonic repertories, but the increased rhythmic freedom of voices in the Ars Nova motet made it particularly important to create a framework for the music, whether the tenors were invented first, as was the normal practice, or not. The complexity of the rhythmic scaffolding in Philippe de Vitry's motet surpasses anything we have seen in the thirteenth century. The work is divided into 78 imperfect longs, and these are arranged (on the level of maximodus) into perfect groups of three. The piece does not start with the tenor, however. First the triplum enters for a length of three longs, and then it is joined by the duplum for three more longs, so a duration of six longs unfolds before the entrance of the tenor. Each of the two statements of the melody in the tenor, known as the *color*, occupies 36 longs (12 × 3). So the total plan of the piece is as follows:

3 + 3 + (color I) 12 × 3 + (color II) 12 × 3

The isorhythmic motet became a vehicle for many kinds of symbolism, including number symbolism. In *Tribum*, the color in the tenor is presented two times, with the second section beginning at measure 43. If the six-long introduction (before the tenor entrance) is subtracted, the piece consists of 72 imperfect longs. These represent the 72 disciples of Christ, or the good men who will triumph in the end over the greedy Fauvel (a horse who has usurped the throne of France). Also discounting the introduction, there are 144 breves, symbolizing the 144,000 saintly elect in the New Testament Book of Revelation 14:1.

The tenor voice does not fall in its usual range, but usurps the territory of the upper voices. In doing so it often rises above the duplum, especially when the text is about "falling." After the second color begins at measures 43–45, the duplum sings "concinat Gallus," which out of context can mean "let the Frenchman sing," but here refers to the crowing of a cock. The triplum then proclaims, "let someone who might fall know" (mm. 46–49). So just as one voice celebrates, the other mentions the cause for celebration: the fall (of Enguerrand). The upper lines not only express their own substance, but make other statements when dovetailing with each other.

The end of the piece is an expanded example of another kind of interaction: simultaneous proclamation, advancing the same theme found in measures 46–49. When "hanging" (*pendencia*) and "joy" (*gaudia*) come together in measures 66–67, the tenor for the second time reaches its highest note, G an octave above the G in the duplum. Shortly afterwards, the word "fall" (*casu*) in the duplum is sung simultaneously with "better [to have] nothing" (*nichil melius*) in the triplum (mm. 71–73). With such wordplay between the voices, the singers of Philippe's motet were able to carry on a musical conversation, rejoicing over the demise of the fox that once gnawed the bones of the French people.

33

GUILLAUME DE MACHAUT (C. 1300–1377)

Dame, de qui toute ma joie vient; Dame, a vous sans retollir (from Remède de Fortune)

Chansons: ballade and monophonic virelai
Mid-14th century

Guillaume de Machaut was the foremost poet and composer of the fourteenth century. He is studied more than any other figure from that era not only because of his genius, but also because his works are completely preserved, many of them in copies supervised by the composer. We also have the advantage of being able to study his way of inserting musical compositions into a poem of his own design. The *Remède de Fortune* (Remedy of Fortune) is a *dit*, a first-person narrative of a didactic nature; it tells the story of a lovesick courtier who overcomes his misfortunes with the help of Lady Hope.

The *Remède* is the only one of Machaut's literary works into which he inserted fully notated compositions throughout. One could write an entire book on the combination of music and poetry in the *Remède*. The charming scenes of courtly life it portrays may reflect Machaut's own experiences, especially in the service of John of Luxembourg, king of Bohemia, and his daughter Bonne, the wife of the man who would be crowned John II of France. The work is dedicated to Bonne, who died in the plague in 1348, months before her husband became king.

33.1 *DAME, DE QUI TOUTE MA JOIE VIENT*: BALLADE

Paris, BN fr. 1584; Paris, BN fr. 1586, f. 47v; from Margaret Switten, ed., *The Medieval Lyric, Anthology II: Guillaume de Machaut, Remède de Fortune* (NEH and Mount Holyoke College, 1988), pp. 78–79. Reprinted with permission. Some of the Switten editions of this work do not include the two-voiced version.

1

Dame, de qui toute ma joie vient,
Je ne vous puis trop amer, ne chierir,
N'assés loër, si com il apartient,
Servir, doubter, honnourer, n'obeïr;
Car le gracieus espoir,
Douce dame, que j'ay de vous vëoir,
Me fait cent fois plus de bien et de joie,
Qu'en cent mille ans desservir ne porroie.

Lady, from whom all my joy comes,
I cannot love you or cherish you too much,
Nor praise you enough, as is fitting,
serve, fear, honor, and obey you;
for the pleasing hope,
sweet lady, that I have of seeing you,
brings me a hundred times more good and joy
than I could deserve in a hundred thousand years.

2

Cils dous espoirs en vie me soustient
Et me norrist en amoureus desir,
Et dedens moy met tout ce qui couvient
Pour conforter mon cuer et resjoïr;
N'il ne s'en part main ne soir,
Einsois me fait doucement recevoir
Plus des dous biens qu'Amours aus siens ottroie,
Qu'en cent mille ans desservir ne porroie.

This sweet hope keeps me alive
and nourishes me with amorous desire,
and places within me everything that is needed
to comfort and bring joy to my heart;
nor does it abandon me morning or evening,
but rather induces me to receive sweetly
more of the sweet goods that Love sends her own
than I could deserve in a hundred thousand years.

3

Et quant Espoir qui en mon cuer se tient
Fait dedens moy si grant joie venir,
Lonteins de vous, ma dame, s'il avient
Que vo biauté voie que moult desir,
Ma joie, si com j'espoir,
Ymaginer, penser, ne concevoir
Ne porroit nuls, car trop plus en aroie,
Qu'en cent mille ans desservir ne porroie.

And since Hope, who is fixed in my heart,
causes such joy within me
when I'm far from you, my lady, if I were
to see your beauty that I desire so much,
my joy, I believe,
could not be imagined, comprehended, or conceived
by anyone, for I would have more
than I could deserve in a hundred thousand years.

Dame, de qui toute ma joie vient is a ballade, one of the three *formes fixes* (fixed forms) characteristic of songs composed in the fourteenth century and later (see Chapter 10 of *Music in the Medieval West*). In Paris, BN fr. 1586 (also known as Manuscript C), which dates from around 1356, the piece has two voices; in some later sources it has four. The two-voice version provides an especially clear understanding of the ballade form, which, like the virelai and rondeau, had its origin in dance and is defined by the use of the refrain. The ballade had become relatively "fixed" by the mid-1300s, thanks largely to Machaut, whose favorite song form it was.

The basic form of the ballade is **aab**; because the piece has three stanzas of poetry, this musical scheme repeats three times. As is often the case with the ballade, there are two different cadences for the **a** section. The first is open, or unstable, demanding resolution; the second ending provided for the musical repeat of the **a** section provides it with a strong, closed cadence on the expected final of the piece. Each eight-line strophe has the rhyme scheme **ababccdD**, with the last line forming a common refrain. Machaut, who wrote both the poetry and the music of *Dame, de qui toute ma joie*, has rounded the musical form by making the last measures of the repeat of the **a** section "rhyme" with the music of **b** at the refrain, and on the final word, "porroie." The music is written so that the semibreve (here worth a quarter note) carries the beat of the measure, three to a breve (worth a dotted half), and the minim (worth an eighth note) now has its own place in the rhythmic scheme.

Just as tempus governs the relationship between the breve and the semibreve, prolation governs the relationship between the semibreve and the minim. Accordingly, *Dame, de qui toute ma joie* is in tempus perfectum (three semibreves to a breve) and prolatio minor (two minims to each semibreve). The emphasis on these smaller note values, and the fact that there are two minims to each semibreve, illustrate the rhythmic flexibility characteristic of the Ars Nova. The featured recording by the Medieval Lyric Project provides a fine opportunity to hear two voices in elegant counterpoint, the lower voice beautiful in its own right as it works in counter-rhythm to the busy upper voice, or cantus.

One can analyze this ballade by tracing the held notes, usually at the ends of lines, and studying their relationships one to the other. Ask yourself if there are progressions that have to do with the harmonies. B♭ is clearly heard throughout the piece as a goal (we have not seen this pitch given such prominence before), with a cadence on the octave at the end, as well as in the repeat of the **a** section. As discussed in Chapter 5 of *Music in the Medieval West*, B♭ was an acceptable pitch in the system of hexachords spelled in the Guidonian hand; Machaut has gone beyond that harmonic understanding, using the pitch not as part of a hexachord, but as a final. Clearly, finals of the modes were no longer all that was available. And where B♭ is a final, the fourth above, E♭, will surely be present, as it is here (sometimes in the score, and sometimes added by the editors). The first statement of section **a** is in G with a cadence on D, here heard as an open or unstable cadence, contrasting with the cadences on B♭. Measures 15–17 lead the ear into thinking that a closed ending is coming, with the tenor holding onto an ornamented B♭, but the cantus leads away from this, forcing the open cadence. By contrast, the second ending of **a** maintains a steady emphasis on B♭, with a run in the cantus from B♭ to the fifth above and back down again. This, too, is how the **b** section ends.

33.2 *DAME, A VOUS SANS RETOLLIR:* MONOPHONIC VIRELAI

Paris, BN fr. 1586, ff. 51r–51v; from Margaret Switten, ed., *The Medieval Lyric, Anthology II: Guillaume de Machaut, Remède de Fortune* (NEH and Mount Holyoke College, 1988), pp. 78–79. Reprinted with permission.

REFRAIN

Dame, a vous sans retollir	*My lady, to you without reservation*
Dong cuer, pensée, desir,	*I give my heart, thought, desire,*
Corps, et amour,	*body, and love,*
Comme a toute la millour	*as to the very best woman*
Qu'on puist choisir,	*who can be chosen,*
Ne qui vivre ne morir	*or who can live or die*
Puist a ce jour.	*in this time.*

1

Si ne me doit a folour	I must not be held
Tourner, se je vous äour,	a fool if I adore you,
Car sans mentir,	for it's no lie
Bonté passés en valour,	that you surpass goodness in value,
Toute flour en douce odour	and in sweet fragrance any flower
Qu'on puet sentir.	that one might smell.
Vostre biauté fait tarir	Your beauty withers
Toute autre et anïentir,	and destroys all other [beauty],
Et vo douçour	and your sweetness
Passe tout; rose en coulour	surpasses all; I see your complexion

Vous doi tenir,	the color of roses,
Et vo regars puet garir	and your glance can heal
Toute dolour.	every sorrow.
Dame, a vous, etc.	*My lady, to you, etc.*

2

Pour ce, dame, je m'atour	Therefore, my lady, I gird myself
De trés toute ma vigour	with all my strength
A vous servir,	to serve you,
Et met, sans nul villain tour,	and I devote without base artifice
Mon cüer, ma vie et m'onnour	my heart, my love, my honor
En vo plaisir.	to pleasing you.
Et se Pité consentir	And if Pity wishes
Vuet que me daigniez oir	to grant that you deign to hear
En ma clamour,	my appeal,
Je ne quier de mon labour	I wish for my trouble
Autre merir,	no other recompense,
Qu'il ne me porroit venir	for no greater joy
Joie gringnour.	could come to me.
Dame, a vous, etc.	*My lady, to you, etc.*

3

Dame, ou sont tuit mi retour,	My lady, in whom are all my resources,
Souvent m'estuet en destour	I most often, far from you,
Pleindre et gemir,	lament and mourn,
Et, present vous, descoulour,	and, near you, I grow pale,
Quant vous ne savez l'ardour	since you don't know the passion
Qu'ay a souffrir	I have to suffer
Pour vous qu'aim tant et desir,	for you, whom I love and desire so much
Que plus ne le puis couvrir.	that I can no longer hide it.
Et se tenrour	And if you show no
N'en avez, en grant tristour	tenderness, in great sadness
M'estuet fenir.	I must end my days.
Nompourquant jusqu'au morir	Nonetheless, until death
Vostres demour.	I remain yours.
Dame, a vous, etc.	*My lady, to you, etc.*

Dame, a vous sans retollir is the simple monophonic song that the narrator of the *Remède de Fortune* writes to display his love and talents after Lady Hope has restored his spirits. The narrative of the poem calls for a hit number at this point, and even today the song's popular appeal comes through loud and clear. Machaut calls the piece both a virelai and a *chanson baladée* ("danced song," an early term for virelai). We will use the term virelai, as it is the name that stuck. It is a joyful song, one that might make Dame Fortune blanch.

Even as they became more complicated in their polyphonic settings, virelais kept a lifeline to the dance, from which they were born. The musical form is **AbbaA** (corresponding to numbers 1–5 in the score), with the capital **A** designating a refrain that serves all three strophes. (The recording by Ensemble Project Ars Nova is accompanied by medieval fiddles to create a sense of the dance, and a group of musicians joins the soloist on the refrain to create a sense of communal song.) The lines are marked by a small melodic figure ornamenting a pitch with its lower neighbor. This neighbor figure can be heard four times in the refrain, as indicated by brackets in the score. The cadence of the **b** section is open, whereas that of the **a** section is always closed. The illumination in the manuscript (Paris, BN fr. 1586, f. 51r) depicts a dance in the round above the music, written in Ars Nova notation, tempus perfectum, prolatio minor.

In all three of the formes fixes, the overall shape of the piece is determined by the nature of the refrain and its location in the scheme. The differences in this regard between the ballade and the virelai are clear: in the ballade the refrain is a single line, the last of a group of eight lines in a poetic stanza. In the virelai, by contrast, the refrain is longer and more dominant, and opens the piece. In the rondeau (see Chapter 8 of *Music in the Medieval West* for a monophonic example), the refrain begins and closes a stanza, and a line from it appears in the middle of the stanza as well.

GUILLAUME DE MACHAUT (C. 1300–1377)

34

Kyrie from the *Messe de Nostre Dame*

Isorhythmic Mass movement

Third quarter of the 14th century

Paris, BN fr. 1584; Paris, BN fr. 1585; from Daniel Leech-Wilkinson, ed., *Machaut's Mass: An Introduction* (Oxford: Clarendon Press, 1990), pp. 183–88. Reprinted by permission of Oxford University Press.

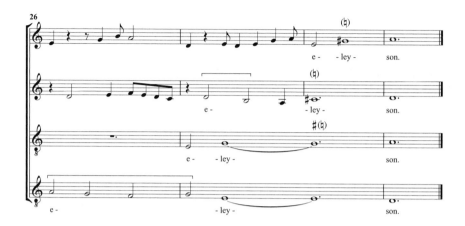

Kyrie eleyson *(3 times)*   Lord have mercy;
Christe eleyson *(3 times)*   Christ have mercy;
Kyrie eleyson *(3 times)*   Lord have mercy.

Machaut wrote much of his music while in residence at the Cathedral of Notre Dame of Reims, in northern France. The *Messe de Nostre Dame* (Mass of Our Lady) is the first surviving cycle of polyphonic Mass movements created by a single composer. He apparently created them to be performed together at Saturday Mass in honor of the Virgin Mary, and after his death to commemorate him and his brother Jean, also a canon at the cathedral. Machaut brought his mastery of the isorhythmic motet (see Anthology 32) to the Ordinary of the Mass; several of the movements are exercises in that form. The Kyrie is a tripartite isorhythmic work, but without the multiple texts that are characteristic of the motet, it becomes an extraordinary display of the late medieval love of combining music and number. In order to make such a piece work, and to clearly bring out the progression of harmonies, the upper voices need to move together with great precision.

    The Kyrie is a four-voice work. The tenor and the contratenor (the lowest voice) work as a pair to form a sonorous foundation for the other voices, with the tenor carrying the famous Kyrie melody *Cunctipotens genitor* (see Anthology 6). In the first Kyrie the chant is divided into seven taleae of four notes each; three of these taleae make a unit for the upper voices, dividing the movement as a whole into two sections of the same number of measures, and one section that is shorter. The editor indicates the divisions by a system of numbering. A capital Roman numeral indicates the major sections. Lowercase numerals indicate the taleae found in the tenor, renumbering them for each major section. It can be seen that the tenor and contratenor offer strong cadences on the start of every new talea, always at the unison, the fifth, or the octave.

Machaut brings great variety to the music, not only by the ways he reworks the parent chant in the tenor in each of the three major sections of the piece (Kyrie I, Christe, Kyrie II), but also through the melodic character of the upper voices, which is different for each section. There is a great deal of syncopation, and the sections become more rhythmically complex as the piece unfolds, until the boisterous end. The passages of playful hocketing in Kyrie II must have sounded especially adventuresome within a sacred work at this time. The Kyrie makes a wonderful contrast with Machaut's Gloria, a work that declaims the long text in simultaneous style, all the parts moving to the same rhythm for the sake of declaiming a long text. (Compare Richard Queldryk's isorhythmic Gloria from the early 1400s, studied in Chapter 11 of *Music in the Medieval West*.)

A comparison of the various modern editions of the Kyrie points to the numerous decisions performers need to make when performing the Mass. It is not possible to know what accidentals would have been employed throughout the work because their use depended on a comprehensive knowledge of fourteenth-century regional practice that is not available to us today. Most editors put suggested editorial accidentals in parentheses above the staff (as in the edition by Daniel Leech-Wilkinson reproduced here). However, Leech-Wilkinson has used a variety of symbols to indicate accidentals: an accidental that is found before a note is in the manuscripts; those which he thinks are plausible are placed above the notes; and those about which he has doubts are placed above the notes, but in parentheses. Another problem is text underlay: where should the words be placed in relation to the notes? The manuscript scores give us no precise guidance. A third decision relates to whether or not to use instruments, either to play the lower parts on their own or to accompany the voices (most musicians today say no).

35

JACOB (JAQUEMIN) DE SENLECHES (FL. 1382–1383)

Je me merveil/J'ay pluseurs fois
Double ballade
Late 14th century

Chantilly, Bibliothèque du Château de Chantilly MS 564, f. 44v; *Codex Chantilly: Bibliothèque du Château de Chantilly, Ms. 564: Facsimile and Introduction*, 2 vols., ed. Yolanda Plumley and Anne Stone (Turnhout, Belgium: Brepols, 2008); from Gordon K. Greene, ed., *French Secular Music*, part 2, Polyphonic Music of the Fourteenth Century, vol. 19 (Monaco: Éditions de l'Oiseau-Lyre, 1981), pp. 62–65. Reprinted with permission.

CANTUS 1

1

Je me merveil aucune fois conment
Homme se vuelt meller de contrefaire
Ce dont n'escrit fin ne comencement
Et quan qu'il fait, raison est au contraire.
D'or en avant voil ma forge desfaire:
Englume ne mertell ne m'ont mestier
Puis que chascuns se melle de forgier.

I am sometimes amazed at how a man wishes to
involve himself in counterfeit of which he does not
write end or beginning, and reason is contrary to all
that he does.
From now on I want to destroy my forge—neither
anvil nor hammer have need of me,
because everyone is getting involved in forging.

2

C'est soctie par peu devisament,
Car cel labour ne leur est necessaire;
Je ne di pas pour celuy qui aprent
Et qui connoist s'il seit bien ou mal faire:
Celui doit on tenir a debonaire.
Mais je ne vueil plus faire ce mestier

Puis que chascuns se melle de forgier.

It takes little reckoning to know it is folly,
because this labor is not necessary for them.
I am not talking about someone who is learning
and who knows if he can do it well or badly: such a
person one must deem of noble spirit.
But I do not want to carry on with this business any
longer,
because everyone is getting involved in forging.

3

Quant on leur dit leur vice evidement,
Qui cognoscent, se ne leur puet il plaire:
Il respondent molt ourguelleusement,
Disant que de doctrine n'ont que faire!
Il doinent aus nouvels fol exemplaire . . .
Pour ce farai soppes en un panier
Puis que chascuns se melle de forgier.

When one tells them of their evident vice,
which they know, although it cannot please
them, they reply most proudly, saying that they
have no doctrine other than to get it done.
They give newcomers a bad example, which is why
I shall make soup in a basket,
because everyone is getting involved in forging.

CANTUS 2

1

J'ay pluseurs fois pour mon esbatement,
Ou temps passé, heu playsir de fayre
Un virelay de petit sentiment
Ou un rondel qui [bien] a moy puist playre.
Mais mantenant je me vueil tout quoy tayre
Et moy lesier ester et reparer
Puis que chascuns se melle de forgier.

I have many times in the past, as a game,
taken pleasure in making a virelai
of little insight or a rondel
which might please me well enough.
But now I want to keep completely silent
and leave myself be and head home,
because everyone is getting involved in forging.

2

Forgier doit chilz qui son entendement
A si agut c'on n'i sceit que refayre;

Mais chascuns vuelt aler primierement
Disant "je sçay" pour loer son afayre
Et pour autruy blasmer en son repaire.
Si ne me vuel je plus enpeschier
Puis que chascuns se melle de forgier.

Only he should forge who has such acute
understanding that the knowledge of everyone else
    is limited to copying his example.
But everyone wishes to go first, saying,
"I know," so as to praise his own business
and to blame others in what they do.
So I do not wish to get involved anymore,
because everyone is getting involved in forging.

3

Il en i a qui vont celeement
Moustrer lour fais a autruy pour parfayre:
Ce n'est pas fayt aseürement
Ne de bon sens, se leur on doit desplayre,
Mais fol cuidier ne sceit ou il repayre!
Pour ce m'estuet bouter en un poillier
Puis que chascuns se melle de forgier.

There are those who go secretly to show what they've
done to others so as to complete them.
This is not done with a guarantee nor from good
sense (although one might displease them), but the
foolish person doesn't know what else to do.
This is why I must knock it on the head,
because everyone is getting involved in forging.

Little is known about Jacob (or Jaquemin) de Senleches beyond the fact that he was prominently associated with the Ars Subtilior (more refined or precise art) of the late fourteenth and early fifteenth centuries. His *Je me merveil/J'ay pluseurs fois* is a double ballade, with two different texts in the upper voices; its basic musical form is **aab**, with the end of the **b** section constituting a refrain. The tenor is without words, and so can be vocalized (perhaps to solfege syllables) or played on an instrument.

Although the entire piece has three stanzas of poetry (as above), only the first one is set to music in the medieval score; the other two are written out by themselves and have to be fitted to the music. The refrain (with the same text and music) that closes the **b** section is one of the most innovative aspects of the piece as a whole. It is a canon at the unison between the two top voices, unfolding a measure apart—a virtuosic display that is delightful to hear. Even more remarkably, the two identical parts are written in different notation: cantus 1 is expressed in tempus imperfectum, prolatio maior, while cantus 2 is in tempus perfectum, prolatio maior. The minim provides an additional level of time below the semibreve.

The interaction between the voices is different throughout from that found in Machaut's *Dame, de qui toute ma joie vient* (see Anthology 33.1). Senleches' ballade lacks the frequent starts and stops, with nervous lines coming together at various points of duration. Instead, one or another of the voices is always in motion, and the only durational resting points are the major cadences at the ends of sections. Although the harmonies are not complex, the rhythms, and above all the expression of the rhythms in notation, make this piece characteristic of the intricate language shared by Ars Subtilior composers.

In addition to black notation with different time signatures, the medieval notator used both red and void, or hollow, notes (as well as particolored notes that will not be discussed here). The modern score uses top bracketing to indicate ligatures, square brackets on the sides to indicate red notes, and bent brackets to indicate void notes. The values of the red and void notes relate to particular levels of time. Given the mensuration signs used in this piece (and each piece may be a world unto itself), red notes have equivalence to black notes on the level of the breve and semibreve, but on the level of the minim, red notes are augmented. In measure 11, a black imperfect breve in cantus 1 (worth six eighth notes) sounds against a red breve in cantus 2. If the latter were a black breve, it would be worth nine eighth notes, but because it is red, the note is worth one-third less, and so the two breves are equivalent.

The tenor is also written in tempus imperfectum, prolatio maior. In the tenor, void notes reduce value on the level of the semibreve. At measure 3, three semibreves, which would be worth three eighth notes each in black notation in the tenor, are each worth two eighth notes (or a quarter note). Because the notes are void, the value is reduced by one-third. The piece is a fine example of the highly ornate Flamboyant style, as discussed in Chapter 10 of *Music in the Medieval West*: the surface details of rhythmic notation overwhelm the workings of the piece as a whole, at least for the very skilled performers who had to deal with the score.

The nature of Senleches' ballade is driven by the text and its many meanings. The piece as a whole offers a lament about modern musicians—in particular, their lack of skill at composing and making appropriate use of the works of others. The times are not what they were, the poet seems to say, and in the refrain the skilled musicians who render the music threaten to quit altogether. Tellingly, Senleches apparently alludes to a ballade entitled *En atendant souffrir* by Philippus de Caserta, a composer active at the papal court in Avignon in the 1370s. The musical allusion occurs at the end of the **a** section of *Je me merveil*, on the word "contrefaire" in cantus 1. The composer is using the work of others skillfully himself, while complaining that others do not and that he will stop giving them his own works to misappropriate.

Senleches' double ballade exemplifies the notational complexity that characterizes the Ars Subtilior. Every performer must realize her or his part from the very difficult notation. Senleches has created an intellectual game that only the performers (or those who have the complete set of parts in front of them) can understand. They triumph over complexity, proud craftsmen who forge music in the workshop of performance. The difficulties of the notation and the rhythmically complex relationships of the voices should not make us think that this music was for musicians alone. *Je me merveil/J'ay pluseurs fois* unfolds with a great deal of repetition; it consists of three strophes, with the rhyme scheme **ab//ab//bcC**. The interplay between text and music creates a sense of sectionality that can be readily heard and enjoyed.

36

MARCHETTO OF PADUA (FL. 1305–1319)

Ave regina celorum/Mater innocencie/Ite Joseph

Latin double motet

Early 14th century, not later than 1305

Oxford University, Bodleian Library Canonici Class. latin 112, ff. 61v–62v; facsimile in F. Alberto Gallo, "Marchetus in Padua und die 'franco-venetische' Musik des frühen Trecento," *Archiv für Musikwissenschaft* 31 (1974): 42–56, pl. 1 and 2; transcription by Michael Long.

TRIPLUM

Ave regina celorum,
pia virgo tenella.
Maria candens flos florum
[Christique] clausa cella.
Gracia que peccatorum
dira abstulit bella
plena odore unguentorum,
stirpis David puella.
Dominus, rex angelorum,
te gignit, lucens stella.
Tecum manens ut nostrorum
tolleret seva tela.
Benedicta mater morum,
nostre mortis medella.
Tu signatus fons ortorum,
manna [das dulcicella,
in te lucet] lux cunctorum
quo promo de te mella.
Mulieribus tu chorum
regis dulci viella
et vincula delictorum
fragis nobis rebella.
Bene [**Dictus** futurorum
ob nos] potatus fella
fructus dulcis quo iustorum
clare sonat cimella.
Ventris sibi parat thorum,
nec in te corruptella.
Tui zelo fabris horum
languescat animella.

Hail, Queen of Heaven,
pious, tender virgin.
Mary, brilliant white blossom of blossoms,
[and Christ's] sealed chamber.
Grace, which removed the
fierce struggles of sinners,
full of the perfume of unguents,
daughter of the lineage of David.
The Lord, King of Angels,
begets you, a shining star.
He remains with you
that He might remove savage arrows from us.
Blessed mother of mortals,
healing remedy of our death.
You, selected a fountain of gardens,
you give us sweet manna,
in you shines the light of all,
which is why I take honey from you;
for women, you lead a chorus
with a sweet vielle,
and you break
the rebellious chains of our sins.
Blessed is He
who drank the bile for us,
sweet fruit by which the shawm of the
just resounds clearly.
He creates the swelling of your womb for Himself,
nor is there corruption in you.
Let every living thing languish
with jealousy for your works.

DUPLUM

[**M**]ater innocencie
Aula venustatis.
Rosa pudicicie,
Cella deitatis.
Vera lux mundicie,
Manna probitatis.
Porta obediencie,
Arca pietatis.
Datrix indulgencie,
Virga puritatis.

Mother of innocence,
hall of delight,
rose of chastity,
chamber of the deity,
true light of cleanliness,
manna of righteousness,
gateway of obedience,
ark of piety,
granter of pardon,
rod of purity.

Arbor fructus gracie,	Tree of the fruit of grace,
Nostre pravitatis.	of our depravity,
Virtus tue clemencie	may the virtue of your clemency
Me solvat a peccatis.	absolve me of my sins.

TENOR

Ite Joseph	Go, Joseph

In both his music and his theoretical writings, Marchetto of Padua articulated the musical culture of the early Italian Trecento (fourteenth century). *Ave regina celorum/Mater innocencie/Ite Joseph* is an "architectural motet," the kind of piece that allows those who study music and those who study architecture to share a common space. Apparently composed for the dedication of the Scrovegni Chapel in Padua on the Feast of the Annunciation in 1305, the music relates to the magnificent cycle of frescoes on the life of the Virgin Mary with which Giotto di Bondone adorned the chapel. (The sole manuscript containing the work is from Padua [c. 1325], also helping to locate it geographically.)

Ave regina celorum is "signed" by the composer through an acrostic: the first letters of each line of the duplum text spell out his name in Latin, MARCVM PADVANVM; whereas the boldfaced first words of the triplum create the *Ave Maria*, putting the composer in the company of the Virgin. (Giotto had included his own portrait in the frescoes, and Marchetto was not to be outdone.) The work is interactive with the chapel for which it was written in other ways as well: the number of perfect longs in the motet, 39, is the same as the number of frescoes in the apse of the chapel. The untexted tenor has recently been identified as an *Ite missa est* setting (on the word "Joseph") borrowed from a Marian Alleluia that describes the Annunciation. The use of this popular tune reinforces the Marian images in the text and relates the piece to the occasion of the dedication. The isorhythmic structure features six taleae, each worth the value of six perfect longs, plus a closing section; there are two statements of the color, labeled A and B in our score.

As in Philippe de Vitry's *Tribum/Quoniam/Merito* (see Anthology 32) and the Kyrie from Machaut's *Messe de Nostre Dame* (see Anthology 34), the isorhythmic scaffolding of the piece creates several levels of time. The tenor is laid out in tempus perfectum, with each long worth three breves (in the transcription, a perfect long equals three tied dotted half notes). Each breve is worth three counts (in the transcription, an unaltered breve equals a dotted half or three quarter notes). At the next level the note values are more fluid. If there are three semibreves, they are represented as three quarter notes, as in measure 15. If there are four, the first two are eighth notes, followed by two quarters, as in the triplum in measure 16. If there are five, the first four are eighth notes, as in the duplum in measure 21. Marchetto uses an Italian adaptation of the Petronian system of calculating semibreves (see Anthology 31).

Ave regina celorum shows how harmonic understandings affected the shape of vocal lines in early-fourteenth-century northern Italy. We know from Marchetto's treatise *Lucidarium in arte musice plane* (Elucidation of the Art of Plainsong), which postdates the motet by some years, that as a theorist he was particularly interested in intervals smaller than the whole tone. The motet embodies this concern in a variety of ways, as do extant fragments of polyphonic Offices from the region. Marchetto considered it crucial that thirds and sixths move directly and smoothly to perfect consonances whenever possible. How they do this can be an aesthetic choice, so strict rules cannot be formulated, but the general idea is for both ornamental notes and tones at cadences to proceed to their goal pitches via half steps through the use of judiciously employed accidentals.

The editor of the motet distinguishes between accidentals indicated in the manuscript (shown beside the notes) and editorial additions (above the notes). For example, after a brief introduction in the duplum, the triplum enters singing "Ave" a major sixth above. The triplum sounds a fifth above the tenor in measures 5–6, and then moves up to create an octave with the duplum (with the tenor at the fifth), at measures 13–14, which will also be the final interval of the entire piece, a strong resting place. It can be seen that the editor has to make adjustments through the use of musica ficta to make these motions work with smooth voice-leading, and without harsh dissonance. The motion from measure 3 to measure 7 in the triplum is from E up to A, and to get there G is sharped; the editor has added a sharp to the C in the tenor in measure 5 to avoid the tritone and to provide smooth voice-leading to the cadence in measure 7. In the next measures, the motion is from A down to E, so the G is made natural. However when the triplum rises for the major cadence at measures 13–14, the editor provides the sharp on F to lead powerfully to G, making a parallel with the notated G♯ in measure 5. The editor also, then, adds a sharp to the C in the tenor at measure 10 to complete the parallel. The use of these accidentals relates to the harmonic goalpost in question, and to whether the line is essentially rising (sharps may be used) or falling (flats or naturals may be used).

As these examples show, the quality of motion in the voices works in tandem with the vertical sonorities. These kinds of decisions, made for the sake of beauty, occur throughout the piece and create a particular melodic character that we have not heard before.

37

ANONYMOUS

Quando i oselli canta

Two-voice madrigal
First half of the 14th century

Rome, Biblioteca Apostolica Vaticana Rossi 215, f. 2v; from W. Thomas Marrocco, ed., *Italian Secular Music*, Polyphonic Music of the Fourteenth Century, vol. 8 (Monaco: Éditions de l'Oiseau-Lyre, 1972), p. 81. Reprinted with permission.

1

Quando i oselli canta,	When the birds sing,
Le pasturele vano a la campagna,	the shepherdesses go into the country,
Quando i oselli canta.	when the birds sing.

2

Fan girlande de herba,	They make garlands of herbs,
Frescheta verde, et altre belle fiore,	with fresh green foliage and other lovely flowers,
Fan girlande de herba.	they make garlands of herbs.

3

Quest'è quel dolce tempo,	This is that sweet time
Ch'amor mi prese d'una pasturella,	that I fell in love with a shepherdess,
Quest'è quel dolce tempo.	this is that sweet time.

RITORNELLO

Basar la volsi e de me de la rocha.	I turned to kiss her and she hit me with her distaff.

The Trecento madrigal (as distinguished from the sixteenth-century genre of the same name) is made up of a number of strophes (*terzetti*) comprising two or more lines, followed by a one- or two-line refrain (ritornello) that is distinct in meter and other musical features from the terzetti. (In this example, it is distinct in theme as well.) This anonymous two-voice madrigal from the Rossi Codex is a study in virtuosic vocal ornamentation, especially in the featured performance by Gothic Voices. Each terzetto is set to the same music. The first and third lines of each terzetto are the same, with the tenor, but not the cantus, repeating the music as well. The restatement of the text in the cantus is completely different, providing two settings of the line—yet another exercise in contrast.

The two contrasting cantus phrases, setting the first line of the terzetto and the third, can be profitably compared, given that they sound against the same musical line in the tenor. The opening phrase of the terzetto is far less decorated than the closing, although both have their longest melismas on the syllable "can-" of "canta." The cantus's third phrase also provides contrast by exploring the higher range as the emotionality of the speaker's delight increases.

The tenor is nothing like the florid cantus, remaining limited in both range and motion. Perhaps we are hearing the influence of a droning instrument in rustic song, maybe even of a bagpipe. The major cadences are three unisons, on A, on G, and on A, with the cantus arriving at the cadence through a florid descent, while the tenor rises to the final pitch of the cadence stepwise.

The ritornello (which is heard only once, unlike the recurring ritornelli of the seventeenth century and later) awakens the listener from the bucolic world of the terzetti. The tonality is different from the start, with a long-held octave on G. To get there, the cantus has to leap up a minor seventh. We have heard that leap before, between measures 7 and 8, but this time it leads to another place altogether, which is precisely the point of the ritornello. Characteristically, the lower voice only drops a pitch; it then moves stepwise up and down from G through B♭ to C, finally cadencing on D. The jagged sounds of the ritornello are reflected in the text, with its theme of abrupt rejection. Here the final melisma becomes a cry of pain, a prolonged "ouch."

Quando i oselli canta gives a taste of improvised secular song, and harkens back to the world of florid organum duplum (see Anthology 13), whether or not the case can be made for a direct heritage. The bald perfect consonances and the circuitous path followed from one to the next by the virtuosic melismatizing of the cantus mark this madrigal as "improvisatory" in character. The text, like that of *Cacciando per gustar* (Anthology 39), plays upon the circumstances of courtly love, its idyllic setting, and the rude awakening that various types of intrusion can present to the lover. Both works provide excellent examples of the humorous effects that medieval poets and composers enjoyed when exploiting convention.

38

FRANCESCO LANDINI (C. 1325–1397)

De sospirar sovente

Two-voice ballata
Mid-14th century

Florence, Biblioteca Medicea-laurenziana, Med. Pal. 87, f. 149v; F. A. Gallo, ed., *Il codice Squarcialupi* (Florence, 1992); from Francesco Landini, *Works*, ed. Leo Schrade, Polyphonic Music of the Fourteenth Century, vol. 4 (Monaco: Éditions de l'Oiseau-Lyre, 1938), p. 80. Reprinted with permission.

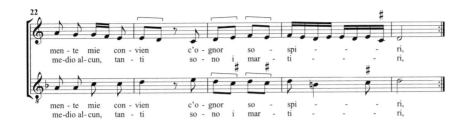

men - te mie con - vien c'o - gnor so - spi - - - ri,
me - dio al - cun, tan - ti so - no i mar - ti - - - ri,

men - te mie con - vien c'o - gnor so - spi - - - ri,
me - dio al - cun, tan - ti so - no i mar - ti - - - ri,

1 (RIPRESA)

De sospirar sovente	To sigh often
Constretto son,	I am forced,
vegiendo per senbiante	seeing in your countenance,
El cor che ti consente	your heart which lets you
Volger gli ochi tuo' vaghi ad altr'amante.	turn your longing eyes to another lover.

2 (PIEDO)

Ricever questo inganno	Suffering this deception
La mente mie convien c'ognor sospiri,	leads my mind to sigh constantly.

3 (PIEDO)

Non trovando all' affanno	Not finding any remedy for my anguish,
Rimedio alcun, tanti sono i martiri,	so numerous are my torments,

4 (VOLTA)

Et assai mi raggiri	and so much you confuse me,
Che ne' pensier' mi	that in my thoughts
paia aver fallato.	I feel like I have made a mistake.
Ma pur s'i' sono errato,	But even if I am wrong,
Piacciati farne chiara la mie mente.	please put my mind at rest.

5 (RIPRESA)

De sospirar sovente	To sigh often
Constretto son,	I am forced,
vegiendo per senbiante	seeing in your countenance
El cor che ti consente	your heart which lets you
Volger gli ochi tuo' vaghi ad altr'amante.	turn your longing eyes to another lover.

The Trecento *ballata* (plural, *ballate*) is a sectional love song, with origins in the dance, like the virelai, its counterpart among the French *formes fixes* (see Anthology 33). *De sospirar sovente* by the Florentine composer Francesco Landini—whose works are abundantly represented in the Squarcialupi Codex—charms the ear from the first listening. The piece consists of four parts: an introductory *ripresa* or refrain; a strophe made up of two *piedi* (feet); a *volta*, set to the same music as the ripresa; and a repeat of the ripresa. So the musical form is **AbbaA**, with **A** representing the refrain.

The two voices in the ripresa join at the beginning of every line and create sonorous harmonies at cadences, each of which is approached by a melisma in the cantus. Phrase by phrase, the voices move as follows in the ripresa: unison to unison; unison to fifth; fifth to unison; staggered unison to octave to octave. Approaches to the cadences are quite different from those in the two-voice madrigal *Quando i oselli canta* (Anthology 37). At measures 4, 8, 13, and 17, the cantus does not approach the cadential pitch from above, but rather from below; and the tenor does not rise to the final pitch at measures 4, 8, and 17, but rather descends. In other words, the characteristic motions of the two voices have been exchanged. Although the piedi are similar in musical character to the ripresa, the cadences fall within the first line of poetry, and there is no sense of closure until the final cadence, which is a unison on D, the fifth of the final G of the ripresa. In this open cadence, too, the cantus rises to the final pitch, although the tenor rises as well. The slight staggering of the rhythms adds some variety to what is essentially a cadence in which both voices resolve upward by a half step.

Using a technique inherited from earlier monophonic ballate, the cantus line in Landini's ripresa takes the ear through many ideas about tripping down the scale to a cadence. It is clear that the musical aesthetic he has learned and come to prize is not content with a simple descent to the final pitch. Landini finds many ways of creating variety and interest. In measures 3–4 he escapes from the final for a moment with a leading-tone ornament, moves down another pitch, and then leaps up a third. In measures 7–8 he moves down a whole step below the final pitch, which is a fifth above tenor A. In measures 12–13 he circles around the final cadential pitch C, once again creating a syncopated double leading-tone cadence, which is varied because the tenor takes off with a new idea.

The different key signatures found in the modern score are also found in the source and are common in late medieval polyphonic works. This phenomenon, known as the partial signature, indicates that some kind of transposition is going on (either modal or hexachordal), although the notes indicated by the signature (in this period, most often a B♭) in the lowest voice (as here) may often be adjusted through the use of musica ficta. We can think of the upper voice as falling in the Dorian mode, with a final of D; and the lower voice as in transposed Dorian, with a final on G, but with pitch relationships that mirror Dorian mode through the introduction of B♭.

At measures 15–17—the final cadence of the refrain, and ultimately of the piece—Landini uses the cadence that would come to bear his name: the tenor moves down to the final, C–B♭–A–G, while the cantus descends first with an ornamented G, then with a syncopated phrase (A to G to the leading tone below G), and finally with a syncopated under-third resolving upward to G. (The last element is the defining characteristic of the "Landini cadence.") Here, as in many of Landini's other ballate, the beguiling variety of the melodic line is generated by the movement toward cadences.

39

ANTONIO ZACARA DA TERAMO
(C. 1350/60–AFTER MAY 19, 1413)

Cacciando per gustar
Three-voice double-texted caccia
Early 15th century

Florence, Biblioteca Medicea-laurenziana, Med. Pal. 87, f. 188v; F. A. Gallo, ed., *Il codice Squarcialupi* (Florence, 1992); W. Thomas Marrocco, ed., *Italian Secular Music*, Polyphonic Music of the Fourteenth Century, vol. 10 (Monaco: Éditions de l'Oiseau-Lyre, 1977), pp. 117–23. Reprinted with permission.

ro. Di fior tro-vai as-sai a-per-ti e chiu-si Ta-
do per gu-star di quel te-so-ro
rot-to!" "A l'a-go-ra fu-sa." "La mer-ce-ri-e mi-nu-ta, Ma-don-

stan-do e o-do-ran-do li più bel-li et u-na vo-ce gri-
Per a-spri mon-ti e bo-schi pe-ri-glio-si D'uno bo-
-na!"

da, "A li gam-ba-rel-li, a li gam-ba-rel-li, a li lat-ta-ri-ni fie-schi!"
schet - to d'ar-bus-sel-li d'o - - ro. Di
"Chi ha de la ra-si-na?" "Chi ha fres-cie o-za-ga-ne vec - - chie?"

"Fie-schi, fie-schi son che an-che friz-za-no!" A li lat-ta-ri-ni fie-schi!"
fior tro-vai as-sai a-per-ti e chiu-si Ta-stan-do e o-do-
"Sals, sals, sal-sa ver-de, mo-star-da!"

PRIMUS AND SECUNDUS

Cacciando per gustar di quel tesoro
Per aspri monti e boschi perigliosi
D'uno boschetto d'arbusselli d'oro
Di fior trovai assai aperti e chiusi
Tastando e odorando li più belli
   et una voce grida,
"A li gambarelli, a li gambarelli, a li lattarini
   fieschi!"

"Fieschi, fieschi son che anche frizzano!"
"A li lattarini fieschi!"
"Tutti gettano la lingua fuori."

Hunting to enjoy that treasure
   through harsh mountains and forests perilous,
in a small clump of golden trees
I found many flowers open and closed,
touching and smelling the most beautiful, and a
   voice cried out:
"Shrimps, shrimps, fresh anchovies!"

"Fresh, so fresh that they're still darting!"
"Fresh anchovies!"
"They all stick out their tongues."

"E son fieschi quissi lattarini!" "And are these anchovies fresh?"
"Dame dui derrate di gambarelli!" "Give me two portions of shrimps!"
"E son fieschi como dici?" "And are they fresh as you say?"
"A la infusaglia dolce." "Sweet lupins!"
"O tu de l'olio, che vallo pe' tetto?" "Hey, you with the oil, how much for a jug?"
"Vo' ne cinque." "I want five."
"A li buoni melangoli! "Fine cucumbers,
Una denaro!" one for one coin!"
"Costa sei solli lo centenaro, e vo' ne dui." "For a hundred it costs six soldi, and I want two of them."

"Saccio che fora trista." "I know that I'll be sorry."
"Se ne vuoi tre per due danari toli tilli!" "If you want three for two coins, get them, keep them."

"Vo' li, vo' li, vo' li?" "Do you want them, want 'em, want 'em, want 'em, want 'em?"

"Vo' ne dare dui." "Would you like to give me two?"
"Chi volli cavalcaci?" "Who wants the caciocavalli?"
"A la cacio sardinale, a lu cacio de la forma!" "Sardinian cheese, cheese from the mold!"
"A lo bono latte." "Good milk."
"No, no, no, no, no, non l'ho." "No, no, no, no, no, no, I don't have it."
"A lo buono caccio fiesco!" "Good, fresh cheese!"
"Non é fiesco como dici." "It is not fresh, as you say."
"Et é buono et é chiaro." "And it's good, and it's clear."
"E chi li vuol li buoni scafi?" "And who wants good fava beans?"
"E chi li vuol li buoni viscioli?" "And who wants good sour cherries?"
"A la ricotta fiesca!" "Fresh ricotta!"
"Al buon olio como l'unto più che l'ambra!" "Good oil, it is like grease, more than the amber!"
"A le buon cerage!" "Good cherries!"
"E chi li vuol le buone ficora?" "And who wants fine figs?"
"E chi li vuol le buone persica?" "And who wants fine peaches?"
"A le castagne rimonde, femmine!" "Boiled chestnuts, women!"
"Anna ca, vien ca!" "Hey, Anna, come here!"
"Fammi bene, cioé forte?" "Give me a good price for this, as it's strong?"
"Compare, vo' me cernere?" "Hey, buddy, do you want to sift through my stuff?"
"Chi altro che farina compra vende, "Who else, who is buying flour, who is selling,
Chi dorme, caccia stuta, e chi accende." Who is sleeping, hunting, snuffing, and who is on fire?"

TENOR

"Ai cenci, ai toppi, ai vetro, ai ferro, ai rame rotto!" "Rags, sacks, glasses, irons, broken copper!"
"A l'agora fusa!" "Needles, spindles!"
"La mercerie minuta, Madonna!" "Tiny merchandise, my lady!"
"Chi ha de la rasina?" "Who has any satin?"
"Chi ha frescie ozagane vecchie?" "Who has ruffs or old ribbons?"

"Sals, sals, salsa verde, mostarda!"

"Chi ha de l'uova?"

"Chi ha de la semola?"

"E son fieschi quessi?"

"A l'olio, a l'olio!"

"Ci, ci sta, che si e scorticato!"

"Boglione sei suolli."

"Anna, va fluor che ti scortichi."

"Non ne vo."

"Come le dai?"

"A l'agli, a l'agli."

"Chi vuo le buone cipolle?"

"Avanti, avanti,

chi si vuol ciurmare?"

"Chi vuol segar li pettini?"

"Chi vuol conciar li pettini da capo?"

"Al dent, al dent!

Chi ha mal dente ha el mal parente,

e chi ha'l mal vicino ha'l mal mattino."

"Chi vuol conciar callare centrari, capisteri,

e comprera treppiedi e coperchie?"

"A l'aceto, a l'aceto,

come'l tossico."

"Chi vuol cernere?"

"Si, madonna, si, salgo su!"

"Gr-, gr-, green sauce, mustard."

"Who has any eggs?"

"Who has any bran?"

"And are these fresh?"

"Oil, oil!"

"Here, here it is, it has been skinned."

"Boglione, I want six soldi for them."

"Anna, get out, or you'll be flayed."

"No, I don't want any of it!"

"How much do you want for them?"

"Garlic, garlic!"

"Who wants fine onions?"

"Come on, come forth,

who wants their fortune told?"

"Who wants to cut the combs?"

"Who wants head-combs mended?"

"Teeth, teeth!

Whoever has a bad tooth has a bad relative,

and whoever has a bad neighbor has a bad morning!"*

"Who wants kettles mended,

buckets and tubs, and to buy trivets and lids?"

"Vinegar, vinegar,

like gall!"

"Who wants to sift?"

"Yes, my lady, yes, I'm coming up!"

*Both phrases are proverbial expressions.

The Trecento *caccia* (plural, *cacce*) had its beginnings as a hunting song in which the voices chase one another—that is, they proceed in canon. In many three-voice cacce, the upper voices are texted, but the tenor is not. In this example by Antonio Zacara da Teramo—perhaps the last known caccia—the top two voices sing one text, the secundus following the primus at a distance of 21 measures, while the tenor sings a different one. The result is an exercise in late-medieval hilarity, joyful in both the musical effects it creates and the ways in which the texts make their meanings by playing off the lively repartee between the voices.

Cacciando per gustar begins with an off-color joke at the expense of the pastoral narrator, who, like so many others of his ilk wandering in and out of medieval literature, is about to have a major surprise. He is in a field of flowers—a euphemism for female genitalia—and about to touch and smell the most beautiful of the flowers when someone yells, "Shrimps!" and he is abruptly transported to a noisy urban marketplace. The musical narrative has a filmic quality, cutting from one scene to another, a technique that continues throughout the conversations in this lively Felliniesque extravaganza.

In order to create a piece that has powerful technical restrictions because of the canon in the upper voices and a complicated relationship between the dovetailing texts and their interactive meanings, it is crucial to have well-thought-out harmonies to support the whole. The static nature of the music is demonstrated in the tenor. It is a D-oriented voice that sounds this pitch at several major points: at the opening, where the primus sounds a twelfth above it; at measure 22, when the secundus enters at the same interval and the primus sounds an octave above the tenor; and at measures 64–65, where the D is held for two bars. The tenor punches out high D at measure 162 and following, as the barking voice tries to sell its wares. In addition, the tenor is laid out in phrases that seem to drive toward D, both harmonically and rhythmically. In measures 14–22, for example, the tenor descends from high to low D, followed by an octave leap up at measure 24. The harmonies are not only made of open fifths and octaves, however; triads also occur, often for extended times, as in the F–A–C of measures 45–47 and the E–G–B of measures 54–55. Yet, static as the tenor might seem from the notes alone, it is kept from dullness in the ways in which character is developed and a lively conversation with upper voices is sustained.

Cacciando per gustar may lack harmonic adventurousness, but this is more than compensated for by the interplay of the three voices, to a degree not found in any other piece we have studied. The upper voices are designed to talk back and forth, and in many places the tenor joins in the conversation. Antonio's setting emphasizes the words and their accents, allowing for various regional dialects, so that the humor experienced at the opening continues throughout the song. At the end of their merry chase, the upper voices close with a woman who needs a man to sift her flour. The voice that begins finishes first, and so has the last word, in the only line not sung by both upper parts: "Who is sleeping, hunting, snuffing, and who is on fire?" The hunt has ended with burning in the top voice, selling in the middle voice, and the tenor repeating, "Yes, my lady, yes, I'm coming up!" Perhaps our interrupted narrator will achieve his goal after all, just not in the way he originally intended.

40

ANONYMOUS

Singularis laudis digna

Three-voice cantilena

After 1347

New York, Pierpont Morgan Library MS 978, f. 1; Ernest H. Sanders, Frank Ll. Harrison, and Peter M. Lefferts, eds., *English Music for the Mass and Offices (II) and Music for Other Ceremonies*, Polyphonic Music of the Fourteenth Century, vol. 17 (Monaco: Éditions de l'Oiseau-Lyre, 1986), pp. 98–110. Reprinted with permission.

1a	Singularis laudis digna	Worthy of singular praise,
	dulcis mater et benigna,	sweet and kind mother,
	sumas ave gratie.	may you accept the "Ave" of our gratitude.
1b	Stella maris apellaris	You are called the star of the sea,
	Deum paris expers paris	you bore God, having no equal,
	loco sedens glorie.	sitting in a place of glory.
2a	Hester flectit Assuerum,	Esther persuaded Ahasuerus,
	vindex plectit ducem ferum	the Avenger smote the savage general
	precis in oraculo.	in the place of prayer.
2b	Tu regina regis regem	You, Queen, direct the king,
	et conserva tuum gregem	and save your flock
	maris in periculo.	in the danger of the sea.
3a	Cesset guerra iam Francorum	Let the war of the French cease
	quorum terra fit Anglorum	and their land become that of the English,
	cum decore lilii.	emblazoned with the fleur-de-lis.
3b	Et sit concors leopardo,	And let there be peace for the leopard,
	per quem honor sit Edwardo	through which let there be honor to
	regi probo prelii.	Edward, king valiant in battle.

The *cantilena*, a work with a sequence-like text usually dedicated to the Virgin Mary and notated in score, is a classically English piece. Each poetic strophe is composed of two versicles, and these are set to repeating music, with the musical form **aabbcc**. The fourteenth-century manifestations of these works feature hallmarks of a sound that would take the Continent by storm in the next century. *Singularis laudis digna* is a three-voice, syllabic, more or less homorhythmic setting of a double-versicle Latin poem resembling a sequence. As the work is through-composed, the setting of each double versicle forms a large section; there are three of these, each with its own musical characteristics. As with a late sequence, the rhythmic Latin text is 8p + 8p + 7pp throughout.

The distinctively English soundscape that emerged in the fourteenth century featured extensive use of thirds and sixths to create a honeyed sonority that can readily be heard and appreciated, especially in the cantilena repertory. *Singularis laudis digna* is filled with examples of this sweet "English sound." The very first measure is a triad (C–E–G), leading to an octave with a third (F–F–A) in measure 2. Each beat of the opening contains a third (or a tenth), making the octave on C, sounding with G, in measure 5 the first resting place or major beat without the interval of a third.

English cantilenas were written out in score, with the text placed beneath the lowest part only. The pieces are strophic and only the first strophe was set to music. Thus decisions have to be made about where to fit the texts in subsequent strophes, and even in the first strophe with respect to the upper voices. The discrepancies you can hear in the text underlay between Christopher Page's recording and the score are not the result of a "mistake" on the part of the performers; they simply indicate that there are different ways of interpreting the evidence.

The use of score notation differentiates some fourteenth-century English polyphonic repertories from those on the Continent, where some form of motet notation was the rule. In motet notation, each voice was written separately on its own set of staves (as with *Alle psallite* in Primer II.4). Early Notre Dame three- and four-voice polyphony started out being written in score notation, but with the advent of mensural notation (and the need to conserve parchment), motet, or choir book, notation became favored for Continental and even some English repertories. This characteristic use of score in English music writing may have encouraged the harmonic practice reflected in *Singularis laudis digna*, but it is not the reason for it, for the English sonority was already well established in popular music making in the early fourteenth century.

The homophonic texture of the cantilena makes the genre particularly good for sounding out the words of the text. This suited the political purposes of the anonymous composer of *Singularis laudis digna*, which fuses veneration of Mary, the queen of Heaven, with praise of an English queen and king. Sustained-note passages alternate with melismatic descending ornaments in one or more voices, prolonging selected syllables of the accentual Latin poetry. In the first section the double versicle is set as follows, with dashes representing melismas:

Singula——ris laudis——digna——
Dulcis——mater et—be—nigna——
Sumas——a—ve gratie

In every case, the longest melismas are placed on nonaccented syllables. The accented syllables are proclaimed with sustained notes or with short melismas of three or four notes in one of the parts. The interplay between the two textures keeps the text from sounding heavy to the ear, yet it is perfectly clear and easy to understand.

The double-versicle structure is used to great advantage for praising Queen Philippa and King Edward III, both major players in various phases of the Hundred Years' War. In section 2 the Old Testament queen Esther is praised in the first versicle and the popular Queen Philippa in the second versicle. (The latter persuaded Edward to spare the burghers of Calais, who had come forth to die in place of the besieged inhabitants of their coastal city.) In the final versicle pair, the English people are described as victorious, whereas the second line of the pair praises Edward: the highly decorated words "Anglorum" and "Edwardo" make the king one with his people.

A Medieval Music Primer

IV. THE LITURGY OF THE ROMAN CATHOLIC CHURCH

Medieval music is imperfectly comprehended from modern scores and notation alone. Performers of the repertories studied in *Music in the Medieval West* and the accompanying anthology, the scholars who write about them, and the editors who prepare the scores learn to read from the manuscripts themselves and make their own decisions based on their knowledge of and close contact with medieval musical artifacts, theory, and practice. This Primer is designed to give all students of medieval music a basic tutorial in using these primary sources.

I. SOURCES

I.1. DATABASES AND REFERENCE TOOLS

Many libraries throughout the world—including such major repositories as the French National Library (Bibliothèque Nationale de France) in Paris and the Bavarian State Library (Bayerische Staatsbibliothek) in Munich, the Beinecke Rare Book and Manuscript Library at Yale University, and the Morgan Library and Museum in New York City—have digitized many of their medieval manuscripts to ensure broad public access. As a result, every teacher and student can work with original sources, bringing a wealth of codices and manuscript fragments into the classroom for group projects and discussions, as well as for individual study. Several online databases have been created as guides to finding and using these manuscripts.

Because the digital landscape is in constant flux, these online resources can only be referenced here in a general way. Many are listed on the author's website, which will be updated periodically. CANTUS is a database for Latin liturgical chant, with a focus on the chant texts for the Office. CANTUS is searchable by textual incipit (the opening few words of a chant text), keywords, saints' names or liturgical occasion, and "chant identification numbers" (drawn from standard chant research resources). CANTUS has many image links, taking the user directly from a chant text to a picture of a medieval source containing that chant. *Oxford Music Online* contains articles with bibliographies on every topic covered in

Music in the Medieval West. In addition this fundamental reference work contains descriptions of the most important medieval manuscripts, including sources for the study of chant, music theory, polyphonic repertories, and vernacular songs.

Although many sites are available for locating digitized manuscripts, printed reference books remain crucial for the study of medieval source materials. An important resource for scholarly purposes is the *Répertoire international des sources musicales* (International Inventory of Musical Sources, or *RISM*), an extensive catalogue of sources, including many medieval books containing the genres studied in *Music in the Medieval West*: tropes, sequences, music theory, polyphonic works, and music for processions.

Another print resource that you will encounter repeatedly in the study of medieval chant is the *Paléographie musicale* (Musical Paleography), a series of noted manuscripts in facsimile with introductions and other materials, including indexes. (Many of the volumes can be read online as well.) The series is published by the monks of the Benedictine Abbey of Solesmes in western France (see §§I.3 and I.4 below), and includes basic sources from several traditions of Western chant, including various dialects of the Frankish (Gregorian), Milanese (Ambrosian), and Beneventan (southern Italian) traditions.

I.2. MANUSCRIPT DESIGNATIONS AND SIGLA

With so many libraries and other repositories possessing medieval manuscripts and manuscript fragments, librarians and scholars have developed ways of referring to sources and to pages within them. A recently developed system based on the *RISM* catalogue creates uniformity: each country has a unique code, and each city and library within that country has its own siglum (identifying letter or symbol). This information is linked to the library's shelf marks, the catalogue numbers associated with individual manuscripts. But most great libraries in the world have long used their own systems of manuscript designations; these are often easier to read than the *RISM* sigla and are commonly used in many fields of study, not just music (the only field in which the *RISM* designations are widely used).

Many medieval manuscripts are numbered not by pages but by folios (abbreviated ff. or fols.; singular, f. or fol.), that is, the front and back of a sheet. To identify a source, then, you must in most cases use the folio number followed by *r* or *v*, to indicate whether you are referencing the front (recto) or back (verso) side of the folio.

Two manuscripts may serve to illustrate the differences between the two ways of referencing sources. The first is a twelfth-century Italian antiphoner (a book containing music for the Office) now in the French National Library in Paris, one of the sources catalogued in CANTUS. To indicate this source according to *RISM*, we would say: F-Pn n.a. lat. 1411. F-Pn is the siglum for France (F), Paris, Bibliothèque Nationale de France (Pn), Département des Manuscrits (Department of Manuscripts); n.a. lat. stands for "nouvelle acquisition latine" (new Latin acquisition). Another way of referring to this same manuscript is Paris, BN n.a. lat. 1411, which is what would be found in many scholarly works of all fields. Once a source has been fully designated, it is common to refer to it thereafter by an abbreviated siglum, such as n.a. lat. 1411.

A manuscript that you will encounter in these pages is D-Mbs Clm 4660 (in the *RISM* designation). This book is in Germany (D, for Deutschland) in the Bayerische Staatsbibliothek in Munich (Mbs), where it is catalogued as Clm (Codices latini monacenses, or Latin Manuscripts) no. 4660. Most English-writing scholars refer to this manuscript as Munich, Bavarian State Library, Clm 4660. In informal discussions, however, it is called *Carmina burana*, a nickname with a history of its own (as discussed in Chapter 8 of *Music in the Medieval West*).

In this anthology and the accompanying book, we refer to manuscripts by their more user-friendly designations, rather than by their *RISM* sigla. We also use the common nicknames for the famous sources we will be studying, as this is how scholars and performers who work with them know them.

I.3. THE *LIBER USUALIS*

The best known and most widespread of modern chant books is the *Liber Usualis* (Book for Common Use, abbreviated *LU*). It contains the chants for Masses of Sundays throughout the year and for major feast days of the temporal and sanctoral cycles in the Roman Catholic Church, following liturgy dating from before the reforms of the Second Vatican Council in the 1960s. It also includes Offices or hours of prayer for a handful of feasts. The first cycle (*temporale*) consists of feasts of the Lord, that is, feasts that commemorate events in the life, suffering, and resurrection of Jesus; the second cycle (*sanctorale*) comprises feast days for the saints.

The musical repertory in the *Liber Usualis* was restored from medieval manuscripts in the late nineteenth and early twentieth centuries by the monks of Solesmes mentioned above. It is worth going to your music library and spending time with the *Liber Usualis*, or downloading the book from the Internet.

Because many of the chants sung on modern recordings are taken from the *Liber Usualis*, we often do not hear the variety of dialects that were present in the medieval repertory. When you work with the *LU* and other modern chant collections, therefore, you should also consult Fr. Jerome Weber's ChantDiscography, an online resource of great value. He provides an index of recorded chant that is continually updated, and, when he is able to ascertain it, the source information as well.

The contents and pagination of editions of the *LU* differ slightly, but all are divided into the same ten sections:

1. Introduction to notation and to calendars
2. Chants for the Mass Ordinary (see §IV.2 below). In this section, the chants are organized by classification of feast, and by genre following the order in

which they are sung in the Mass. Kyries, for example, come first because they are the first of the Ordinary chants to be sung. The numbers are often used to designate the pieces; for example, the Kyrie *Cunctipotens Genitor* is also known as Kyrie IV, its number in the *LU*.

3. Tones for the psalms (see §III.3) and other formulas for reciting texts, followed by plans for three hours of prayer: Lauds, Vespers, and Compline (see §IV.3)

4. The temporal cycle of feasts, running from Advent (the season before Christmas) to Sundays after Pentecost. Chants found in this section are "proper" to the feasts (see §IV.2).

5. Feasts for commons of saints; for apostles, martyrs, and others; for church dedications; and for votive Masses. (Common chants are those used for particular categories of saints.)

6. The sanctoral cycle of feasts, beginning with saints whose feasts fall in Advent. (At the end of the *Liber Usualis* you will find an index of feasts, with all the saints represented in the book listed by name.)

7. The Mass and Office for the Dead, including the sequence *Dies irae* (Day of Wrath), dropped from the Roman rite in the reforms of the Second Vatican Council (1962–1965)

8. Appendix, including the Te Deum and other miscellaneous chants

9. Indexes (very useful, for example, for finding incipits of psalms)

10. Later supplements, which vary according to region

I.4. THE *GRADUALE TRIPLEX*

The Solesmes editions were officially endorsed by the Catholic Church in 1903. Since the Second Vatican Council of the 1960s and its attendant liturgical reforms, a new series of chant books has come out, some of which are useful for the study of medieval repertory. An introduction to these books is found in Peter Jeffery, "The New Chantbooks from Solesmes," *Notes* 47 (1991): 1039–63. Among the most important of these newer collections is the *Graduale Triplex* (*GT*).

The *Graduale Triplex* juxtaposes music as found in earlier Solesmes editions with hand-drawn reproductions of the medieval notation, following some of the most important early chant manuscripts. The three Mass Propers for Easter found in Anthology 3 are taken from this source. Example P1 shows two Easter chants expressed in the square notation associated with the Solesmes method of chant interpretation (see §II.1 below for an overview of chant notation). Above and below it have been provided the neumes of early medieval manuscripts for the sake of comparison. The following manuscripts, indicated by their common abbreviations (see §I.2 above), are as listed found in the preface to the *GT*, the first three being the sources most commonly used for the neumation supplied for the chants. The *PM* references are to facsimiles in the *Paléographie musicale* series:

L Laon 239, early 10th century; *PM*, vol. 10

C St. Gall 359, early 10th century; *PM*, series 2, vol. 2

E Einsiedeln 121, early 11th century; *PM*, vol. 4

G St. Gall 339, first half of the 11th century; *PM*, vol. 1

H St. Gall 390–91, late 10th or early 11th century (Hartker Antiphoner); *PM*, series 2, vol. 1

B Bamberg 6, late 10th century; facsimile: *Die Handschrift Bamberg Staatsbibliothek Lit. 6*, Monumenta Paleographica Gregoriana, vol. 2 (Munsterschwarzach, 1986). The letters MRBCKS refer to six early manuscripts containing texts for the Mass chants, edited by René-Jean Herbert, *Antiphonale Missarum Sextuplex* (Brussels, 1935).

Working with your teacher, or by yourself (if you are feeling adventuresome), use the *GT* as a guide to locate chants in some of the earliest manuscripts in this list (the most commonly referenced of them are online). Every medieval chant in the *Graduale Triplex* is supplied with the following information: the sigla of the manuscripts from which the neumes have been taken, and the page and folio number of the chant in those manuscripts. Using these numbers to find particular folios within medieval manuscripts online, it is easy to compare early versions of the chants to those in modern books. There are many differences. For example, Offertory chants have verses in the early sources, a feature that had died out in most regions by the twelfth century. There are no Offertory verses in the *GT*, nor would there be in most medieval chant books from the early twelfth century forward. Also in early books, the temporal and sanctoral cycles are mixed rather than separated out, as in later medieval books and in the *Liber Usualis* and the *Graduale Triplex*.

We can use the *GT* to compare a chant featured in both Chapter 3 and Anthology 3 to medieval versions of the chant. Already in the ninth century, the Easter chant *Resurrexi* was categorized as an Introit in the fourth mode, which has its final on E, and a reciting tone of A (see §III.2 below). In the score as given on pages 196–97 of the *GT* (Ex. P1), most of the music necessary to sing this chant is written out. The Introit (the opening chant of the Mass liturgy) for Easter Sunday includes several parts—first the Introit antiphon (an antiphon is a short chant, usually sung with a psalm or a psalm verse), then its psalm verse ("Domine probasti me," Psalm 139 [138]:1–2). The performer must know that the verse should be followed by the intoned Doxology, or *Gloria Patri*, a short prayer text addressed to the members of the Trinity which always forms the last verse of an intoned psalm or canticle ("Glory be to the Father, and to the Son, and to the Holy Spirit; as it was in the

Example P1: *The Introit* Resurrexi *and the Gradual* Haec dies, *from the* Graduale Triplex, Abbey of St. Peter of Solesmes Monks, pp. 196–97. Reprinted with permission of Abbaye Saint-Pierre.

AD MISSAM IN DIE

I have arisen and am still with you, alleluia: you have put your hand on me, alleluia. Your knowledge has become wonderful, alleluia, alleluia. Lord, you have tested me and known me; you have known my sitting down and my rising up.

beginning now and forever, Amen" [Gloria Patri et Filio et Spiritui Sancto; Sicut erat in principio, et nunc, et semper, et in saecula saeculorum. Amen]), followed by a repeat of the antiphon. To sing the *Gloria Patri* here, the performer would fit the words to the same tone used for the psalm verse. The *GT* provides other useful information as well. For instance, it gives the psalm and the verses from which the chant text is taken. For each chant it shows which of six very early collections of chant texts contain the piece, and it provides notation from medieval manuscripts. In the case of *Resurrexi*, the neumes in black are as found in Laon 239, and below the line in red as found in Einsiedeln 121, with folio or page numbers for each manuscript provided in a small box along with the manuscript sigla.

Medieval musicians in the early Carolingian period would not have written down as much information as is found in the *Graduale Triplex*. It is instructive to find this same piece in St. Gall 359 from the early tenth century, and compare it to the example in the *GT*. The psalm is not written out in St. Gall 359. It can be surmised that the cantor was expected to have a *tonary*, a book listing the modes of chants (see Chapter 3 of *Music in the Medieval West*), from which he could determine how to sing the psalm. As he knew the psalm tones (see §III.3 below) by heart, he would be able to fit the words to the appropriate memorized tone, and could generate new pieces from this information as well, if he wished. It can be seen by comparing the contours of the Introit antiphon that the same melody is found in all sources represented here. *Resurrexi* belongs to one of the oldest layers of the chant repertory and is fairly fixed in its text and pitches, compared to some of the repertory we will study from the tenth century and after.

II. MEDIEVAL NOTATION

II.1. NEUMES AND SQUARE NOTATION

The version of the hymn *Ave maris stella* studied here, from the *Liber Usualis*, is written in square notation (Ex. P2; see Chapter 1 of *Music in the Medieval West*). This is a modern version of the notation that evolved in Europe in the twelfth and thirteenth centuries and came to be used in many regions, especially west of the Rhine. For anyone who reads modern musical notation, square notation is not difficult to transcribe or sing from. The staff has four lines and two clefs are used, C clef and F clef, indicating which line stands for C or F. Medieval musicians used both of these clefs, depending on the range of the chant they were notating, helping them make efficient use of the valuable parchment on which the music was copied. Even if the music moved up or down dramatically, they might keep the notes within the same area of parchment just by using a different clef.

The hymn is in mode 1, designated by the number written below the word "Hymn" (see §III.2 for a discussion of the church modes). In this version, the first

Example P2: *Square-note version of* Ave maris stella *from the* Liber Usualis

A - ve má-ris stélla,   Dé - i Má-ter álma,   Atque   semper Vírgo,   Fé-lix caéli pórta

Hail, star of the sea, tender mother of God and ever virgin, happy door of heaven.

thing you see on the staff is a C clef, followed by a succession of square neumes. The shapes of the neumes found in square notation developed out of earlier ways of writing music, more specifically out of French neumes. Very early neumes, which probably evolved out of signs used by grammarians, are directional, with the acute accent, or upward sign, slanting up to the right, and the *gravis* or grave accent sign, which means "lower," slanting downward to the right. Hence the acute directionality came to be expressed by the *virga* ("rod"), representing a relatively higher note. The *punctum* (dot) and *tractulus* (dash) represented notes of the same or lower pitch. Many neumes of two, three, or more notes appear to be derived from combinations of these foundational note shapes: acute and *gravis* or *virga* and *punctum* or *tractulus*. These signs developed differently in each region; below, after the discussion of square notation, we will look at the notational style from the area around the Swiss monastery of St. Gall.

Example P2 is written in square notation. The first note is a *punctum*, a simple square representing a single note over the syllable "-la" in "stella." The first note is a *virga*, which looks like a *punctum* with a downward stem. This represents the highest note in a grouping known as a *climacus* (from the Greek for "ladder"), since the *virga* is followed by three descending *puncta*, shown as lozenge-shaped notes. Neume shapes that are created by combining two or more signs are known as ligatures (from the Latin verb *ligare*, to unite). Ligatures or ligated neumes were necessary when a vowel was sung to more than one note. Hence a melodic style in which many of the syllables are set to ligatures of two or more notes is called "neumatic." When the average syllable is set to a single note, the style is called "syllabic." When some syllables are sung to a great many notes, the style is called "melismatic."

The two most important ligatures consist of two notes each. The *pes* or *podatus* (from Latin and Greek words for "foot") can be seen on the syllables *-ve*, *-ris*, and *Ma-*. The lower note is sung first, then the higher one. It was originally formed by a *gravis* joined to an acute, meaning "lower, then higher," and looking like the shape of a foot. In *Liber Usualis* notation it looks like a *punctum* with a *virga* connected to it above. The *clivis* (possibly from a Latin word for "hill" or "incline") is the opposite of the *pes*, a higher note followed by a lower note. It was originally formed from an acute joined to a *gravis*, forming a hill-like shape. An example can be seen on the syllable *al-* in the second phrase. A somewhat jazzier note is the *quilisma* (from a Greek word for "rolling"). It originally resembled a sign used in medieval Latin to represent a question mark. The *quilisma*, a special type of *pes*, originally represented a quivering or trembling sound, which usually ascended a half step to the note following. In modern recordings following the Solesmes method, however, it is usually sung merely as a short, light note, with some lengthening of the note before. The first example in *Ave maris stella* is the second, jagged note over the syllable "-go" of "Virgo."

You can now transcribe *Ave maris stella* from the *Liber Usualis* or sing it directly from the score. Other versions of this same melody abound in the medieval sources. (See Example 1.3 in Chapter 1 of *Music in the Medieval West* for a version of the chant as sung at the Cathedral of Notre Dame in Paris.)

Other commonly used neumes in square notation appear in the score of the Easter Introit *Resurrexi* (see Ex. P1, and Anthology 3). In addition to the two-note *pes* and the *clivis*, it includes several three-note neumes. The *torculus* (on the syllable "-sur-" of "resurrexi") looks like a *punctum*, a *virga*, and a *punctum*; the *porrectus* looks like a *virga*, a *punctum*, and a *virga*. (The word "sum" is set to a melisma consisting of a *pes* and a *porrectus*.) A three-note neume that occurs often, for example on the first syllable of "isti" and the second syllable of "super" looks like an ornamented form of the *scandicus* (see Table P1). But in the St. Gall neumes it

Table P1: *Square neumes and equivalents in modern notation and in St. Gall neumes and French neumes*

NAMES OF SYMBOLS	BASIC ST. GALL NEUMES	SQUARE NOTATION	MODERN NOTATION
1. *virga*			
2. *tractulus*			
3. *punctum*			
4. *gravis*			
5. *clivis*			
6. *pes*			
7. *porrectus*			
8. *torculus*			
9. *climacus*			
10. *scandicus*			

is actually a *tractulus* followed by a *quilisma-pes*. The *climacus* is sometimes joined with other neumes to make a smooth grouping, for example on "-cta" of "facta," where the *climacus* begins with a *pes* instead of a *virga*. The dots on final neumes are a Solesmes convention signifying a lengthening. In early medieval notation, a similar effect was represented by the *episema*, a bar, as can be seen above the *clivis* on "-ia" of the final "alleluia."

Like *Ave maris stella,* most well-known pieces of medieval music have come down to us in varied forms. As a result of this, and of the nature of the notation and the loss of direct contact with medieval practice, many decisions must be made by the editor and performer, even with the simplest of pieces. Medieval square notation as used for most chant repertories tells us little about the rhythm, for example. (Not until the development of the rhythmic modes in the thirteenth century, as described in §II.3 below, did it become possible to notate the relative durations of notes.) The performance practice most widely used in the twentieth century, developed by the monks of Solesmes in France (see §I.4 above), assigns approximately equal value to every note. The classic "equalist" or "Solesmes style" of singing chant also groups the notes into units of two and three pulses. It has no basis in medieval practice, but it does achieve the softly undulating line that can be heard on numerous recordings. An accessible introduction to this approach is *A Gregorian Chant Master Class* by Theodore Marier, a handbook and CD featuring the singing of the nuns of the Abbey of Regina Laudis in Bethlehem, Connecticut. The film *Work and Pray: Living the Psalms with the Nuns of Regina Laudis* offers many examples of singing in the Solesmes style.[1] The *Liber Usualis* also contains a useful introductory section titled "Rules for Interpretation."

Today, singers experiment with alternative approaches to rhythm and expression. Although the ways of interpretation are many, in general performers try to use the ligatures of the notation to group the notes, and pay close attention to the accentuation and other features of the texts as well. The singing of Richard Crocker, featured in the recordings for Anthology 3, is based on his interpretation of medieval neumes. It is especially interesting to follow his recordings along with the *Graduale Triplex*.

II.2. ST. GALL NOTATION

The early-tenth-century manuscript St. Gall 359 is a cantatorium, a book containing the chants for soloists at the Mass liturgy. The notation in this source demonstrates how neume shapes appeared at the Abbey of St. Gall in modern-day Switzerland, a major center for the production of musical manuscripts in the Middle Ages. The Easter Gradual *Haec dies*, as presented in the *GT*, is written in

---

[1]*Work and Pray: Living the Psalms with the Nuns of Regina Laudis*, written and produced by Margot Fassler (New Haven: Yale Institute of Sacred Music, 2004), distributed by W. W. Norton & Company.

square notation. But above the staff are neumes from the tenth-century MS Laon 239, from northeast France; below the staff of square notation are St. Gall neumes, as found in St. Gall 359, which will be discussed here. (A portion of *Haec dies* is shown in the original notation from St. Gall 359 in Fig. 3.2 of *Music in the Medieval West*; or you can find the digitized manuscript online and enlarge the neumes for close study.) As can be seen by examining the neumes from St. Gall 359, the notation functioned only for singers who already knew the chant by heart, as the neumes are not "on the line"—that is, they are not precisely heightened so that specific intervals and pitches can be read from them. The early-tenth-century cantor-scribe who prepared St. Gall 359 doubtless sang softly as he wrote, or at least heard songs he knew well in his mind.

The very first neume in *Haec dies* is a *clivis*. As can be seen in Table P1, a *clivis* represents two notes, moving downward. To make a *clivis*, the scribe drew an upward-slanting *virga* and then went down to make a *gravis*; this created a hairpin shape that says "higher to lower." The opposite kind of neume, the *pes*, reverses the procedure: *gravis* then *virga* for "lower to higher." A *pes* appears above the word "quam" in the chant *Haec dies* (see Ex. P1). The scribe began by drawing a short, downward-moving *gravis*, then hooked around and slanted upward to the right in a *virga*: the result is two notes, the second of which moves upward from left to right and is therefore higher in pitch.

Three major three-note neumes are used in *Haec dies*, as found in the *GT*. The *climacus* ("ladder") indicates three notes progressing downward in pitch; this shape occurs right after the *clivis* of "Haec," the first word in the chant. As you can see by following along in the St. Gall notation below the staff of Example P1, or in Figure 3.2 of *Music in the Medieval West*, to draw this neume, the scribe made a *virga* (the higher note) followed by two lozenge-shaped *puncta* (lower notes). On the "di-" of "dies" we have another *climacus*, followed by a *porrectus*, which is made of a *virga*, a *gravis*, and a *virga*, so it represents a higher note followed by a lower note, followed by a higher note. On the "-cit" of "fecit" one can see a *torculus* ("twisted") after the two comma-like notes (clearly visible in Fig. 3.2). How did the scribe make this neume? He began with a *pes* (lower to higher), and then descended again with a *gravis*, keeping his pen on the parchment throughout. The result is a group of three notes, the second of which is higher than both the first and the last.

Notice the little "t" above the initial *clivis* of *Haec dies* in the St. Gall notation; it indicates the Latin word for "sustain." Above the next group of notes is a small "c" with a very long tail; this means "quickly," and the scribe lengthens the tail to show that all five notes—those of the *climacus* and the next *clivis*—should be speeded up. He can also use a nearly horizontal bar called an *episema* to express holding a note longer in order to emphasize it. One of these can be seen at the end of the *virga* on the "-es" of "dies," another above the last *clivis* of "exsultemus," just before "et laetemur." The ability to indicate that some notes should be held longer provided a way to mark musical phrase endings, but also a way to emphasize certain words while proclaiming the text, as in the word "bonus" in *Haec dies*. Clearly, at St. Gall in the early tenth century, chant was not sung with every note having the same duration. But what the precise rhythmic values were, neither this scribe nor any other tells us. In manuscripts from other regions of Europe, away from St. Gall, the opening few notes of *Haec dies* suggest several possible performance practices. There was no one way.

In order to transcribe *Haec dies*, you will need a version that is written in heightened (diastemic) neumes, as in the square notation found in the *GT*. In general, heightening did not happen in western Europe until the early eleventh century, although there were earlier attempts to use letter notation to express pitches and intervals (as in the pair of ninth-century theoretical treatises studied in Chapter 3 of *Music in the Medieval West*). When the diastematic neumes of a chant are compared with the earlier neumes that are not heightened (adiastematic), we can usually tell that the melodic contour is the same. Like the square-notated version of *Haec dies* in the *GT*, later versions are guides for deciphering the earlier ones, and we are able to transcribe the earlier notated works because of the fixity of the repertory and the survival of later copies in heightened neumes. With *Haec dies*, comparison of the square notation in the *Liber Usualis* to the unheightened neumes found in St. Gall 359 proves that this is the same melody. Only the heightening in later manuscripts allows transcription from the earlier notation. Thus the repertory of Old Spanish chant, which survives in unheightened neumes alone, has been lost because it was never recorded in a later, precisely heightened version. For further study of the many dialects of chant notation, students are referred to the excellent collection of plates from medieval sources, with discussions and some transcriptions, in David Hiley, *Western Plainchant: A Handbook*.[2]

II.3. THE RHYTHMIC MODES

The rhythmic modes are patterns of long and short notes first embodied in the ligatures of square notation. The modes are expressed in feet, each of which has three beats. Melodies written in the modes fall into phrases called *ordines* (singular, *ordo*) that characteristically (when "perfect") begin and end with the same note value (Table P2). Thirteenth-century theorists classified the ordines by the number of complete statements or feet of a modal pattern they contained (not counting the rest). So, for example, the third ordo of mode 1 contains three complete long-short feet, as can be seen in Table P2. At first, the rhythmic modes appear to have been understood in the same patterns that underlie accentual Latin verse, but use long and short notes to create the patterns, as can be seen in Table P2. The patterns found in the ligatures of the first layers of Notre Dame polyphony from the early thirteenth century (see Chapter 9 of *Music in the Medieval West*) have nothing to do with note shapes.

---

[2] *Western Plainchant: A Handbook* (Oxford: Oxford University Press, 1993); see pp. 405–41.

Table P2: *The Modal Patterns, with Characteristic Ordines*

MODE	METRICAL PATTERN	PERFECT ORDO	PATTERN OF LIGATURES	MODERN EQUIVALENT
1	Trochaic: long-short	Third		
2	Iambic: short-long	Third		
3	Dactylic: long-short-short	Second		
4	Anapestic: short-short-long	Second		
5	Spondaic: long-long	First		
6	Tribrachic: short-short-short	Third		

The ordines and their rhythmic interpretations as found in ligature patterns drive the aesthetic of early modal repertory. In the beginning, the characteristic foot of modal notation was a two-beat long followed by a single-beat breve. The idea of a ternary long being "perfect" came later in the thirteenth century, and would be a crucial concept for the development of mensural notation. The notation of the thirteenth century, and its movement from modal to mensural, added a crucial element to western notation: the ability to express rhythm precisely.

In the middle of the thirteenth century, notators began to think of expressing the modes and the values of which they are composed in terms of notes with particular shapes, long (*longa*) and breve (*brevis*), corresponding to the *virga* and *punctum* of square notation and particular ligature shapes as well. This innovation was born of necessity when texts were added to melismatic passage of music originally expressed exclusively in ligatures. As the ability of note shapes to stand for longs, breves, and even shorter notes increased, mensural notation was born (see §II.4 below).

II.4. MENSURAL NOTATION

Early mensural notation is also called Franconian notation. The name Franconian comes from the German theorist Franco of Cologne, who worked in Paris in the third quarter of the thirteenth century, and was one of several who categorized and explained mensural notation. As will be seen in our transcription exercise below, the rhythmic modes are also fundamental to mensural notation in this period. As the notation developed in the fourteenth and fifteenth centuries, however, the rhythmic modes no longer mattered.

Franco tried to embody the rhythmic modes through use of individual longs and breves as well as by particular ligature patterns. Rests also become codified in the system, depending on how many lines of the staff they cover. By the end of the thirteenth century, Franco's innovations had developed even further, so that longs, breves, and semibreves all had particular shapes. The following rules apply to the transcription of the note shapes, especially as regards a group of breves between two longs. In the third quarter of the thirteenth century, the idea of perfection became very important: feet were seen as perfections, and a perfect long as a three-beat note. Each of these beats is called a *tempus*; and a perfect long has three *tempora* (plural of *tempus*). Rules for transcribing Franconian notation include the following:

1. A long is perfect (three beats) if followed by another long, or by two or three breves.

2. If a long is followed by one or by more than three breves, then it is made imperfect (worth two counts) by the first breve.

3. If there are several breves between two longs, they must be placed in groups of three. If there are two left over, then the second of these is altered, to be worth two counts.

4. If one breve remains, it will make the following long imperfect.

Perhaps the most famous motet in the so-called Montpellier Codex (Montpellier HS 196) is the much-performed and recorded *Alle psallite cum luia* (Ex. P3). The piece is actually a polyphonic Alleluia with an added text (a trope). It probably originated in England, where the composition of Ars Antiqua liturgical polyphony continued unabated in the second half of the thirteenth century (see Chapter 11 of *Music in the Medieval West*). With its abundant repetition and imitation, *Alle psallite* is a good piece to practice transcribing from mensural into modern notation, since if you get a bit of it right, you can transcribe the entire piece.

To be able to render late-thirteenth-century mensural notation in modern form, remember that everything is calculated in feet, or groups of three *tempora*, each of which constitutes a perfection. The shapes of the noteheads (longs and breves) matter, but so too do whether or not they have stems, and the sides on which the stems are placed. Semibreves are indicated by an upward stem on the left of a square note, and relate to breves in the same ways that breves relate to longs. To transcribe *Alle psallite*, start with the tenor. Set up your page in $\frac{6}{8}$ time, so a perfect long is worth the value of a dotted quarter note and a breve has the value of an eighth note (unless the principle of alteration applies). The piece on the manuscript page is expressed in motet notation, with the triplum voice on the left, the duplum (or motetus) on the right, and the tenor across the bottom of the page. You will need a score of three staves. Although the manuscript uses both C clef (for the upper voices) and F clef (for

Example P3:

(a) Alle psallite *in mensural notation from the Montpellier Codex*

(b) *Transcription by Yvonne Rokseth*

the tenor), you can transcribe the music using a G clef, if you like. The first note of the tenor is a D. It is a perfect long, followed by a Franconian ligature shape indicating long-breve-long, hence the first long of the ligature is imperfected by the breve and the second long is perfect. Next come two longs on E and D, both of which are perfect and thus worth the value of a dotted quarter note. Then a line slashes through three lines of the staff; this is a rest, and because it covers three lines, it is perfect—that is, a dotted-quarter rest (shown here as a quarter plus an eighth rest). This pattern repeats throughout most of the tenor, forming a kind of foundational foot (*pes*) for the entire work, with the two more-rhythmically lively voices unfolding above in imitation.

Now you basically know all that is necessary to transcribe the tenor of *Alle psallite*. (Use Yvonne Rokseth's transcription of the piece in Example P3b as a guide.) As the two upper voices are imitative, if you get one right, you have the piece nailed. The first line gives you everything you need to do the entire piece. Since the upper voices are written with C clefs, the first note of the triplum is D, an octave above the tenor. Having transcribed the tenor, you should be able to do this line in the following feet: perfect long; perfect long; imperfect long and a breve; imperfect long and a breve; perfect long; two semibreves and an altered breve; perfect long; and perfect rest. What follows should come fairly easily, and again you have Rokseth as your guide.

III. MEDIEVAL MUSIC THEORY AND PRACTICE

III.1. THE GREATER PERFECT SYSTEM

In *De institutione musica* (Fundamentals of Music), Severinus Boethius (c. 480–c. 524) explains the Greater Perfect System with the lowest pitch at the top and using a set of four tetrachords to make up a two-octave scale, or gamut. As shown in Example P4, the Greater Perfect System illustrates some of the common theoretical terms. Beginning with B above A (at the top of Ex. P4), each tetrachord has four pitches, and the relationship of pitches within each tetrachord is always semitone-tone-tone (ST-T-T). The first two tetrachords in the system are conjunct, that is, they share a pitch (E). (The transcription of Boethius's system of tetrachords given here is conventional: in early medieval music, pitch is a relative concept and is not associated with absolute frequencies.) The next tetrachord is disjunct, beginning with B an octave higher. The final tetrachord is once again conjunct, E being shared. Each tetrachord has a Greek name describing its position relative to the others.

The journey from Boethius's exposition of the Greater Perfect System, to the modes used by music theorists in the ninth century (see §III.2 below), to later understandings of pitch and scales is long and complex. However, the concepts of tetrachord,

Example P4: *Boethius's view of the Greater Perfect System (adapted from Charles M. Atkinson,* The Critical Nexus: Tone-System, Mode, and Notation in Early Medieval Music *[New York: Oxford, 2009], 12)*

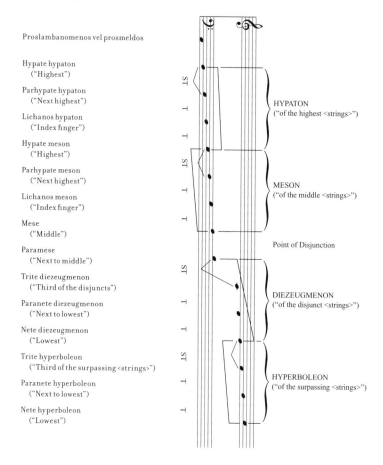

tone, semitone, disjunct, and conjunct are fundamental to understanding medieval music. According to Pythagorean number theory, the whole tone has a specific ratio (9:8), but the semitone does not. To this day, tonal systems and understandings are governed by how one measures the semitone. In Boethius's system, it comes out to 256:243—not a ratio easy to calculate on a monochord (see Chapter 2 of *Music in the Medieval West*). Diatonic scales are made up of a combination of whole steps (each one tone) and half steps (each one semitone), but the precise measurement of the steps (tones) and half steps (semitones), as well as the relationships between the steps of particular scales, depend on theories of tuning.

Boethius defined another important concept, *species*, as an arrangement of tones and semitones having "a unique form according to one genus" of tetrachord (either diatonic, chromatic, or enharmonic), based on the arrangement and size of steps. This concept, which was part of Greek music theory, allows for steps larger than a whole tone and smaller than a semitone. However, the four tetrachords in Boethius's Greater Perfect System are of the same diatonic species, ST-T-T, as can be seen in Example P4. This is a diatonic system.

III.2. THE CHURCH MODES

The medieval modes, often known as the church modes today, are a system of scales whose character, like that of the tetrachords in the Greater Perfect System, is determined by a unique relationship between tones and semitones. As can be seen in Example P5, the eight modes are arranged in pairs (and later in the Middle Ages, these came to be called *maneriae*; singular, *maneria*); the higher and lower modes of each pair are called authentic and plagal, respectively. Every mode has a principal note, or final. The pairs of the scales are usually numbered as follows: protus (modes 1 and 2; final of D); deuterus (modes 3 and 4; final of E); tritus (modes 5 and 6; final of F); and tetrardus (modes 7 and 8; final of G). Each mode has a commonly used pseudo-Greek name: Dorian and Hypodorian (modes 1 and 2), Phrygian and Hypophrygian (modes 3 and 4), Lydian and Hypolydian (modes 5 and 6), and Mixolydian and Hypomixolydian (modes 7 and 8).

In addition to the final, each mode has a characteristic octave pitch range, which may be exceeded by one or two notes, and a reciting tone, to be used in intoned psalmody of various types in both the Mass and the Office (see §IV.2 and §IV.3 below), and in both antiphonal and responsorial psalmody. Note that the scales break at the fifth and fourth above and below the finals, putting great emphasis on the "perfect" intervals of octaves, fifths, and fourths. Medieval music theory is a reflection of the sonic ideas of the age, as is the music itself.

As shown in Example P5, the reciting tones of authentic modes generally lie a fifth above the final, and those of plagal modes are a third below the reciting tone of the corresponding authentic mode. However, exceptions are made to deal with the pitch B, which forms a tritone with F and so was deemed unsuitable as

Example P5: *The modes and maneriae*

MANERIA	CATEGORY	RANGE AND RECITING TONE		MODE/GREEK NAME
Protus final of D	Authentic	D to d	A	1 (Dorian)
Protus final of D	Plagal	A to a	F	2 (Hypodorian)
Deuterus, final of E	Authentic	E to e	C	3 (Phrygian)
Deuterus, final of E	Plagal	B to b	A	4 (Hypophrygian)
Tritus, final of F	Authentic	F to f	C	5 (Lydian)
Tritus, final of F	Plagal	C to c	A	6 (Hypolydian)
Tetrardus, final of G	Authentic	G to g	D	7 (Mixolydian)
Tetrardus, final of G	Plagal	D to d	C	8 (Hypomixolydian)

a reciting tone. This is particularly true of deuterus scales, where the expected reciting tone is B, the fifth above E. Instead, it has been moved up to C and the reciting tone of the corresponding plagal scale has been moved to A, the third below. Tetrardus scales present a problem as well. The reciting tone for the authentic scale of the pair is D, the fifth above G, but the third below D is B. Hence the reciting tone of the plagal scale with a final of G has been moved to C.

III.3. THE PSALM TONES

Each of the eight modes is associated with a psalm tone, a formula for singing psalms in the Office and antiphonal chants of the Mass, although the Introit tones are slightly more elaborate. Each of the psalm tones used for the Office is based on its reciting pitch (or *tenor*), the note that is used for proclaiming most of each verse of the text. However, just as a sentence requires punctuation, so do the recitation of psalm verses to their tones. Accordingly, there are formulas for openings (intonation), midpoints (mediant), inflections of the tenor to cover especially long texts (*flex*), and endings (termination) of each verse, and these are slightly different for each of the tones (Ex. P6).

Example P6: *The psalm tones*

In medieval monasteries and cathedrals, there were two basic ways of singing psalms, antiphonally and responsorially. Two sets of tones were used for both ways of singing in the Office, and these constitute the workhorses of medieval music: one set is for the antiphons, another for the verses of great responsories (to distinguish them from the short responsories also sung in the Office). Only the tones for the antiphonal psalms of the Office are discussed here (see §IV.3 for discussion of the great responsories).

The tones for antiphonal Office psalmody are slightly simpler than those used for Mass Introits and Office canticles, and each tone offers singers a way of inflecting the verses of the text—a kind of musical punctuation. Example P7, which shows verses from Scripture adapted from medieval theoretical teaching practice by Peter Jeffery, offers an easy way to memorize the eight psalm tones, their reciting pitches, and their formulaic inflections. The first tone, for example, is memorized using a verse from Matthew 6 that has the word "first" in it. Present in this little exercise is

Example P7: *Verses from medieval poems adapted to the psalm tones by Peter Jeffery*

the opening intonation formula (on "first seek"), the reciting pitch (A), the mediant (on "kingdom of God"), and the termination formula (on "added unto you"). The ninth psalm tone is the *peregrinus* or wandering tone, which was used for Psalm 114 (113), the first two verses of which are illustrated here. It can be seen that the reciting pitch wanders: it is A in the first half of the verse and G in the second half. The two verses remind us that in Office psalmody the opening intonation is only used for the first verse of the psalm.

In both medieval manuscripts and modern books, you will see the letters EUOUAE, with pitches above them, following the psalm intonation. These are the vowels of the final words of the Doxology ("*se-cu-lo-rum a-men*"). They provide the termination formula, or *differentia*, used to end each verse and to connect the tone to its antiphon at the end of the psalm. This is the same kind of information provided in the psalm tone poems of Example P7, but those give just one end formula for each tone, whereas for most tones there are several possibilities, and the EUOUAE designation tells the singer which one to use. The tones are varied just enough to keep the singer alert, and are related to the accents of the Latin as well as to counting back from the final accents. You can see how this intonation process works in Anthology 4, which pairs the Office psalm *Laudate Dominum* with the mode 7 antiphon *Ecce apparebit Dominus*. The nuns of the Abbey of Regina Laudis sing this entire psalm with *Ecce apparebit* in the film *Work and Pray*, demonstrating the alternation between the two sides of the choir, verse by verse, that is a crucial feature of the performance practice (see §II.1 above).

III.4. A LESSON WITH HUCBALD

According to Boethius's description (see §III.1 above), the Greater Perfect System was built out of tetrachords. Medieval theorists took the tetrachord as the basic building block of a system of their own, loosely modeled upon the Greater Perfect System, but they related that tetrachord to the modes. The theorist, poet, and composer Hucbald of St. Amand (c. 850–930) attempted to give authority to the pairs of scales found in the church modes by using their finals (D, E, F, and G) as the basis of a system also mentioned in the *Enchiriadis* treatises (see Chapter 3 of *Music in the Medieval West*). He gave each pitch what he thought was its Greek name. Thus, in Hucbald's account the new system seemed to be constructed out of the elemental pitches of the scales used for Gregorian chant, as found in the four pairings (he uses the word "tones").

> Passing over the first three notes [of the Greater Perfect System, A, B, and C], the next four, namely the lichanos hypaton [D], the hypate meson [E], the parhypate meson [F], and the lichanos meson [G], are used in constructing the four modes or tropes. These nowadays are called "tones"

and are the protus, deuterus, tritus, and tetrardus. This is done in such a way that each of these four notes reigns over a pair of tropes subject to it, namely a principal one, which is called the "authentic," and a collateral one, which is called the "plagal."[3]

Imagine yourself in the classroom of a Carolingian music teacher. He has just explained that the relationship between Hucbald's four "reigning" notes is T-ST-T, as opposed to the ST-T-T arrangement of pitches in Boethius's tetrachords. Hucbald believed that the Greek system began on A. If you build upward from A, making tetrachords using the pitch relationships T-ST-T, you can construct the system that Hucbald describes, provided you understand the difference between conjunct and disjunct tetrachords. Conjunct tetrachords share a note; that is, the last note of one group of four pitches and the beginning note of the next-higher tetrachord are the same. Disjunct tetrachords do not share notes.

Now we can see how Hucbald uses the "tetrachord of the finals" to construct a two-octave scale, or gamut. He believed his system was consonant with Greek theory as inherited from Boethius, but was also made from the most basic building blocks of Gregorian chant. In Example P8, you can see Hucbald's tetrachords, identify which are conjunct and disjunct, and locate the whole-step and half-step patterns. Hucbald's system enables us to begin to understand how early medieval musicians thought about the church modes, the pairs of scales that are fundamental to understanding medieval music theory (see §III.2 above).

Example P8: *Hucbald's tetrachord of the finals (from Fiona McAlpine,* Tonal Consciousness and the Medieval West *[New York: Peter Lang, 2008], 46)*

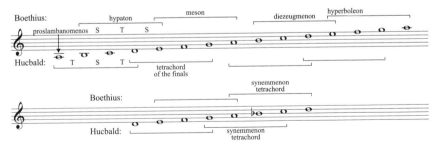

[3] Hucbald of St. Amand, *Melodic Instruction (De harmonica institutione)*, in *Hucbald, Guido, and John on Music: Three Medieval Treatises*, ed. Claude V. Palisca, trans. Warren Babb (New Haven: Yale University Press, 1978), 13–46, at 38.

IV. THE LITURGY OF THE ROMAN CATHOLIC CHURCH

IV.1. THE CAROLINGIAN (FRANKISH) MASS

The medieval high Mass, the kind celebrated on Sundays and major feasts, was a major musical production that unfolded in every church, cathedral, and monastery. It required architectural spaces, furnishings, books (increasingly), vestments, candles, and above all people to sing, for every part of it was proclaimed in song, including the intonations of the texts. Table P3 depicts the Mass as celebrated in Carolingian times, from the ninth century forward, with additions representing later developments. In the right-hand column, a brief statement concerning the allegorical meanings of liturgical action is given, following the early-ninth-century commentator Amalar of Metz, who was the most copied and influential commentator on the liturgy and its meanings from the entire Middle Ages. (Musical additions were usually not extant for the entire lives of each chant genre; for example, Introits were troped in many regions in the ninth through eleventh centuries, but after this time most Introit tropes died out.)

The Mass has two major sections, the Liturgy of the Word and the Liturgy of the Faithful. The chants sung in these two parts are listed in the leftmost column, with the kinds of musical additions or commentaries traditionally added to them in italics.

There were also two kinds of antiphons, both highly ornate, sung at Mass in some churches: processional antiphons and antiphons before the Gospel (not listed in Table P3). These antiphons are not sung with a psalm, and are free-standing pieces meant to accompany some sort of action.

IV.2. THE MASS PROPER AND ORDINARY

Liturgical chants fall into two major categories, Proper and Ordinary. Proper chants are those whose texts change in accordance with particular feasts and seasons; they constitute the oldest layer of chant in the Frankish repertory. Proper chants are primarily sung with psalmodic texts, but they proclaim the texts in three different ways: antiphonally (Introits and Communions), responsorially (Graduals, Alleluias, and Offertories) and *in directum* (verse by verse, as in the Tracts). Several of these genres of chant have a way of being *troped*, or supplemented by additional texts to comment on their meanings (the Graduals and Tracts are not troped). Each genre of Proper chant has its own way of employing the modes, and many have particular formulas that are characteristic of the genre. The Alleluias constitute the youngest layer of Proper chants, and the sequences that developed out of them are even later. In the sequences, which were composed from the ninth through the fifteenth centuries and even later, we find the only chant genre that can be seen to change over time, as musical taste and styles changed. Yet some of

Table P3: *The Mass of the Roman Rite, as Understood in the Ninth and Tenth Centuries*

Sung Parts of the Mass in Francia, c. 850, and Select Commentary on Chants and Readings by Amalar of Metz

PROPER CHANTS (TYPE OF PSALMODY) *NATURE OF COMMENTARY*	ORDINARY CHANTS *NATURE OF COMMENTARY*	PRIEST'S PRAYERS	READINGS	AMALAR'S COMMENTS SUMMARIZED (FROM HIS COLLECTED WRITINGS)
		LITURGY OF THE WORD		
Introit (antiphonal) *interlinear tropes*				Prophetic voice announcing the coming of Christ
		Collect		
	Kyrie (*primarily prosulae*)			Like Isaiah 33:2: "Lord, have mercy on us who wait for you."
	Gloria (*primarily interlinear*)			The priest intones the chant, and suddenly a multitude of angels replies (Luke 2:13).
			Epistle	Compares to voice of John the Baptist: a forerunner to the Gospel.
Gradual (responsorial) *only rarely troped*				The choir of apostles responds to Christ.
Alleluia (responsorial) *primarily prosulae*				The angel of great counsel Isaiah 9:6; a "new song" to the Lord
Sequence (developing in the ninth century)				
Tract (*in directum*); substitute for Alleluia in solemn times *no tropes*				May be penitential (Moses in Exodus 19:32) or joyful (Daniel in Daniel 6)
			Gospel	Christ addresses the people.
	Credo *not troped*			After Scripture, a confession of faith

(Continued)

LITURGY OF THE FAITHFUL

Offertory (responsorial) *Some introductory Prosulae for some melismas*				The bread and wine to be offered are like the clothing and vestments offered by people in Jerusalem, and the chant is like their song.
		Preface		
	Sanctus *interlinear tropes*	Canon (spoken by the celebrating priest)		Sanctus from Revelation; Benedictus means that Christ will come to judge the living and the dead.
		Pater Noster		
		Peace		
	Agnus Dei *interlinear tropes*			A chant for the people about to take the body of the Lord
Communion (antiphonal) *interlinear tropes*				A reciprocal voice, responding as in Luke 24:30–35: the disciples return from Emmaus and recall seeing the Lord as they broke bread.
		Post-Communion		
	Ite missa est *some tropes; some prosulae*			When this is sung by the deacon, the people's minds turn to that fatherland where the Lord has gone, and long for it.

the oldest and best-established sequences remained in the repertories of some regions for centuries, and even after the reforms of the sixteenth-century Council of Trent.[4]

Ordinary chants are chants whose basic texts do not change throughout the year, although they may be commented upon with various kinds of tropes. Ordinary chants do, however, have different melodies, and these are often seasonal, or became so in the later Middle Ages. Some portions of the Ordinary have

---

[4] See Richard Freeman, *Music in the Renaissance* (New York: Norton, 2013).

fairly large repertories of melodies, and others, especially the Credo, very few. But whatever the case, the Ordinary chants are a younger repertory in general than the Proper chants. The style of music they use is, for the most part, later than that employed in some genres of Proper chants. They tend to have been born after the modes were well established, and so use the full range of modal theoretical understanding. Moreover, they are more likely to be regional in their melodic uses and in the ways they are commented upon.

IV.3. THE DIVINE OFFICE

In *Music in the Medieval West*, we explore several ways in which the nature of the Mass chants suited the action of the medieval liturgy, with chants designed both to explain Scripture and to express the meanings of the eating of a ritual meal at the altar. The medieval Office was very different in character from the Mass. There were far fewer types of music in general, the main ones being antiphons for the singing of psalms and canticles, and responsories, elaborate chants sung at the close of an intoned reading. Responsories consist of a respond, sung by the choir (and made up of a psalm verse, part of which also acts as a refrain), and a verse, sung by a soloist. In manuscripts, these two parts are labeled R and V. Sometimes they are also performed with half of the Doxology, depending upon their position within the Office liturgy. The Office was also used as a narrative vehicle, and many parts of the Office for major feasts are arranged to express the story of an action in the life of Christ or of one of the saints (or a group of saints). Many Office responsories were versified, employing various poetic strategies. In the earlier Middle Ages the poetry was accentual, but not usually rhyming. In the later Middle Ages, new Offices might also be made up of rhyming stanzas of various types. Rhymed Office chants were written by the thousands—so abundant are they that many have never been studied or even catalogued.

The eight hours of prayer, which collectively constituted the Divine Office, were a central part of the daily liturgy in both monastic churches (overseen by an abbot or abbess) and secular churches (regulated by a bishop and his entourage of administrators). Devoted to prayer and the singing of psalms, the hours were celebrated at specific times of the day as follows: Matins (early morning), Lauds (sunrise), Prime (6 a.m.), Terce (9 a.m.), Sext (noon), None (3 p.m.), Vespers (sunset), and Compline (9 p.m.).

Table P4 depicts the Office as sung for Sundays and major feast days in cathedrals. Although the basic structure of the Office, like that of the Mass (see §IV.2 above), was fixed, certain elements of the singing and intoned readings varied in accordance with the rhythms and themes of the church calendar. So the definitions of Proper and Ordinary discussed in relation to the Mass liturgy and its music relate to the Office as well, although in somewhat different ways. The ferial Office consisted of those psalms and antiphons sung during days when no major feast was being celebrated; you can find the ferial psalms for Lauds, Vespers, Compline, and the so-called Little Hours (Prime, Terce, Sext, and None), as well as for Sunday and all the other days of the week, in the *Liber Usualis* (see §I.3).

Table P4: *The Office (Sundays and Major Feasts)*

First Vespers (identical in structure to Second Vespers, but with different chants and psalms, as appropriate to the feast)

Matins OPENING	1. Versicles: *Domine, labia mea aperies*, with response Psalm 51 (50):17, *Et os meum annuntiabit laudem tuam* (Lord, open my lips, and my mouth will declare your praise); and *Deus in adiutorium meum intende* (God, come to my assistance), with response *Domine ad adiuvandum me festina* (Lord, make haste to help me) 2. Invitatory psalm: Psalm 95 (94), *Venite exultemus Domino* (Come, let us praise the Lord), sung to a tone 3. A hymn
THREE NOCTURNS	1. Three psalms with antiphons and three lessons from Scripture, each prefaced by a blessing and followed by a great responsory. The third responsory, at least, was sung with half of the *Gloria Patri*. 2. Three psalms with antiphons and three lessons from the lives of church fathers or saints, each prefaced by a blessing and followed by a great responsory. The third responsory, at least, was sung with the first half of the *Gloria Patri*. 3. Three psalms with antiphons and three lessons from a church father or pope, each prefaced by a blessing and followed by a great responsory. The third responsory, at least, was sung with the first half of the *Gloria Patri*.
TE DEUM LAUDAMUS	(Monastic use would have a total of 12 psalms with antiphons and 12 lessons with great responsories.)
Lauds (main musical elements)	Versicle/response: *Deus in adiutorium*, etc., and *Gloria Patri* (the Doxology) Five psalms with antiphons (or with one antiphon for all five) Hymn Canticle: *Benedictus*, with antiphon (Song of Zechariah, Luke 1:68–79) Prayer *Benedicamus Domino*

Prime (main musical elements)	Versicle/response: *Deus in adiutorium*, etc., and *Gloria Patri* Hymn Psalms with one antiphon Chapter (three texts according to season) Short responsory Kyrie, Pater noster, Credo Collect *Benedicamus Domino*
Terce, Sext, and Nones (main musical elements)	Versicle/response: *Deus in adiutorium*, etc., and *Gloria Patri* Hymn Psalms with one antiphon (three portions of Psalm 119 [118] for each hour) Reading Short responsory (sung to a tone) Prayer *Benedicamus Domino*
Second Vespers (main musical elements)	Versicle/response: *Deus in adiutorium*, etc., and *Gloria Patri* Five psalms with antiphons (or with one antiphon for all five; might share the Lauds antiphons) Great responsory (for major feasts in some churches) Hymn Versicle and response *Magnificat* with Proper antiphon (Song of the Virgin Mary, Luke 1:46–55) Kyrie, Pater noster Prayer *Benedicamus Domino*
Compline (main musical elements)	Versicle/response: *Converte nos Deus salutaris noster/Et averte iram tuam a nobis* (Change us God, our salvation; and turn your anger from us); *Deus in adiutorium*, etc., and *Gloria Patri* Psalms 4, 91 (90), and 134 (133), with a single antiphon Reading Short responsory Hymn Versicle *Nunc dimittis* (Song of Simeon, Luke 2:29–32) Kyrie, Pater noster, Credo Prayer *Benedicamus Domino* Antiphon for the Blessed Virgin Mary

The celebration of Matins is more complicated than Lauds, Vespers, and the Little Hours. For each Sunday, there was a particular set of psalms, readings, and responsories, and these were divided into units known as *nocturns*, as can be seen in the outline above. For any ferial day of the week following, Matins would consist of three readings and responsories and three psalms with antiphons, taken from one of the three nocturns of the preceding Sunday. But on major feasts, instead of the ferial Office, Proper readings and chants would be sung throughout. There were elaborate rules for dealing with the clash of feasts that sometimes happened, especially given that many feasts of the temporal cycle moved as they depended upon the ever-changing date of Easter. Sometimes when two major feasts collided, one would not be celebrated but would instead be commemorated by giving it a memorial, perhaps consisting of a three-lesson Matins. The canticles of Lauds, Vespers, and Compline were fixed, but the antiphons were Proper, giving the reciting of these important texts a festive coloring. The fixity of the canticle texts in the medieval Office helps to explain their great popularity as texts for choral music.